THE
NATION
AND ITS
CITIZENS

Praise for the book

This is a book of considerable theoretical acuity, courage and scholarship, which shows how important it is to view the nation as a modern construct, contrary to all the claims currently in vogue. Nationalism is both cultural and political, and can refer to a movement, doctrine, ideology, sentiment or identity, either singly or in combination. All of these aspects are given deep and thoughtful interrogation. This makes the book a very important study that helps us better understand the rise and spread of authoritarian nationalisms and how to join the struggle to make India, and the world, more inclusive, humane and just.

Achin Vanaik,
Retired Professor of International Relations and
Global Politics, University of Delhi

This important and timely book provides a critical account of the often tortuous relationship between the nation and its citizens. The author deploys his wide-ranging and granular scholarship of the recent history of the Indian republic, to illuminate the urgent needs of the future. This is a book that needs to be widely read.

Sanjay Kak,
Documentary Filmmaker and Writer

THE NATION AND ITS CITIZENS

TALES OF BONDAGE AND BELONGING

SUKUMAR MURALIDHARAN

First published by
Rupa Publications India Pvt. Ltd 2022
7/16, Ansari Road, Daryaganj
New Delhi 110002

Sales Centres:

Allahabad Bengaluru Chennai
Hyderabad Jaipur Kathmandu
Kolkata Mumbai

Copyright © Sukumar Muralidharan 2022

All rights reserved.

The views and opinions expressed in this book are the author's own and the facts are as reported by him which have been verified to the extent possible, and the publishers are not in any way liable for the same.

No part of this publication may be reproduced, transmitted, or stored in a retrieval system, in any form or by any means, electronic, mechanical, photocopying, recording or otherwise, without the prior permission of the publisher.

ISBN: 978-93-5520-638-1

First impression 2022

10 9 8 7 6 5 4 3 2 1

The moral right of the author has been asserted.

Printed in India

This book is sold subject to the condition that it shall not, by way of trade or otherwise, be lent, resold, hired out, or otherwise circulated, without the publisher's prior consent, in any form of binding or cover other than that in which it is published.

CONTENTS

Introduction: Bondage and Belonging   *vii*

1   Identity and Citizen Loyalty   1

2   Nation in Action: The Rituals of Democracy   25

3   Violence and Forgetting   64

4   The Many Perceptions of India   118

5   Nation, State and Civil Society   168

6   Networks of Populism and the Unequal Nation   209

Acknowledgements   255

Index   257

INTRODUCTION
BONDAGE AND BELONGING

It is difficult to precisely date, though the signs perhaps start emerging from about the second decade of the millennium. That is when the optimism about a shrinking world, where nations would get ever more closely integrated in values and material interests, begins to evaporate. In its place comes a growing sense of disenchantment, variously expressed. There were growing animosities between nations, and rapidly polarizing emotions within them. Nationalist observances, once a place for the comfortable affirmation of a sense of mutual belonging, began to acquire a new stridency, an insistence on enforced uniformity. On the other side was growing anxiety that the nation had not quite delivered on its promises to citizens.

Amidst the growing clamour that citizens who have been left out should take back their country, there is another strain emerging that puts down all the troubles of the nation to its easy attitude towards difference. National salvation is seen in the imposition of rules of uniformity. In place of the easy comfort of mutual belonging, the new nationalism advocates a form of bondage to fixed ideas and identities. A vivid illustration of the new path to national salvation is the imposition in India of certain ritual, dietary and even sartorial codes on all who seek to belong. Expressions of a different identity are now sought to be banished from the public space.

Scholars on nationalism have always recognized a difficulty in reconciling the everyday life of the community with the larger construct of the nation, which, by its nature, is a community of anonymity. Nations negotiate that contradiction between the familiarity of everyday life and the remoteness of the larger collective through a number of ritual observances, such as honouring the national anthem and saluting the flag.

These national rituals are designed to appeal to all and invite their proud and willing participation. Yet, occasions could arise when they are given an inflection not uniformly acceptable, when symbols of identity become sources of discord.

Nations are creations of consent, normally arrived at after complex negotiations among citizens. Some of that spirit of thinking through complex issues was demonstrated when India's Constituent Assembly met, after the trauma of Partition, to decide on the foundations upon which the nation could be constituted. It was, as a legal scholar has said, 'India's founding moment'.[1] There was a spirit of adventure there, constrained by worries over the violence in which the nation had been birthed. Some members of the Constituent Assembly insisted on a maximalist charter of rights, while others cautioned against excessive ambition.

Consensus requires a willingness among citizens to take the successes they have and live with failures that seem unavoidable. But the consensus among the elite has to be underwritten by the people. And one of the processes through which that linkage is established is the universal franchise.

As the Constituent Assembly prepared to adjourn after agreeing on the basic law that would govern India's life as a nation, Dr B.R. Ambedkar, a figure revered in history as the architect of the Constitution of India, delivered a speech that continues to resonate through India's modern history. The principles embodied in the Constitution were those of the generation that had drafted it. Yet, each generation, he said, with a bow towards Thomas Jefferson, one of the founding fathers of the United States of

America, could be regarded as a 'distinct nation'. Each generation, in turn, could bind itself by 'the will of the majority' but had no such right to impose its will on the 'succeeding generation'.[2]

Constitutions evolve and likewise do nations. Nations are creations of history. They live their lives in historical times and in the memories that citizens carry of lived and unlived experiences. Nationalist lore, invariably, is rich with embellishments and erasures of real-life experiences. History is often written as the unfolding of events leading to the formation of the nation. But time does not end with the creation of the nation. The nation, rather, is a lived experience of citizens in historical time, continually being made and remade through their actions.

How does a nation ensure that this infinity of actions by citizens not aware, except in an abstract sense, of each other's existence does not result in disorder? There is a system of law and its enforcement that the State holds in reserve to ensure the sustenance of order, but nations are, above all, held together by consent. It could be a consensus evolved over the years or one learnt under the active tutelage of the State. Every nation seeks that balance between a cohesive civil society held together by unwritten rules and the overarching power of the State to impose its will in the name of the collective good. Some require a firm hand at the helm, while others are able to function in perfect harmony with the coercive apparatus of the State virtually invisible.

Even when invisible in its everyday life, the nation can never exist without the State, the political sovereign that embodies the popular will. How the State is constituted and invested with its powers is key to how the nation chooses to see itself. The State also fashions the relationship between the nation and its external environment. Indeed, every nation seeks, as it pursues its own life, to also shape the environment it lives within. Sustaining social order and calm within the nation also requires a stable order without. And that linkage between the internal structure of a nation and its external relations would be impossible without the agency of the State and the instruments of persuasion and coercion it holds in reserve.

Nations that came on the global map first—Britain, France, most of Europe, the United States (US) and Japan—succeeded to a greater extent in shaping their external relations to suit their interests. But a time came when their coexistence within spheres of influence fashioned for themselves became impossible, and they began to tread on each other's toes. When persuasion fails, coercion remains the only option. And that is when war, often the crucible of the nation state, breaks out. The twentieth century saw two great conflagrations between nations, both to this day remembered as 'world wars', though active belligerents were few. Most people were recruited into the war effort against their will. They, indeed, had no say in the matter, since the prevailing wisdom—embodied in the charter of the fancifully named League of Nations—was that not all people had risen to the state of maturity where they could take charge of their destiny. The immature, in fact, had to be guided in matters large and small by the enlightened European powers.

The second of the world conflagrations birthed many of the nations that make up today's world map. And the decades that followed, though marked by intermittent flare-ups in various corners of the globe, marking a continuous record of warfare, did not amount to a serious disruption of the world order. But there were nations that sat at the high table and determined the fate of others.

As the novelist Milan Kundera wrote, commenting on the last frantic negotiations between the European powers prior to the Second World War, there have always been two kinds of historic nations, which could, in shorthand (though with some imprecision), be called the large and the small. It is a typology that was starkly represented at the Munich conference of 1938,

Introduction: Bondage and Belonging

when a cabal of great powers determined 'the fate of a small nation to whom they denied the very right to speak'. There are, says Kundera, nations that are 'seated in the negotiating chambers' and those 'who wait all night in the antechambers' to be told what fate is in store for them. What distinguishes the two types is something far deeper than the 'quantitative criterion of the number of their inhabitants'. There are some nations for which 'existence is not a self-evident certainty but always a question, a wager, a risk', since 'they are on the defensive against History', deemed not to have a right to exist except at the sufferance of the bigger powers.[3]

Two major poles emerged following the second great global conflagration, determining between them, the range of choices available for the new nation states. In several instances, the new nations were turned into battlefields between competing interests and ideologies, and choice was effectively taken away from them. Some like India managed to chart an autonomous course, making patchy and sporadic progress towards the aspirational status of a 'great nation' while constantly dealing with internal discord. Through the 1980s, as the socialist alternative went into a slow process of disintegration, ending with its catastrophic collapse in 1991, the world was increasingly told that there is only one way open to any nation that seeks greatness.

The liberal democratic credo insists that every nation is free to choose its pathway to progress. It also asserts, on the other side, that its way is the only way. In 1989, the political scientist Francis Fukuyama could boldly proclaim 'an unabashed victory of economic and political liberalism… [and] the triumph of the West'. Mankind had reached the 'end point of [its] ideological evolution' and that lay in the universal acceptance of western liberal democracy as the final form of human government'.[4]

That forecast did not weather well. Early in 2022, Fukuyama revisited this prognosis in a spirit of seller's remorse, admitting that he had been remiss in many respects. Liberalism was a celebration of equal rights for all, yet, in the three decades that it had held untrammelled sway over the world, it had contributed to the growth of inequality to a truly shocking degree.[5] Alibis were offered aplenty, though Fukuyama's moment of epiphany was long in the making.

Since the early 1960s, the Munich Security Conference (MSC), an annual platform for the movers and shakers of international strategic studies and policy, has offered a moving image of thinking on the issues involved. The reports produced at each of these events provide a good index of how the guardians of the international order have responded to growing signals of the crisis. In 2015, the report was titled *Collapsing Order, Reluctant Guardians*.[6] The following year, it was *Boundless Crises, Reckless Spoilers, Helpless Guardians*.[7]

A few years on, the conference chose a provocative and interesting play on words. The dominant mood globally at the time, it decided, was 'Westlessness'. The West itself, though celebrated as a paradigm of the values the entire world should aspire to, was losing its anchorage. Indeed, after being the agency of nationalist consolidation in all corners of the globe, the West seemed adrift, facing a backlash not just from former colonies but from within. And much of this backlash claimed the mantle of nationalism.

A 'spiritual disunity' confronted the West due to 'the rise of an illiberal and nationalist camp within the Western world'. An 'increasingly vocal group' was demanding that the West redefine itself, asking that it break free from 'liberal-democratic values', and recast itself on 'ethnic, cultural, or religious criteria'. This was an understanding that marked a sea change from a 'liberal' understanding. Proponents of this 'closed' interpretation believe that the West is threatened by 'outsiders' with different religious beliefs or cultural backgrounds. Western societies have been too weak, even suicidal, 'undermining themselves by societal

Introduction: Bondage and Belonging xiii

liberalization, the empowerment of women, and immigration'.[8]

As the West suffers this existential crisis, the rest of the world tries to create itself afresh. Every nation makes a promise to its citizens to safeguard individual liberty and ensure opportunity. The balance between the two could vary. Some nations may offer greater opportunity in exchange for a sacrifice of individual liberty; some struggle to reconcile the two; while others achieve both with a measure of ease.

Citizens in India, through its 75 years of existence as an independent country, have, at various times, been called upon to make sacrifices. There have been long periods of time when the expansion of opportunity had to stand aside, since individual liberty was the priority, punctuated by one notable instance—an ill-remembered Emergency in the mid-1970s—when the nation was identified with a leader and gained priority over individual liberty.

With all these sacrifices, if basic questions of identity are being litigated afresh in the Indian nation today, there probably is a reason. And that is a failure to deliver on all the promises made at the time the nation emerged after two centuries under the colonial yoke. India adopted some features of the nation state that the colonialists had enforced and suffered the serious dislocation of a partition based on religion. But it made a promise to itself—to be a nation for all.

That was the promise built into the Constitution, but it was long in the making. From the time in the late nineteenth century when ideologies emerged insisting that the roots of India as a nation lay in the distant Vedic past, the forces of unity had fought a serious battle against the forces of fissiparousness. That battle was lost in the cataclysm of Partition.

The invocation of that original source of Indian nationalism triggered an equal and opposite reaction from people of the Islamic faith. But the greater traditions were handed down in debates over how India could fashion a relationship between society and State that was uniquely suited to its circumstances. There was Mahatma Gandhi, who disdained the coercive power of the State and insisted on reviving what he thought were the inherent harmonies in society; Rabindranath Tagore, who found the construct of the nation itself alien to India; and a wide array of thinkers in the nationalist stream, including Jawaharlal Nehru and Subhash Chandra Bose, who thought that India could fashion itself into a nation state feasibly representing all. Then there was Ambedkar, who saw the multiple fractures within Indian society and insisted on a State armed with sufficient powers to reverse these abuses handed down by history.

India's independence was a revolution half-consummated. The greater revolution was supposed to be the embrace of the values of the republican Constitution, embodying the vision of liberty, equality, fraternity and opportunity for all. It required an active engagement of the State—constituted as an embodiment of the general will—with society. How that engagement has been shaped is part of the story of where India's aspirations to be a nation that belongs to all stands today.

The chapters that follow seek to explore this range of themes, beginning with that elusive attribute of 'identity' and the centrality of the nation to an individual's sense of being. Nations are affirmed in a variety of daily rituals, some involving the cooperation of all its citizens, often unknown to each other, and occasionally involving competition. The competitive phases are typically contained within defined limits, never breaking out in conflict, perhaps only renewing the foundations of cooperation every few years. Nations are often created in the crucible of conflict, and till the violence subsides, require a strong hand at the helm to prevent enduring damage to the foundations. But once the violence subsides, the State can sheathe its sword, allowing citizens to evolve consensual modes of pursuing their daily lives. The remembrance of certain conflicts and the effacement of others from the collective memory are part of how nations define themselves. There is, of course, nothing fixed or immutable about this, and the episodes from history that a nation chooses to foreground in public memory are often an index of who holds power within.

The nation is also an economy, a system of mutual interdependence or division of labour. There is an agreed system of allocation of functions within the nation and a pattern of sharing the fruits of collective labour. This is underwritten by consensus but held together by the mostly unseen power of the law. When dissonances emerge, they could be settled through established institutional processes, but there could be occasions when these might escape the conciliatory power of existing institutions. That perhaps is one of the factors behind the new discord that has emerged between nations and within them in recent times. In many of them, there is a cry to 'take back' the nation from the elites who have disregarded the 'real' people for far too long. This populist war cry, heard with increasing frequency across the world, could fundamentally reshape the nation state as it exists today. Prognoses on where this will lead might be hazardous, but understanding the situation as it is today would be to learn how to deal with the likely challenges.

Notes

1. Khosla, Madhav, *India's Founding Moment: The Constitution of a Most Surprising Democracy*, Harvard University Press, 2019.
2. 'Constituent Assembly Debates On 25 November, 1949', https://tinyurl.com/ysu7c9h4. Accessed on 30 May 2022.
3. Kundera, Milan, *The Curtain: An Essay in Seven Parts*, Faber & Faber London, 2007, p. 33.
4. Fukuyama, Francis, 'The End of History and the Last Man', *National Interest*, Summer 1989, pp. 3–18.

5. Andrew, Anthony, 'Liberalism and Its Discontents by Francis Fukuyama review—a defence of liberalism...from a former neocon', *The Guardian*, 8 March 2022, https://tinyurl.com/2evsfd44. Accessed on 30 May 2022.
6. Munich Security Conference, *Munich Security Report 2015: Collapsing Order, Reluctant Guardians?*, https://tinyurl.com/38mc34dh. Accessed on 30 May 2022.
7. Munich Security Conference, *Munich Security Report 2016: Boundless Crises, Reckless Spoilers, Helpless Guardians*, https://tinyurl.com/3pftcw4y. Accessed on 30 May 2022.
8. Munich Security Conference, *Munich Security Report 2020: Westlessness*, https://tinyurl.com/kankkca9. Accessed on 30 May 2022.

1
IDENTITY AND CITIZEN LOYALTY

For all the energy spent in its interpretation, 'identity' remains an elusive concept. Historians argue over when the construct became an ingredient in political mobilization, and political scientists wonder about its unique power to move masses. As an aspect of life really lived, identity is deeply infused with affect and emotion. 'Who am I?' is a question every thinking adult asks several times in a lifetime in a quest that often, if not always, remains unfulfilled. Life is limited in time, and all who ask the fundamental identity question are usually worrying about how they will defeat that finitude. Generational succession is one way an individual leaves an imprint that goes beyond his finiteness, but that is often a meagre reassurance.

Apart from finitude, every individual must cope with the constant awareness of the limited space she inhabits. If it is a god she owes her existence and identity to, he has created only a limited expanse of habitable land on planet earth. And even if space and time are not knowable in their origins, the limits any individual can lay claim to are evident. The primary question of identity—'Who am I?'—is typically posed alongside another: 'Where do I belong?'

This is a quest in part for a world, a territorial expanse on God's finite earth, where an individual can assert a rightful claim. Patriotism was an answer to both the deep questions of identity—a mood consciously and constantly evoked during India's freedom struggle. For Sarojini Naidu, who addressed that question during the early years of the freedom movement, the answer was obvious: patriotism was a way of showing love for the land one is born to, by living in harmony and goodwill with all others similarly situated.[1] In more contemporary times, patriotism is portrayed as an unsullied form of love, wishing the best for the land one is born into and the people one lives amidst, uncorrupted by competitive jealousy at others' success.[2] The latter, indeed, is identified as the undesirable emotion promoted by the doctrine of nationalism.

In his classic 'Notes on Nationalism', George Orwell attributes the 'rise and spread' and indeed 'worst follies' of nationalism to the 'breakdown of patriotism and religious belief'. Patriotism differs from nationalism, despite their interchangeable usage, simply in being about 'devotion to a particular place and a particular way of life'. It is the best way the patriot would choose to live his life, without wanting to 'force [it] on other people'. Nationalism, in contrast, is 'inseparable from the desire for power'. The nationalist is driven by the quest for 'power and prestige', both for himself and for the 'nation or other unit in which he has chosen to sink his own individuality'. Patriotism, in contrast, is by its very nature 'defensive, both militarily and culturally'.[3]

This is an interesting contrast between words often freely switched. It is important, however, to interrogate how well it fares in an actual encounter with reality. Can patriotism, as a purely defensive doctrine, survive without an active patrolling of the borders of the community and the ability to repel potential threats to its way of life? Can patriotism survive in hermetic isolation, assured of internal harmony, with all potential for conflict neutralized?

Patriotism is a term that comes with a heavy burden of custom, sharing a common root with the term 'patrimony' or property. How easy would love of the land be for those who have no part in its ownership? It seemed almost self-evident to Voltaire, as he wrote in the middle of the eighteenth century, that property and ownership were truly of the essence. 'What therefore is the patrie (or homeland)?' Voltaire asks, before providing the answer:

> Wouldn't it be by chance a good field, about which the owner, lodged comfortably in a well-kept house, would be able to say: 'this field that I cultivate, this house that I built are mine; I live here under the protection of laws that no tyrant can break. With those who own, as I do, fields and houses assembled for their common interests, I have my voice in this assembly, I am a part of the whole, a part of the community, a part of the sovereignty: there is my patrie.[4]

The point is underlined at the expense of a baker's assistant who enters Voltaire's plot, and despite a lack of property and means, affects a sense of great attachment to his homeland. His pretensions are roughly dealt with: a neighbour asks him what he means by his 'homeland'. Could it be the village where he was born, which he has 'never seen again since'? Could it be the street where his parents lived, before they 'were ruined', reducing the young man to 'stuffing little pies for a living'? If neither of these, could his homeland be the town hall where he could not even expect to be a minor functionary? Or the church where he could not gain a place as a choir-boy?[5]

Observing the serious confusion of the young man at all these questions, a bystander observes that in a 'country spread over a fairly large area, there were often several million people with no homeland'.[6]

This inattention to the aspirations and interests of the 'lower orders' seemed natural to the ideologues of democracy in the late eighteenth century. For thinkers of Voltaire's generation, the land was a gift whose fruits could be enjoyed within the family. A 'homeland' was made up of 'several families', and in an extension of the loyalty owed one's family, it was possible to display the same pride with the 'town' or 'village'. Yet, the 'larger the homeland becomes, the less you love it', simply because 'a love that is divided is a love that is weakened'.[7]

Being a patriot, for Voltaire, meant wanting 'one's city to prosper through trade and be powerful through arms'. One could not win without the other losing. And there was no way this could be achieved except through a 'human condition' that revelled in another's misery: 'to want your country to be great is to wish your neighbours ill'. 'World citizenship' was a possibility, but one that could be claimed by someone who could accept a homeland that would never 'be larger, or smaller, or richer, or poorer'.[8]

Such modesty of ambitions was exactly what seemed impossible in France, even as Voltaire wrote. Indeed, the emerging classes of seafaring merchants, master craftsmen and townsmen were, at that juncture, chafing under the restraints imposed by the old aristocratic order. The Ancien Régime with its entrenched privileges, its taxes and tithes, its fragmented legislative bodies and institutions of administering justice, fettered the ambitions that just then seemed eminently realistic. It was a time when provincial estates wielded enormous power in the governance of daily lives, and localism reigned supreme.

In the event, it took the French Revolution, the upheaval of 1789, followed by many rounds of fission and fusion within the larger revolutionary current, and finally Napoleon Bonaparte's coup d'etat of 1799, for these issues to be resolved. It took this prolonged political churn, a period marked by turbulence within, the threat of armed intervention from abroad and a violent backlash and virtual 'reign of terror' to eliminate all threats to the incipient nation. The birth pangs of nationalism are rarely, if ever, painless.

The nation that emerged from the French Revolution was, in the perception of its main architects, a community of values. Within a matter of months, it was transformed, in the public imagination, into a community of language and identity. The *patrie* was briefly acknowledged to belong to all citizens, but now transformed into the sole property of those who shared a linguistic inheritance. A key moment in this transition was when the political gains of the revolution were threatened by intervention from beyond the boundaries of the nation by agencies whose enmity to the ideals of the revolution was identified with an alien language. French was the only language in which those values could be expressed; no other language, the revolutionaries proclaimed, could quite get that same resonance.

The French Revolution was no singular event. It was many revolutions enfolded within a sequence that began with the storming of the Bastille in 1789. A key moment in its progression was the Jacobin ascendancy, beginning in 1791, after which the next phase of the 'revolutions within the French revolution' began. By this time, the 'fate of France', Albert Soboul observes, no longer lay in the hands of the masses or the politicians. Rather, the commanders overseeing military campaigns, notably Napoleon Bonaparte, began to emerge as the decisive players.[9]

The Nation and Conquest

Is there anything inherent in the logic of nationalism that impels a country into external conquest when it is unable to settle differences within? For so long as the French nation state had the aspiration of belonging to all, it explicitly renounced external aggression or conquest, which would have been grievous violations of the rights it was committed to upholding. But the French nation state soon began a retreat from all its radical promises on citizenship rights. In particular, the values of 'liberty, equality, fraternity' that it blazoned as eternal commitments were proving very difficult to live up to. France then became the eager and active agent of overseas conquests, its purpose ostensibly being the lofty one of bringing less fortunate people into the orbit of its republican ideals.

Napoleon's military project, which depended on linking up with Tipu Sultan (or Citizen Tipu Sahib as he may have preferred being addressed) and pushing back against the growing British dominance in India, suffered a serious defeat in Egypt. But the cultural invasion fared somewhat better in Egypt. In the chaos of the Ottoman disintegration and the disarray of squabbling Mamluk tribes, the example of order that the French nation provided became the template for Egyptian politics.[10]

Britain set the template in India, the continent Napoleon failed to reach. The colonial state introduced categories of administration as it enforced a process of modernization on India. Nationalism came to India first as a form of nostalgia for the ancien régime, a longing that was defeated in the bloodbath that followed the 1857 Uprising. The ancien regime was overturned in India not by native revolutionary impulses but through the harsh repression of a colonial power that successfully recruited elements of Indian society to its cause. Nationalism was variously inflected and did not remain a singular ideal in the themes that the new Indian elite embraced. Yet, an element that perhaps remained common to its various later mutations, except the Gandhian, was the urge to emulate the material success and prolific cultural output of the West.

The Bonds of the Nation

What is the nature of the bonds that patriotism or nationalism promotes? Harmony is rarely an innate and spontaneous response towards all who are situated within the land an individual may call his or her own. In the real world, harmony and disharmony are constant companions, and one gains its ability to bind only in contrast to the other's power to divide. Here, as with so much else, the lethal pandemic that swept the globe beginning in early 2020, has provided many teachable moments. Taking the entire spectrum of sentiment—from fellowship to its opposite—a day in the life of the recent pandemic instanced two extremely contrary occurrences.

In the affluent Hauz Khas area of India's national capital, Delhi, a grocery storekeeper declined to serve a customer on grounds of her faith. This was at the time when a congregation of the Muslim faith in another part of the city was being blamed in frenzied media coverage—falsely as it turned out, though with little demur from the political leadership—for being a deliberate effort at spreading the virus. The customer, whose faith was evident from her sartorial style, was berated as a 'big M' and physically blocked from securing the items she sought. Her daughter, waiting outside, intervened with a warning that the storekeeper could be liable to criminal prosecution. She was reportedly 'cursed' and told that she would 'remain unhappy for generations'.[11]

Not far away, in Jaipur city, a man died of causes unrelated to the virus, and his cremation was organized by neighbours from another faith. It was a time when handling the dead was a stigmatized activity, since funeral rites were regarded as a possible source of infection. The numbers who disregarded the potential risks to pay their respects to a dead person were a demonstration of fellow feeling that went beyond immediate worries about personal safety. It also transcended the bonds of faith.[12]

There is something ineffable about this sentiment called fellow feeling; it is triggered in certain circumstances, while others bring forth its opposite. Because it is so difficult to grasp, the fellow feeling that unites people in loyalty to a nation is usually expressed through shared rituals. The singing of the national anthem before major sporting events is one such ritual of loyalty. Another could be the ceremonies organized on recognized days of national remembrance, such as the anniversaries of India's independence and its subsequent adoption of a republican constitution.

Protocols for these occasions are typically laid down, though in the broader arena, societies often feel free to improvise while staying within the spirit of the observances. On India's Republic Day in 2018, activists of the Bajrang Dal, a youth organization from the ideological fraternity that claims a brand of nationalistic assertion called Hindutva,[13] took out a *tiranga yatra*, a motorcycle procession celebrating the national tricolour, in the district town of Kasganj in Uttar Pradesh. They paused as they drove through a Muslim neighbourhood where a solemn flag-raising event was underway, to demand that slogans attacking Pakistan be raised. Violence flared following tense exchanges; gunshots rang out and one person lay dead. The only firearms that were brought to the confrontation, later photographic evidence showed, belonged to the Bajrang Dal side. A brutal retaliation followed nonetheless, with several shops belonging to people of the Muslim faith being vandalized and set afire.[14]

Late in February 2020, violence erupted in a rough and rather impoverished neighbourhood of Delhi. Protests against amendments to India's citizenship law had been running for weeks together and had captured several key locations in the national capital, when they ran into a countervailing mobilization by partisans of India's ruling party. As the violence escalated, a particularly heinous sequence was captured on video: five grievously injured Muslim youth shown sprawled on the road with policemen crowding around, beating them and forcing them to sing the national anthem. One of the youths, Faizan, died a few days later.[15]

These two instances, when symbols and rituals of nationalist fellow feeling have been rather perversely interpreted, need to be distinguished from each other. One speaks of discord within society, of a nationalist ritual becoming the setting for hostility between two categories of citizens; the other speaks of tension between officials of the Indian state and a group of citizens identified by religious identity.

Scholarship on the nation, which has proliferated since the

1980s, concurs on the impossibility of studying the subject without bringing the State[16] into focus. The nation could exist as an abstract or aspirational ideal but gains firmness and realization only in the State. The State is an embodiment of the collective sovereignty of the citizens of a nation, the ultimate safeguard for every citizen, formally entitled to a full spectrum of rights. If the first line of defence of citizen rights is the sense of fellow feeling and mutual empathy, the final guardian is the coercive power of the State, embedded in the law. The State works not on fellow feeling but on the principle of equal distance from all citizens.

Hindutva is a construct of nationalism derived ostensibly from a primordial past, and since 2014, when a party committed to that doctrine assumed untrammelled power in India, certain demonstrative public rituals have come to be seen as de rigueur in the affirmation of loyalty to the nation. Among these is the veneration of the nation as a caring maternal figure, expressed through the slogans '*Vande Mataram*' or '*Bharat Mata ki Jai*'. Chanting these is often held by ruling party vigilantes as a threshold requirement for enjoying liberties available under India's republican constitution.[17] The stipulations also extended to the dietary sphere, for instance, in the demand that every citizen swear off bovine meat. Real or perceived violations—more the latter, some of them involving persons of the Muslim faith engaged in dairying as a trade—were known to invite summary punishment and brutal public chastisements that often resulted in death.[18]

While this epidemic of lynching in the cause of bovine honour raged, a movie actor from the southern state of Karnataka had a criminal complaint of sedition—one form of crime against the nation—slapped against her for suggesting that India's western neighbour Pakistan was not a hellhole of a country as the Indian media was wont to portray it but a regular place like India inhabited by very similar people.[19] There was some irony there. In the first amendment to the Indian constitution, enacted within months of its entry into force, words either written or spoken, that jeopardized friendly relations with foreign states were characterized as one possible circumstance in which free speech could be restrained. The amendment was introduced and passed because a newspaper affiliated with Hindutva had been publishing content that seriously endangered ties with the state of Pakistan, when a cooperative relationship was essential to deal with the human tide flowing both ways across newly drawn borders.[20] The constitutional amendment did not weather well. In more recent times, as with the legal action initiated against the Kannada movie actor, an opposite principle seemed to be gaining traction: that hostile rhetoric against Pakistan is an obligation of Indian citizenship. Sheer absurdity ensured that the legal action against the movie actor got nowhere, but in terms of the public stipulation of citizenship duties, it lives on in the prosecutions launched against Indian citizens for their overt support of Pakistan in cricket encounters.[21]

Individual Identity and Mutual Dependence

As the Covid-19 pandemic tightened its grip globally in 2020, sending the world into spasms of anxiety, healthcare workers everywhere became the focus of public expectations and hopes. With all the knowledge accumulated over the years as a professional group, they struggled everywhere against the sheer magnitude of the viral threat. But they were never seen to fall short in terms of courage and commitment, or the willingness to risk personal safety for the larger cause.

What is it that impelled this professional group to a task that took, among its ranks, a toll in lives yet to be fully reckoned? Modern societies function on a division of labour, and an individual's position in this distribution of tasks—essential, life-sustaining, recreational or cultural—is often their identity.

Scholars have sought to define that elusive attribute, identity, as the reason a person has to do something. These are matters that are often an unreflective instinct and sometimes consciously thought through.[22]

It is never easy distinguishing between these two categories of response. Classical moral philosophy, in many ways the foundation for the discipline known today as economics, provides an answer, after a fashion. In his classic work *The Wealth of Nations*, which spends little time trying to understand what a nation really is, Adam Smith is concerned rather with the conditions for economic progress. And these he sees in an innate tendency in humanity to 'truck, barter and exchange' one thing for another, that, in turn, promotes the division of labour in society. Self-interest is the motive, he argued, and though every man 'has almost constant occasion for the help of his brethren', it would be 'in vain for him to expect it from their benevolence alone'. Indeed, said Smith in a line that has become a teachable aphorism for the economics discipline: 'It is not from the benevolence of the butcher, the brewer, or the baker, that we expect our dinner, but from their regard to their own interest.'[23]

In the context of the Covid-19 pandemic, was the commitment and dedication shown by the medical community all about serving their self-interest? Was it about ensuring that their food on the morrow would be available from the communities serving those needs? Smith the political economist perhaps thought so, though that was decidedly not his belief two decades prior. In *The Theory of Moral Sentiments*, Smith the moral philosopher chose to state his basic premise in the very first sentence: 'How selfish soever man may be supposed, there are evidently some principles in his nature, which interest him in the fortune of others, and render their happiness necessary to him, though he derives nothing from it, except the pleasure of seeing it.'[24]

Was the dedication of the medical community then about the

pleasure of seeing sufferers of the coronavirus infection recovering and resuming their healthy lives? Does the vision then begin with the local community and end there, or stretch beyond that into a wider fraternity? Is this benevolence limited in some way to the local area, the region or the nation? Or does it, as the Cuban doctors who volunteered for duty on the frontlines of the pandemic showed, affirm a more universal sense of solidarity without borders?[25]

Roughly two centuries after Smith, with all the detours taken in that time by social and political theory, Dr B.R. Ambedkar sought, in the context of a debate over the future political map of India, to revisit the themes of empathy and fellow feeling. In 1955, the year before his death, as public agitation raged over mapping the Indian nation as a mosaic of linguistic states, Ambedkar intervened with a forceful plea that culture was an essential ingredient of stable political organization. Political stability could only be assured when boundaries between provinces and nations were drawn in accordance with cultural affiliations. A State, said Ambedkar, 'is built on fellow-feeling', and this was a 'double-edged' sensibility, since it came with a sentiment of 'anti-fellowship' towards those outside the bonds of group solidarity. There was, said Ambedkar, no intrinsic propensity for enmity between cultural groups, except when they were compelled by circumstances to live in proximity and share among themselves the cycle of governmental activities.[26] Conflict would then inevitably arise over the purposes political power should serve.

The Citizen in Freedom and Unfreedom

Freedom, in a liberal-democratic framework, could be construed in both the negative and positive sense. Every person is 'free to do' what he wants; but also has the right to be 'free from' interference or encroachment into a realm of personal autonomy.[27] Compelling a fellow citizen to chant a slogan in veneration of the nation as a threshold requirement for his enjoyment of all rights is an obvious encroachment into another's freedom. In resolving this issue, most judicial bodies opt for the course of restraint: explicit acts of veneration are not called for in the normal course, so long as overt disrespect is avoided. In 1985, in a case involving the public ritual of the national anthem, the Supreme Court of India held that members of the Christian sect, the Jehovah's Witness, were at liberty not to join the singing on grounds of religious belief as long as they maintained a respectful public attitude through the rendition of the anthem. Overt expressions of respect were not imperative, but explicit actions suggesting disrespect would attract punitive sanction.[28]

The cases from Delhi and Kasganj, as cited before, convey a singular message. A notion may be gaining ground in India, which insists on citizenship and its attendant rights being earned. Beyond all the formal requirements for citizenship rights, it is necessary also to fulfil certain expectations of public conduct. Not everybody merits freedom, particularly if she is unable to continuously affirm the sentiments of Hindutva and practise the daily habits of living it demands.

'The nation is a daily referendum', said the nineteenth-century French ideologue and philologist Ernest Renan.[29] But in contrast to his sense, which was about national solidarity being affirmed through ordinary acts of belonging, of observing certain norms of fellow feeling, the mood in India since Hindutva assumed political power is to demand proactive and affirmative declarations of loyalty, though only from persons of a particular religious faith.

Recent scholarship has spoken of the nation as an invention. It is not an essential part of the quest for identity but a creation of circumstances. It is infused, moreover, with an element of 'artifact and social engineering'. A remembered history is important, but so too is a forgotten history. Renan put it rather well: 'The essence of a nation is that all of its individuals have many things in common; and also that they have forgotten many things...every French citizen must have forgotten the St Bartholomew's Day massacre and the massacres in the Midi in the 13th century.'[30]

This is a curious formulation, where the ideologue of the French nation is reminding its citizens of events in their history they are enjoined to forget. It was this curiosity in the imagination of the nation that Ambedkar drew attention to in his work written shortly before Independence and Partition on the demand for Pakistan. 'Forgetfulness and I shall even say historical error', he wrote, 'form an essential factor in the creation of a nation; and thus it is that the progress of historical studies may often be dangerous to the nationality'. By this touchstone, Ambedkar ruefully observed, 'the Hindu view that Hindus and Mussalmans form one nation falls to the ground', since 'the two communities can never forget or obliterate their past'. For both the Hindus and Muslims of colonial India, the 'past is imbedded in their religion, and for each to give up its past is to give up its religion'.[31]

A decade after Independence, the socialist leader Ram Manohar Lohia, reviewing a book by Maulana Abul Kalam Azad on India's march to freedom, cast a retrospective eye towards the cataclysm of Partition. He focused on how perceptions of history sustained the estrangement:

> The force that separates most is a particular view of history...There would be no Hindu-Muslim problem today or when partition was effected if Hindus and Muslims had been able to interpret their history unitedly and learnt to live in peace...The Hindu and Muslim views of their common history have differed in the past as they do today and that is a main cause of their separation in identity and action.[32]

The Indian Constitution as Statute of Limitation

The Indian constitution was one effort at forgetting the embitterment of the past, enshrining in collective memory its many glories and moving towards a future of equality and opportunity for all, irrespective of identity. This was not a nation given by history but constructed on the promise of the future. The nation was to be invented and affirmed in everyday life by its rituals—the singing of an anthem, the saluting of a flag, and the trek to the ballot box to elect an authority that would govern a part of the civic life. It was also to be celebrated in collective achievements in culture, sport and science.

Every nation invites the equal participation of all citizens in the daily affirmation of its rituals. Yet, there could be moments when certain social classes are deliberately kept out. The Sri Lankan republic's commemoration of the day in 2009 when it defeated a long-running war of separatism elicits distinctly mixed emotions among the nation's Tamil minority. The Columbus Day observance in the US is a day of mourning for indigenous communities, who mark it as the beginning of their near extinction in successive waves of genocidal violence.

There could be occasions when certain social groups within the nation could simply opt out of the customary nationalist observances. In India, in the mid-1980s, various political entities that drew their support from citizens of the Muslim faith chose to boycott the Republic Day observances to protest an event in Ayodhya, which led to a monument of Islamic provenance being converted into a Hindu place of worship.[33]

Ayodhya was the moment in independent India's history when a fresh identity was actively sought for a nation unable to create the material circumstances in which all citizens could enjoy the promises of equality and opportunity. The ghosts of history, only partially placated, returned to haunt the politics of the nation.

There had, till then, been a consensus around the institutions of the Indian state as fair and reliable arbiters in every manner of conflict. Growing State incapacity in matching the revolution of rising aspirations caused an erosion of this faith. Through the 1980s, Ayodhya began looming larger in the national firmament, not as a physical location or a locus of popular faith but as a metaphor for all that could possibly go wrong in a post-colonial State, all that could threaten the coexistence of cultural diversities within a nation. The Ayodhya moment in Indian history begins in the early-1980s, and the fever mounts and convulses the entire body politic in the years that follow, arriving at a final catharsis late in 1992.

'Secularism' was the shorthand term evolved for the brand of nationalism that India adopted, which assured all citizens of equality irrespective of identity. It was not a principle that escaped persistent challenge, notably on the grounds that it was indifferent to native cultural idioms. Secularism against primordial culture—that was the first of the challenges the principle had to face. The notion that social identities are as old as history has a powerful influence. Scholarly works that draw attention—as the historian E.J. Hobsbawm[34] has—to the 'shifting, fuzzy and ambiguous' nature of the criteria utilized in identity fixation invariably elicit a reaction of outrage or disbelief. Certain claims of identity are considered intrinsic to social existence, and any interrogation of their foundations would be dismissed without so much as a pretence at reasoned argument.

It is this seemingly axiomatic, self-evident character of the 'Hindu' appellation, and its apparent centrality to the existence of the vast majority in India, that has contributed very significantly to the effort to redefine the character of the nation. Hindutva began to be projected as the basic identity of the Indian nation, given since primordial times, which the practice of secularism since Independence had negated. The battle to regain the birthplace of a founding hero of the Hindu faith at Ayodhya was also about restoring the original genius of the Indian nation.

Ayodhya lost its resonance once the monument that had supposedly usurped the hallowed space was effaced. For long, the main vehicle of Hindutva ideology, the Bharatiya Janata Party (BJP), failed to pierce the threshold of a quarter of the votes cast nationwide. In 2014 came the breakthrough when it won a majority on its own in the Lower House of Parliament, with over 30 per cent of the national vote.[35] Five years later, it won a renewed mandate with an even greater share of the national vote, gained primarily at the expense of the numerous parties that had proliferated across the political map, representing specific regional interests within the larger national conversation.

A nation remains viable so long as it can negotiate a viable civic compact between its diverse groups. The most enlightened civic compact that a modern liberal-democratic nation state can put in place is premised, in a very basic sense, upon respecting and safeguarding cultural autonomy in a private space. In the public sphere, the only identity the citizen of a modern nation state has, by this criterion, is her civic self, respectful of constitutional rights, never pushing them to breaking point. This separation of the public and private spheres is a necessary part of the civic compact the modern nation state rests on. Alongside, citizens are supposed to function with an awareness of their civil rights and an abundant measure of respect for other's rights.

In periods of expanding economic opportunity, the identity questions remain subdued, since there is, seemingly, room for everybody to seek a place in the sun. Identity, in fact, remains unimportant, since the nation looks capable of credibly delivering on its promises of equality and opportunity.

In its effort to construct a hegemonic identity for all Indians, Hindutva, even if unwittingly, unleashed a multitude of little identities. Conceptually, political thinking responded to the proliferation of identities by devising the doctrine of casteism, considered quite distinct of religious sectarianism. Hindutva mobilization, conveniently represented under the shorthand of Ayodhya, was the force that ran into the immovable object of 'Mandal' in the 1990s. One sought to cement a sense of unity among a diversity of social classes by emphasizing their collective interests against an alien 'other'. The ideology of Mandal politics, named after a politician who led an official commission inquiring into caste-based preferences in public employment, asserted quite a different viewpoint—that far from providing a common basis for action to retrieve the spirit of nationalism, Hindutva was, in fact, a dagger in the soul of democracy.[36] To have even a moderate chance of success, a constitutional order needed to provide sufficient redress for the system of graded inequality that Hindutva rested upon.

The opposition seemed, for a while, to be fundamental, and it was, in fact, one of the principal forces driving politics through the two decades following the 1992 demolition at Ayodhya. But the Mandal proponents turned out to be a fractious crew and the lower-caste coalitions that cut at the foundations of Hindutva proved all too prone to fission. At a point when their fortunes seemed to be on the wane, many of the breakaway groups, which remain anchored in specific configurations of caste loyalties in their pockets of influence, made common cause with the Hindutva party. The alibi proffered for this opportunistic shift in allegiance was the supposed quest of good governance, a neutral, politically untainted principle.

Mandal seemed, for a while, to afford an opportunity for a broad-ranging coalition of the underprivileged castes that would impart a new energy to participative democracy. But in subsequent years, it fell away in narrow sectarianism, creating the conditions for widespread public disillusionment and the reconstitution, across the nation, of a coalition born in the malaise of endemic political instability. The party of Hindutva promised a wider consolidation by drawing in diverse social groups, based upon the tenuous fiction of primordial belonging. Since the premises of this switch of political affiliations could not stand up to rigorous interrogation, it required the constant identification of the other, an alien faith that could solidify the internal cohesion of the group claiming the mantle of the nation.

Conflict can be a force that binds, but when its basis is in caste, it will most likely remain confined, perhaps with a few repercussions in other parts of the linguistic cultural area but rarely beyond. If fellow feeling is cemented by contrast with the other, then the complex patchwork of castes in India provides no foundation for crafting a unified structure of governmental authority through electoral competition. The religious other, identified by its alien presence in the mythopoeic history of the nation, provides richer potential. With its presence in isolated pockets scattered across the country, the minority faith affords a template for creating new political solidarities through negative association. The 'we' who are the nation are bound by a sense of fellow feeling forged in our shared identification in not being what 'they' are.

Religious strife in any one region strikes up resonances in others. The experience of the Ayodhya campaign was all about how violence against the religious minority in one part of the country caused a wide-ranging contagion, invading regions and metropolises that had been free of the menace for decades. The nation is built on the premise that the State, which serves as the embodiment of the collective will of citizens, holds a monopoly over legitimate violence. The endemic violence that certain regions of India suffered spoke of a State that was tolerant of the breaching of this ostensible monopoly by agents in civil society. When the victims share particular attributes, as with being the religious minorities or those disadvantaged by caste, it fuels a belief that the nation understood in terms of a civic compact belongs to a relative few, that its civic institutions do not work for the powerless.

The chapters that follow explore these issues from the theoretical and historical perspectives, in the belief that these would have a bearing on how India as a nation negotiates the pathway ahead. We will explore the values, norms and social commitments that were embedded in the Indian constitution and how well politics, in its subsequent course, has lived up to them. We also will seek to advance some hypotheses on how identity, that most powerful construct in modern politics, is crafted. If politics is all about a contest of symbols, these chapters will seek to break down the symbols that have contended in the public sphere for popular allegiance, how some have waned in their power, while others have gained. Nationalism is expressed in daily acts of belonging that underscore what it is and what it is not. It also runs in tandem with the competitive ethos, the contestation for electoral success. Far from being fixed and invariant in its essence, nationalism is constantly being redefined in this whirl of life as actually lived.

Notes

1. Quoted in: Habib, Irfan, *Indian Nationalism: The Essential Writings*, Aleph Book Company, New Delhi, 2019.
2. Shashi Tharoor in his book *The Battle of Belonging* (Aleph Book Company, New Delhi, 2020, p. 66) quotes an American political theorist to make the point that patriotism is 'one of the basic human sentiments': 'If not a natural tendency in the species, it is at least a proclivity produced by realities basic to human life, for territoriality, along with family, has always been a primary associative bond'.
3. Orwell, George, 'Notes on Nationalism', The Orwell Foundation, https://bit.ly/3iOaGAA. Accessed on 30 March 2022.
4. Voltaire, 'Homeland', *Voltaire: Political Writings,* Cambridge University Press, 1994, pp. 25–30.

5   Ibid.
6   Ibid.
7   Ibid.
8   Ibid.
9   Soboul, Albert, *Understanding the French Revolution*, Peoples' Publishing House, Delhi, 1989, p. 168.
10 Strathern, Paul, *Napoleon in Egypt,* Bantam Books, New York, 2009.
11 Ravi, Sidharth, 'Grocery store owner "insults" mother-daughter over religion', *The Hindu,* 14 April 2020, https://tinyurl.com/3zsmfs9w. Accessed on 23 June 2022.
12 Mohammed Iqbal, 'Muslims conduct Hindu man's funeral rites', *The Hindu*, 13 April 2020, https://tinyurl.com/2uk5bhy2. Accessed on 23 June 2022.
13 Hindutva will be a subject for further discussion later in this book. For now, it is sufficient to understand it as a contemporary political doctrine that claims the nation exclusively on behalf of the faiths that originated in its territory. The political doctrine of Hindutva is most often sourced to the militant ideologue Vinayak Damodar Savarkar and his brief pamphlet, *Essentials of Hindutva*. Ostensibly written in 1921–22, when the author was undergoing a life term in the Andamans penal colony on charges of sedition against the King Emperor, the book was published pseudonymously and had an underground existence for long. To its limited credit, it has not caused as much embarrassment to contemporary exponents of the doctrine as *We, or Our Nationhood Defined*, a 1936 work by Savarkar's fellow traveller for part of the way along the extremist fringes of nationalism, M.S. Golwalkar. In his biography of Savarkar, *Echoes from a Forgotten Past* (Penguin Random House, Delhi, 2019), Vikram Sampath accords primacy to Chandranath Basu, a Bengali writer from the late nineteenth century, in inventing the term Hindutva, though the full elaboration of the concept was uniquely Savarkar's. The origin of the Indian nation, for Savarkar, is in the Arya culture and civilization, heralded in the verses of the classical Sanskrit

text, the Rig Veda. Embarrassingly for contemporary proponents of the ideology, Savarkar's exegesis of the foundational texts pays unwitting homage to the Aryan invasion hypothesis. Though part of the historiography of preceding champions of Hindu nationalism, the Aryan hypothesis proved a burden in later years for all who sought primordial bonding as a condition for nationalist belonging. Later chapters will provide greater elaboration of these themes.

14   Mahaprashasta, Ajoy Ashirwad, 'Kasganj: The Anatomy of a Communal Riot', *The Wire*, 7 February 2018, https://bit.ly/3NHpn6H. Accessed on 1 April 2022.

15   'India: Protests, "Shoot the Traitors": Discrimination Against Muslims under India's New Citizenship Policy', Human Rights Watch, 9 April 2020, https://bit.ly/3uHt1VH. Accessed on 1 April 2022.

16   In this and all subsequent references, the word 'State' when capitalized will refer to the political sovereign that claims the right to rule over the nation. In its lower-case usage, it will refer to the territorial entities, the states, for instance, that constitute the Indian Union.

17   Bose, Sugata, *The Nation as Mother and Other Visions of Nationhood*, (Penguin, 2017) offers a history of this strain of thinking. He highlights how the worship of the nation as mother, through compositions in poetry and the visual arts, escalated through the early years of the twentieth century, creating waves of anxiety among the people of the Muslim faith, who could not quite associate with the imagery. It was a controversial matter all through India's freedom struggle, and Jawaharlal Nehru and Rabindranath Tagore were both on record disapproving of the imagery as a nationalistic trope. This matter is also explored in this author's essay, 'Patriotism Without People, Milestones in the Evolution of the Hindu Nationalist Ideology', *Social Scientist*, vol. 22, no. 5–6, May–June 1994, pp. 3–38.

18   'India: Vigilante "Cow Protection" Groups Attack Minorities', Human Rights Watch, 18 February 2019, https://bit.ly/3JXaLhp. Accessed on 1 April 2022.

19 '"Sedition" charge against actor Ramya for "Pakistan is not hell," remark', *Indian Express*, 23 August 2016, https://bit.ly/3iX5GK9. Accessed on 1 April 2022. Sedition under the colonial law introduced by the British was about crimes against the supreme sovereign, represented by the Crown. Many among India's freedom fighters were convicted under this clause of colonial law, and at the time of Independence, there was a powerful current of opinion calling for the deletion of this clause from the statute. Yet, it was retained with particularly fateful consequences for more intolerant times.

20 On this and the larger story of the First Amendment, see Singh, Tripurdaman, *Sixteen Stormy Days*, Penguin Random House Delhi, 2020.

21 Poddar, Umang, 'What laws are being used to book those who celebrated Pakistan's cricket win over India?', *Scroll in.* in 29 October 2021, https://bit.ly/3uNA5zY. Accessed on 1 April 2022.

22 Appiah, K. Anthony, *The Lies That Bind: Rethinking Identity*, Liveright (W.W. Norton), New York, 2018, p. 25.

23 Smith, Adam, *The Wealth of Nations*, Edwin Cannan (ed.), Random House, 2000, p. xviii.

24 Smith, Adam, *The Theory of Moral Sentiments*, Penguin Classics, 2010, p. 1.

25 Augustin, Ed, 'Cuba Has Sent 2,000 Doctors and Nurses Overseas to Fight Covid-19', *The Nation*, 22 May 2020, https://tinyurl.com/52753kjc. Accessed on 22 June 2022.

26 Ambedkar, B.R., 'Thoughts on Linguistic States', *Dr Babasaheb Ambedkar, Writings and Speeches*, Volume I, Vasant Moon (ed.), Education Deprtment, Government of Maharashtra, Mumbai, 1979, pp. 143–44.

27 This is the well-known formulation by Isaiah Berlin that broadly distinguishes between an individual's 'freedom to' do anything he chooses, and his right to be 'free from' any manner of interference or encroachment into a domain of personal autonomy.

28 Singh, Yash, 'Bijoe Emmanuel v. State of Kerala', Indian Law Portal,

8 July 2020, https://bit.ly/3jbDZxr. Accessed on 1 April 2022.
29. Cited in: Anderson, Benedict, *Imagined Communities: Reflections on the Origin and Spread of Nationalism,* Verso, London, 1983, pp. 199–201.
30. Ibid.
31. Ambedkar, B.R., 'Pakistan or the Partition of India', *Dr Babasaheb Ambedkar, Writings and Speeches,* Volume 8, Vasant Moon (ed.), Education Department, Government of Maharashtra, Mumbai, 1990, p. 37.
32. Lohia, Ram Manohar, *Guilty Men of India's Partition,* Kitabistan, Delhi, 1960, p. 5.
33. Ahmed, Farzand, and Ajay Kumar, 'Call by section of Muslim leaders to boycott Republic Day functions raises a storm', *India Today,* 11 December 2013, https://tinyurl.com/ycwxxxrt. Accessed on 23 June 2022.
34. Hobsbawm, E.J., *Nations and Nationalism since 1780: Programme, Myth, Reality,* Cambridge University Press, Cambridge, 1992, p. 25.
35. Misra, Satish, 'Understanding the rise of the Bharatiya Janata Party', *Observer Research Foundation,* 21 September 2018, https://bit.ly/3j1bimp. Accessed on 1 April 2022.
36. Muralidharan, Sukumar, 'Mandal, Mandir aur Masjid: "Hindu" Communalism and the Crisis of the State', *Social Scientist,* vol. 18, no. 10, October 1990, pp. 27–49.

2
NATION IN ACTION: THE RITUALS OF DEMOCRACY

The nation is often a creation of adversity, of certain social strata seeking to break out of the restraints of a social order. The French nation came into existence in the adversities of the Ancien Régime and the irresolvable conflicts between the aristocracy, clergy and monarchy. However, the nation then prospered, even as it brought 'other' people under its colonial sway. It also alternated between popular rule and various forms of monarchy until firmly embracing the republican format in 1871, eight decades since the Revolution.

Like the French, the US too began with lofty promises of equality but then prospered from slavery, a particularly base form of exploitation. The British subjugated a greater number in the service of their conception of nationhood, always torn between Crown and country. In none of these canonical instances were the principles of liberty and equality, one of the fundamental premises of nation-building, even remotely fulfilled.

India, likewise, embarked upon its pathway towards sovereign nationhood with similar promises to itself. For most members of the Indian Constituent Assembly, the republican Constitution adopted by unanimous acclaim in November 1949, was both point of arrival and departure. It was the culmination of a prolonged struggle for national freedom and precursor to a social revolution that would rapidly efface all inequalities. However, Dr B.R.

Ambedkar, after the lone and, in most part, losing hand he played in forging the nation's freedom contract, had no such illusions. Though widely revered today as an architect of India's republican constitution, Ambedkar himself did not regard that as a notable accomplishment. In his valedictory address at the conclusion of the final session of the Constituent Assembly, he warned of many challenges ahead. While promising a 'political democracy', the Constitution did not yet ensure a social democracy enshrining the essential virtues of 'equality, liberty and fraternity'. As he then said:

> In politics we will be recognising the principle of one man one vote and one vote one value. In our social and economic life, we shall, by reason of our social and economic structure, continue to deny the principle of one man one value. How long shall we continue to live this life of contradictions?[1]

Caste was a distinctive feature of Indian society, a system that Ambedkar described as 'graded inequality'. If the nation was built on the notion of the free and sovereign individual, caste with its ascription of roles and status threatened its very foundations. Ambedkar recognized that the democratic franchise could tame the iniquities of caste, but this could not be taken for granted. Rather, it called for stringent safeguards beyond the guarantee of a vote for every citizen. Ambedkar never flinched from his insistence that the untouchables, as he boldly called them, deserved separate political recognition. From his 1919 submission to the Southborough Commission on franchise reform to his insistence during the 1930 Round Table Conferences, he constantly ran into the opposition of Mahatma Gandhi, who swore that he would rather give up life itself than permit the sundering of the Harijan from Hinduism.[2]

The compromise devised was about assured rather than separate representation. The southern states were already embarked upon that path. However, following the collision between Gandhi and Ambedkar, a diverse mosaic of policies came into existence across the country, assuring the lesser castes, variously described and characterized, a share in the executive and legislative branches.

Caste oppression was part of the history that India as a republic chose to acknowledge, though with the reassuring conviction that it would soon be forgotten. Caste and religious communities were embedded in the franchise system drawn up under the Government of India Act of 1935, and even while adapting this template into its voluminous administrative section, the Indian constitution took care to purge what the majority of the Constituent Assembly had begun to see as the more divisive aspects. The problem of religion had been resolved, after a fashion, by the partition of India, though this was far from a clean break and the toxic residue was to resurface many years later.

Caste, moreover, was accepted very grudgingly. A few years later, as he looked back at those early deliberations, Ambedkar remarked with irony that for all the common sense gleaned about caste from real-world experience, empirical verification was impossible because the census had turned a blind eye to it. The 1951 Census, the first of independent India, omitted an enumeration by caste. Lofty notions of shared identity, citizenship and equality were advanced as the rationale, but for Ambedkar, the whole process carried the whiff of escapism:

> The Home Minister of the Government of India who is responsible for this omission was of the opinion that if a word does not exist in the dictionary, it can be proved that the fact for which the word stands does not exist. One can only pity the petty intelligence of the author.[3]

The gulf in perceptions was wide, and Ambedkar ascribed the evasive attitude of independent India's early political leadership to bad faith. In the absence of strong positive evidence though, this evasion could be put down to naivety. Perhaps the belief that caste could be wished out of existence through administrative action was rooted in the boundless optimism of Independence and the investment the nation was making in the ethic of modernization.

Constitutional Patriotism as an Ideal Too High

If the legislative consensus involved at least the recognition of caste as a transient inconvenience, India's newly instituted Supreme Court proved impatient about waiting through a transition. When called upon to decide how far preferences for castes categorized as 'depressed' or 'socially and educationally backward' were consistent with constitutional promises, it decided in favour of the abstract principle of equality, wishing away the lived reality of inequality.[4]

Prime Minister Jawaharlal Nehru, furious at this, among other acts of what he called the lawyerly 'purloinment' of the great constitution India had given itself, moved swiftly to introduce an amendment to the article on equality.[5] As the architect of a model of 'constitutional patriotism'—well before the term acquired formal definition in the work of the German philosopher Jürgen Habermas—Nehru believed very firmly that India as a nation could put behind the traumas of religious strife and caste oppression. The Constitution marked India's new life as a nation. The suppression of certain aspects of the past was about inventing a future of equality and opportunity for all. Irrespective of any other marker of identity, every individual was, above all, an equal citizen of the republic.

The first amendment enacted to the Indian constitution tried to indemnify special protections granted to the lesser castes from judicial review. Since the equality clause had been quite literally interpreted by the Supreme Court to strike down the preferential quotas introduced for those traditionally disadvantaged by caste, the first amendment introduced a non obstante (or notwithstanding) clause. Nothing in the equality clause of the Constitution, the first amendment said, would prevent the State from introducing special preferences for socially and educationally backward classes. But few such formal arrangements in law were deemed necessary to repair the religious divide. In some degree, Partition was thought to have resolved the issue of religion-based difference.

An official theology of the national movement was then taking shape, putting down the cataclysm of Partition to Muslim League intransigence in the face of every good-faith effort at reconciliation by the Congress. The official theology of the nation involved a stigma that the very substantial Muslim minority in India were left to bear. 'Secular' nationalism, though, promised an opportunity to leave behind the bitterness of the past.[6]

Indian secularism was not as firm as the US constitution in mandating the separation of religion from politics. The first amendment to the US constitution prohibited any law on the establishment of religion, part of the emerging nation's assertion of identity as a haven for refugees from economic deprivation and religious persecution in Europe. The disestablishment clause[7], as it has come to be called, also carried resonances of the rebellion against the British Crown, which embodied the religious authority of the Church of England.

Secularism in India was conceived more ambiguously. It was written into the Constitution in 1976 by the ill-remembered Emergency regime. Though the Constituent Assembly witnessed a lengthy debate on religion in public life, the outcome, finally, was uncertain. The freedom to profess, practise and propagate all religions was written into the Fundamental Rights, limited only by the dictates of 'public order, morality and health'. But then, a principle of State primacy over religion was established by an article enabling the regulation of 'economic, financial, political, or other secular activity that may be associated with religious practice.'[8]

Constitutional articles that prohibited religious instruction in publicly funded educational institutions bowed towards the principle of disestablishment. Yet, these were immediately afterwards diluted by another article permitting every denomination or sect to establish and maintain educational and charitable institutions. Immediately afterwards, an article prohibiting any tax or levy on a religious basis shifted the balance back towards a principled distance between Church and State.[9]

There were varying inflections placed on the principle of secularism through the Constituent Assembly debate. A first draft of the Constitution conceived of strong provisions on minority rights as a necessary part of the guarantee of equality. In the aftermath of Partition, Sardar Vallabhbhai Patel sounded the retreat because of what he described as 'changed circumstances'. Minority representation was discussed and set aside as a superfluity, since fair outcomes were guaranteed by the principles of equality before the law and equal access to public services and employment. Separate communal electorates, a grim legacy of the colonial years going back to the first concessions made by the British Raj to local representative bodies, were best forgotten in the new order.[10]

Equality embraced the right to be different, though not a difference in rights. Exceptions would apply only for classes of citizens suffering a deficit of social and cultural capital that were not remediable through the guarantees of equality and fair opportunity.[11] But with all this, the Constitution felt compelled to create a rubric of minority, though defined in a very slippery fashion.[12]

Equal citizenship based on a charter of rights was a principle the Constituent Assembly members, mostly upper caste with no great self-awareness about their privileges, could easily embrace. And the ambiguous mix of principles they wrote into the Constitution was fertile ground for a practical idiom of politics marked by religious confessionalism in varying proportions. This was a brand of politics dignified by the slogan '*Sarva Dharma*

Samabhava', or equal opportunity for all religions, rather than a strict doctrine of separation. Equal opportunity to every manner of confessionalism, in a competitive political system, tends to tilt towards majoritarianism. Some hints of this possible threat to equality as a principle were available in early executive actions.

Vigilantism and the Citizen

Beyond the privileged perimeter of the Constituent Assembly, in the real world of dislocation and trauma, local vigilantism, triggered by the turmoil of Partition, sought to inscribe a narrower identity on the incipient nation. The surreptitious introduction of idols into the Babri Masjid at Ayodhya, where a dispute over building rights on an adjacent site had simmered since the late nineteenth century, was one such act.[13]

It is on record that Prime Minister Jawaharlal Nehru wrote insistently to the chief minister of Uttar Pradesh at the time, Gobind Ballabh Pant, demanding that the idols smuggled into the Babri Masjid be removed. Less known is his suggestion, in a 1949 letter to a Cabinet colleague, of a wider problem involving the expropriation of Muslim places of worship.[14]

Nehru's insistence on the reversal of these intrusions gradually receded from the attention span of governments at state and local levels. Ayodhya, like numerous other incidents from the time, faded into the far recesses of political attention, since nation-building had assumed an importance that promised to reduce it to triviality. The Nehruvian promise that modernity and expanding opportunity would create the Indian nation and the sovereign, civic individual, making every smaller identity irrelevant, kept the nation engaged for a while.

Democracy is an ideal that all nations like to embrace, even when they negate its principles as a matter of casual routine. The soundness of democratic practice, finally, is determined by local factors, since that is where citizen engagement begins. In the early years of India's independence, the pioneering sociologist M.N. Srinivas rendered an account of how local relations of power were being adapted into the politics of universal franchise. Srinivas found, after extensive fieldwork in his native Mysore region (in the state now known as Karnataka), that decisive power lay with the 'dominant caste', which was, as he elaborated in a 1955 essay, one that enjoyed strength in numbers while also wielding 'preponderant economic and political power'. Power relations were transformed and integrated into the electoral system, Srinivas found, through the 'vote bank' mechanism. Dominant castes were able to create 'fresh opportunities for the crystallisation of parties around patrons', each of whom controlled a 'vote bank' that could be placed 'at the disposal of a provincial or national party for a consideration which is not mentioned but implied'.[15]

Writing around the same time, Ambedkar seemed, from a politically more engaged perspective, to have in mind a like phenomenon. 'Politics is nothing if not realistic', he wrote, 'There is very little in it that is academic'. Politics could be discussed in academic terms, but there was finally no escape from the 'social structure' to which the constitutional plan is 'sought to be applied'.[16]

A debate was then underway over the linguistic reorganization of the Indian map, an idea that Ambedkar endorsed with an important caveat: every linguistic state, he said, would likely be the arena of one or the other dominant caste, which could potentially leverage social, economic and ritual status to constitute itself into a 'communal majority'. Once established in that position, these castes were all too likely to 'run away with the title deeds given to a political majority to rule'.[17]

How does the subsequent political life of India square up against these early enumerations of the opportunities embodied in the Constitution and the potential threats inherent in society?

Nation in Action: The Rituals of Democracy

India held its seventeenth general election to the Lok Sabha in 2019. Just prior to the dissolution of the sixteenth Lok Sabha, the incumbent government introduced three legislative initiatives that gave ample suggestion about its likely campaign pitch in pressing a claim to a second term.

Cumulatively, the three affirmed the Hindutva construct of nationalism and reproached all other parties for abandoning that basic identity in their anxiety to play the politics of appeasement. A concurrent judicial manoeuvre sought to reclaim the Ayodhya site—to proclaim the symbolic triumph of one faith over another.

None of the legislative measures introduced on the eve of the election was taken to fruition before polls. That seemingly was not the purpose, which was, if anything, to lay out a road map for the ruling party, were it granted a renewed mandate. After failing to hustle the Ayodhya issue through its appeal process in the Supreme Court, the Modi government briefly considered an ordinance to appropriate the land under dispute for the purpose of a temple.[18] That plan, however, was abandoned, seemingly because the executive pre-emption of a matter under judicial consideration may have been a risky flirtation with impropriety. If Ayodhya's likely impact on the course of the general election remained unquantified, the projection of the issue front and centre was a strategy the BJP sought to capitalize on.

Secularism in its uniquely Indian variant, which allowed the free play of varieties of confessionalism in the political arena, was now all about majoritarian assertion. The BJP's legislative initiatives in the last months of the sixteenth Lok Sabha clearly signalled that.

At the moment of its birth, the Indian republic adopted a definition of citizenship that was agnostic towards religious identity. A law enacted in 1955 formalized the conditions under which citizenship would be a birthright, and certain others in which it could be obtained by registration. Identity criteria were absent in the latter, a residence requirement was sufficient. An amendment proposed in 2016, referred to a select committee and reintroduced in January 2019, allowed a fast track to citizenship for members of six religious communities—Hindu, Christian, Buddhist, Sikh, Zoroastrian and Jain—admitted as refugees from three neighbouring countries of predominantly the Muslim faith.[19]

In another signature initiative, the BJP government introduced a bill that would make summary divorce under Muslim customary law—the pronouncement of the triple talaq—a criminal offence. The Supreme Court, in a majority ruling in August 2017, held the practice in breach of the basic rights of the female partner, giving anybody subject to summary divorce the remedy of civil litigation. The proposed amendment added the jeopardy of imprisonment on criminal charges, potentially depriving the male partner of access to his livelihood while imposing on him the civil liability of paying maintenance.[20]

The numbers failed to materialize at this point. Both bills had initially lapsed, since passage through the Rajya Sabha was uncertain. Passage of the bills may not have been the priority at the time, since the more important object may have been political signalling for the upcoming general election.[21] A third legislative initiative from the government in the dying days of the sixteenth Lok Sabha was nothing less than a constitutional amendment, creating a new class of entitlements for citizens who met an undefined criterion of poverty. Affirmative action, or assured opportunities in education and public-sector employment, is a time-honoured remedy for deficits of social and educational capital, but poverty-based preferences were contrary to clear judicial precedent. In its most authoritative ruling on the matter, the Supreme Court had held in the case of Indira Sawhney versus Union of India, in 1992, that reservations on an income criterion did not meet the test of constitutional validity.

Early in the year 2019, before the formal notification of the general elections to the Lok Sabha, Prime Minister Narendra Modi addressed a rally in his home constituency in the city of Varanasi. Like all politicians entering a tough campaign after a term in office, he was eager to claim significant achievements. He also seemed in retributive mood, reserving his most severe strictures for those using caste in political mobilization. He drew upon the example of Sant Ravidas, the mediaeval poet and social reformer, an icon of cultural identity for several among those denied a place in the traditional Hindu caste hierarchy, or the Dalits in today's political lexicon. 'Irrespective of caste, creed and other factors, all should get benefit of government schemes', Modi said after the ceremonial inauguration of a project commemorating Ravidas's birthplace in Varanasi.[22] This was a coded reference to a grievance that forward castes, as they are called, have for long nursed. Traditional caste privilege was often a passport to economic status, though there were several who ended in straitened circumstances after waves of disruptive change. It has been an oft-voiced grievance among those losing out in life's lottery that the Other Backward Classes (OBCs) are granted an assured share in public employment despite having all the means required for economic mobility.

Politics of Backwardness

Politics had been anxious to assuage this grievance, but measures to bring in preferences on grounds of economic disadvantage faltered at the threshold of constitutional validity. Early judicial orthodoxy held that special provisions for Socially and Economically Backward Classes (SEBCs), which is the officially mandated term, were an exception to the assurances of articles 14, 15 and 16 of the Constitution: equality before the law, freedom from discrimination and fair opportunity in public employment. In a later, more reflective phase, the Supreme Court held that reservations for those disadvantaged by caste were not an exception but a stronger affirmation of the constitutional principles. Equal treatment of unequals would be a perpetuation of inequality: the constitutional mandate went beyond the objective of avoiding fresh inequalities, in demanding that inequalities handed down by history be remedied. Within this paradigm, economic disadvantage would be redressed by the redistributive policies the State was ordained to follow under the Constitution. A special dispensation was required only where inherited deficits of social and educational capital made certain classes of citizens incapable of drawing the benefits of an economic justice agenda.[23]

In obvious disregard of the rich background of affirmative action policy, the Modi government, early in 2019, rushed through its constitutional amendment, as the sixteenth Lok Sabha was about to pass into history. A new class of entitlements came into existence for citizens meeting an undefined criterion of material deprivation. This did serious violence to the principles on which affirmative action had been built, since, as the constitutional lawyer Suhrith Parthasarathy observed, economic disability has always been viewed as 'a transient criterion', not one that put people into 'a definite group requiring special privileges'.[24]

The quota for Economically Weaker Sections was, expectedly, soon listed as a constitutional challenge before the Supreme Court. The court declined a stay in a ruling that K. Chandru, a former judge of the Madras High Court, called out for its profound illogic. The 'twin test of social and educational backwardness'—a principle the Supreme Court had once insisted on—stood diluted. Virtually '80 per cent of the population' would be entitled to reservations in accordance with the newly specified income and property thresholds. But since communities notified as SEBCs would be barred from availing the new provisions, this was effectively a 10 per cent reservation for upper castes, a quantum of privilege they would be ineligible for 'even on population basis'. With no foundation in the logic of affirmative action, Chandru concluded, the only rationale for Modi's promotion of the constitutional amendment was its potential contribution to his re-election cause.²⁵

There is no way to estimate the electoral advantage Modi gained through this legislative initiative. It was, in little time, overshadowed by a supposed military confrontation with Pakistan.²⁶ As he concluded his campaign, Modi struck a supremely confident posture, dealing rather brusquely, at a rare unscripted media interview, with the suggestion that his move on reservations was all about garnering electoral capital, particularly after a sequence of adverse results from state-level elections in December the previous year. 'Journalistic limitations', Modi alleged, were responsible for this misperception. The legislation introduced in the Lok Sabha in January 2019 had been preceded by 'two years of deliberations'. Change was triggered by the spectacle of the 'Maratha, Jat, Gujjar and Patidar agitations'. If that manner of unrest were to persist, asked Modi, 'Where will the country go?'²⁷

Modi's first term as prime minister, beginning in 2014, had seen a succession of agitations over reservations, which had peaked in 2016 and then subsided.²⁸ Modi's response to a question posed in 2019 is notable for the aggrieved castes he identifies. Except for the Gujjars, the other three classes named have been identified in sociological research as 'dominant' in their respective areas.²⁹ And even as Modi spoke out against caste discrimination, BJP-ruled states of Haryana, Gujarat and Maharashtra were eagerly committing themselves to quotas in public employment for precisely these classes of citizens.

Soon after the elections in 2019, when it was confirmed he had earned a decisive mandate, Modi addressed elected members of his party and its allies in the central hall of India's parliament. After the ovations and welcomes, he spoke for an hour and a quarter in Hindi, touching in the early part on the tendency for elections to create schisms: 'An election creates distance and erects walls. But the 2019 election has dismantled walls and joined hearts.' The supposed 'minorities' of the country had, for many years, been exploited at the polls for the numbers they could add to vote tallies but betrayed of their rights. The BJP, though, would 'regain the trust of all', irrespective of who they voted for.[30]

A prominent leader from a BJP ally in Bihar, a state where politics conventionally has been studied almost entirely in terms of caste determinants, soon afterwards proclaimed that the 2019 outcome marked the death of a variety of identity politics, eponymously named after B.P. Mandal, the chair of an officially mandated commission on backward classes. The Mandal Commission's singular recommendation was to extend the scope of affirmative action to classes that had failed to make the cut when eligibility was decided in the early years of India's independence, based on the 1931 Census. From the time this recommendation was notified as official policy in 1990, the term 'Mandal' has been associated with the fragmentation of politics into microscopic identities. The 2019 general elections did not negate caste as a 'hard reality', in the judgment of this senior BJP ally, but governance quality and other circumstances, such as rising female participation, had helped 'transcend' the arithmetic of caste.[31]

A Disappearing Act by Caste?

Was the 2019 election result about the disappearance of caste or the restoration of the natural hierarchy? For long years after Independence, the Congress, as inheritor of the mantle of nationalism from its leadership of the struggle against colonialism, remained under secure upper-caste leadership. Yet, it could count on the allegiance of a substantial number among Dalits and Muslims, enabling it to stitch together winning coalitions. This was a time when caste was not seen as a greatly influential factor in politics, since leadership was in line with the naturally ordained scheme.

The 2019 election result, the sociologist Satish Deshpande

argues, was conditioned by the fission and fusion of larger caste categories. Political competition birthed the category of 'Maha Dalit' from the 'Dalit', and 'Most Backward' from the OBC, engendering 'split groups' that had to be 'fused at a higher level for a party to win by mustering a majority'. Far from the marginalization of caste, this process suggests its maturity into a highly 'transactional and mobile category', with coalitions fissuring into smaller units and fusing afresh in the electoral arena. The BJP, in 2019, proved the most adept at the game: 'It recognised frictions within larger clusters and promised things to those dissatisfied with the existing situation. The BJP read the situation better and practised a more refined, targeted form of caste politics.'[32]

Following the early years of equanimity, the splintering, partial reconstitution and subsequent fragmentation of the Congress coalition caused years of instability. Political alliances were in a continuous state of flux as coalitions formed and fell apart in the quest of power. Through seven general elections, beginning in 1989, no party could manage a sufficiently broad coalition of social forces to win a majority in Parliament. The scenario changed with the BJP's win under Modi in 2014 and was underlined by the more definitive outcome of 2019.

If Mandal has truly been laid to rest, as the BJP partisan asserted in the euphoria of the 2019 win, the immediate implication would be relative political stability, no grounds for celebration in itself, since stability is no assurance of justice. The BJP ally's acclaim, though, goes beyond the shallow longing for political stability, suggesting that Indian politics is on the pathway towards a mode of electoral competition in which citizens shed sectarian interests to embrace a wider civic norm of good governance.

Has the BJP really been transformed as a party? Well before the 2019 election cycle began, two political journalists carried out a fine-toothed analysis of the leadership tiers of the BJP and found that it remained 'a Brahmin–Baniya club', or to translate that term of art into ordinary language, a coalition of the upper castes traditionally associated with the ritualist and mercantilist functions within the social order. With all the strategies adopted to broaden its appeal, the party remained 'predominantly upper-caste' in its organizational structure. An 'in-depth analysis of the caste profile of the BJP's organisation structure' had found, in fact, 'that over three-fourths of the party's office bearers at the national level are upper caste and over 60 per cent of its national executive is drawn from the general category'.[33]

The new normal of the transcendence of caste may well be a rather thin camouflage for the restoration, particularly in the Hindi belt, of upper-caste dominance. The representation here of Scheduled Castes (SCs) and Scheduled Tribes (STs), or Dalit and Adivasi in more explicit language, has remained fairly constant through the years, reflecting their inability to expand beyond reserved seats. Upper-caste representation, with just a few fluctuations, fell between 1989 and 2004, before picking up dramatically in 2009, sustaining itself in 2014 and then marginally diminishing in 2019. OBC representation rose again, with minor fluctuations between 1989 and 2004, and fell sharply in 2009, before recovering through the next two electoral cycles.[34]

This indicates that till 2009, OBCs were gaining or losing inversely as the forward castes in the Hindi belt. Muslim representation trended roughly in the same direction as the OBCs till 2004. In 2009, both OBCs and Muslims suffered a sharp drop in representation, cumulatively totalling 20 seats in the Lok Sabha, while the upper castes increased their representation by 23. In 2014, upper castes maintain their numbers, though Muslim representation fell by six, while OBCs increased their seats by seven.[35] These numbers point towards the creation of a new electoral template of upper-caste alliance with the OBCs. In 2019, the OBCs increased their seats, though only marginally, while upper-caste representation fell by eight seats. In rather hostile circumstances, in a challenge however feeble to the consolidation of upper-caste and OBC votes, Muslim representation increased from four in the Hindi belt to 10. This limited recovery of Muslim representation in 2019 occurred at the expense of the upper castes. Indeed, the entire gain of six seats that candidates of the Muslim faith registered was within the largest state of the country, Uttar Pradesh—from zero representation in 2014 to six seats in the Lok Sabha in 2019.[36] This was the consequence of an alliance between two long-estranged parties, the Samajwadi Party (SP) and the Bahujan Samaj Party (BSP) that had famously joined forces once before, in 1993, to push back the BJP when its victory in the first Vidhan Sabha election after the demolition of the Ayodhya mosque seemed almost foreordained. Unlike then, the alliance had only limited success in 2019, showing how the dynamics of caste alliances had been transformed from the ground up in the intervening quarter century. A consolidation of the SP and BSP constituencies may have been a conceivable political project in the early 1990s, but the subsequent fission and fusion of caste groups made it an alliance of limited strategic utility in 2019.

Return of the Hard-Line Agenda

Soon after the electoral triumph, the Modi government turned its focus to the legislative initiatives put on hold since the last days of the earlier Parliament. In August 2019, it pushed through the law criminalizing summary divorce through the triple talaq.[37] Days later, it contrived, through a contentious manoeuvre, to have both houses of Parliament declare the pretence of autonomy granted India's only Muslim-majority state, Jammu and Kashmir (J&K), a thing of the past. In December 2019, it secured the passage of the Citizenship (Amendment) Act (CAA), which created a fast track to Indian citizenship for refugees of six defined religious groups, not including Islam, from three neighbouring countries of predominantly the Islamic faith.[38]

A selective morality spoke out loud in the concern shown for refugees from Muslim-majority countries in India's neighbourhood. Early in 2018, contesting a petition to halt the forced repatriation of Rohingya Muslim refugees who had fled military atrocities in Myanmar, the government submitted to the Supreme Court that India could not become the 'refugee capital of the world'. Since then, there has been a pattern of hostile actions against Rohingya refugees across settlements in India.[39]

Alibis could be offered for this pattern of behaviour, none really viable.[40] In the assessment of a formally accredited United Nations inquiry, the Rohingya are refugees from a cycle of violence that has 'all the hallmarks of genocide'.[41] Leaving aside this ethical concern, India's reluctance to bear the Rohingya refugee burden could be a consequence of economic incapacity—except that this plea would not square with India's eagerness to accept people of six other faiths with a fast-track offer of citizenship.

The CAA was one among the two instrumentalities deployed to alter the conditions of citizenship entitlements in India. A quite distinct process—the National Register of Citizens (NRC)—had been underway in the northeastern state of Assam, as part of an accord concluded in 1986, following years of agitation against supposed infiltrators by a student body claiming to represent truly native people. The NRC had been delayed long years because of the sheer complexity of separating citizen from immigrant in a region of shifting topographies and diverse ethnicities, where identity papers are a rarity for current, not to mention past, generations. When the first iteration of the NRC was completed in July 2018, no fewer than four million of Assam's recorded population of 33 million was confronted with the prospect of a stateless future. In neighbouring West Bengal, there was an explosion of fury, since most of those threatened with this grim prospect were of Bengali ethnicity and the Islamic faith.

Nation in Action: The Rituals of Democracy

The first draft of the CAA, introduced in December 2017, threatened to undo all the political capital the BJP had gained with the NRC exercise. Assamese ethnic nationalism had secured the reward of the NRC but was fearful of losing some supposed gains. Even with the exclusion of Islam, it was seen as a sufficient threat if people of other faiths, believed to have trickled over the border from Bangladesh, were granted citizenship. The NRC may have been a strategic choice the BJP made to run the gauntlet of Bengali ire for the political reward of consolidation in Assam and other northeastern states, where immigration triggers deep sensitivities. But soon afterwards, the CAA overturned that calculation. The Asom Gana Parishad (AGP), successor to the student body that negotiated the Assam Accord, pulled out of its alliance with the BJP amid a wave of protest, though the estrangement was brief.

In course of the 2019 election campaign, Prime Minister Modi and his loyal understudy Amit Shah, then president of the ruling party, seemed to hit upon a new scheme—of the CAA and NRC in combination being a sorting mechanism between citizens and others. In border regions of mixed ethnic demography, Shah spoke of illegal infiltrators as 'termites' attacking the vitals of the nation.[42] The BJP manifesto for the election spoke of the 'huge change in the cultural and linguistic identity of some areas due to illegal immigration', and the consequent 'adverse impact on local people's livelihood and employment'. As a remedy, the BJP vowed to 'expeditiously complete the National Register of Citizens process in these areas on priority'. Following this, the BJP manifesto vowed that the NRC would be implemented 'in a phased manner in other parts of the country'.[43]

On the campaign trail in West Bengal, Shah was reported saying that 'every single infiltrator' would be removed, except those of the Buddhist, Hindu and Sikh faiths. At about the same time, the official Twitter handle of the BJP posted a vow to 'ensure implementation of NRC in the entire country'.[44] These were not mere flourishes reserved for the campaign trail. Ensconced after the election in the home ministry, effectively then the second-most powerful position in the Modi government, Shah served up the same narrative within Parliament. It was July 2019, and the first full session of Parliament since the Modi government began its second term, an occasion conventionally used to lay out priorities. And Shah was emphatic about removing illegal immigrants through an NRC of widening expanse. The government would ensure that no illegal immigrant would be registered under the NRC, he vowed. 'The NRC is part of the Assam Accord and was also in [BJP's] election manifesto based on which the government has come to power. The government will identify illegal immigrants living on every inch of the country's soil and will deport them as per the international law.'[45]

It is easy to see why the envisaged process of sorting between immigrant and citizen stirred deep anxieties. The CAA is neither about refugee rights nor the expression of a humanitarian instinct: the text of the amendment does not once use the word 'refugee'. India is not a signatory to the Refugee Convention, extended without geographical limitations in 1967, after its initial formulation in 1951, to address Second World War dislocations in Europe. India, indeed, does not have any manner of law for refugees, only exceptions decreed by executive fiat to the definition of an 'illegal migrant'.

Refugees are identified as exceptions to the provisions of immigration law. In this conflicted scenario, the CAA came as a rude intrusion, waiving the 'illegal migrant' tag for persons from three neighbouring Muslim-majority countries, subject to them being from six identified religious groups. While introducing the Bill in Parliament, Shah spoke of a 'minority' from neighbouring countries of Muslim predominance as a 'reasonable classification', permitting a special provision, without violating the equality stipulation in Article 14 of the Indian constitution.[46] There was unintended irony in the sharp contrast between this concern for minorities in countries where Islam is the dominant faith and the BJP's insistence within the domestic context that India's minorities did not merit any distinct status.

Equality in the Constitution trumps identity. An individual at birth was deemed to gain an identity through various rituals specific to her community. Rituals of the community did not yet give her the full range of entitlements promised by the State, since citizenship is conferred through the bureaucratic process of registration. From a study by the Census Commissioner and Registrar-General of India, we know that in 2001, three decades after birth and death registrations were made mandatory, a mere 58 per cent of all births had been registered.[47] In other words, almost half the population born at the turn of the century, all of whom would have attained voting age by the 2019 general elections, were devoid of the evidence testifying to their arrival on earth. Their identity as citizens eligible to vote would have been negotiated along the way, each person concluding a separate bargain with local authorities.

Improvements since the dawn of the millennium were no more than marginal. The Registrar General found that by 2010, 82 per cent of births were being registered.[48] Yet, a *Rapid Survey of Children*, carried out by the Ministry of Women and Child Development, found that only 72 per cent of births had been registered over the year 2013–14. More critically, only 37 per cent of the sample could produce a birth certificate when asked. The numbers that failed both tests were fractionally below the national average among both the Hindu and Muslim faiths, marking one dubious respect in which the Indian state has delivered on its promise of equality before the law. The average was pulled up by smaller minority faiths like Christianity, Jainism, Sikhism and neo-Buddhism.[49]

In the context of the NRC proposed alongside the 2021 Census, the CAA could conceivably have been a filter through which undocumented persons of certain faiths could be saved from a limbo of statelessness. For people of the faith that is the CAA's singular omission, disenfranchisement and disentitlement were a very concrete prospect. When the protests began after the amendment to the citizenship law, there was a different story emerging. Modi first denounced the agitators as 'recognisable by their clothes', in one of many ways to ostracize and isolate the protests.[50] He then took the plea that the CAA does not threaten any person with the loss of citizenship, since its intent was the reverse: to confer citizenship on the persecuted in neighbouring countries.

In December 2019, as the protests across the country gained momentum, Modi addressed a political rally in Delhi. His government never had the slightest intent of implementing an NRC, he declared, except in Assam, where an obligation had been handed down and enforced by a Supreme Court diktat.[51] This erasure of the whole record of campaign utterances by Modi's closest political associate and the explicit mandate that the BJP had assumed in its election manifesto passed without serious comment.

Good faith being nowhere in evidence in these reassurances, the protests continued, eliciting a furious response, particularly in states ruled by the BJP. Over 30 people were killed in police crackdowns on protesters in Uttar Pradesh, Assam and Karnataka. In Delhi, a state ruled by a rival party, though with the Union Government controlling law and order, the police raided the Jamia Millia Islamia, a university steeped in India's Islamic modernism, cutting a swathe through the library, roughing up students and breaking and overturning furniture. Police action in Uttar Pradesh was much more severe.[52]

Following the attack on Jamia Millia, residents of the adjacent neighbourhood of Shaheen Bagh spontaneously assembled to register their protests at a busy intersection. In quick time, the spontaneous gathering of local residents acquired a small makeshift pavilion and began attracting visitors and expressions of solidarity. Similar gatherings soon sprang up in other parts of the country.[53] Global public opinion was captivated by the protests and, in most part, repulsed by India's effort to tamper with its citizenship law. The government's embarrassment only mounted as the Shaheen Bagh vigil extended into the last week of February, when US President Donald Trump was scheduled to visit Delhi.

The virulence of the public rhetoric from the governmental side began rising at this time. A young MP of the ruling party gave out a call to 'shoot the traitors'. Soon afterwards, though no clear linkage can be established without the rigorous police investigation that was conspicuously absent, there was a clumsy bullet fired at the Shaheen Bagh protesters by a rootless vigilante. A few days later, another BJP functionary, with a senior police officer standing by indulgently, sent out the threat that if the demonstrations in various locations in Delhi were not cleared up within a specified deadline, he would take matters into his own hands.[54]

That was the trigger for days of violence across a vast stretch of Delhi's eastern suburbs, mostly home to the working class and the poor. All the abuses of fair policing principles seen in Uttar Pradesh through the first phase of the protests in December were reprised in Delhi through the February riots. Police were often inciting the rioters and joining them in inflicting violence on Muslim lives and property.[55]

A familiar book of rules was brought into play in the aftermath: of ignoring provocative words and violence from the majority side and targeting the minority in ways that went beyond fair law enforcement. Petitions by spirited public individuals and civil rights activists, demanding criminal cases against the BJP leaders who had instigated violence, were left to languish in the labyrinthine pathways of the Indian judicial process. Arrests were made on the basis of wildly conflicting eyewitness accounts. Perhaps because of the mere fact that global attention was focused on the official response to the violence, there was an effort to apprehend at least a token number from the majority side: nowhere near proportional to their actual involvement in the violence but seemingly just enough to deflect scrutiny.

The pretence at even-handed administration of justice was not sustained for long. Around the middle of July 2020, the press reported worries in the higher echelons of the police hierarchy over 'resentment' at the arrest of 'some Hindu youth' from Delhi's riot-hit areas. Worries were acute enough for a senior police officer, with overall responsibility for criminal investigations, to send out a circular advising caution: 'Due care and precaution', he warned, should be taken in effecting arrests.[56]

Just two weeks afterwards, the Delhi High Court, in hearing a petition questioning the fairness of the investigations, asked the police administration about the 'necessity' of such a circular. This manner of instruction in criminal cases was perhaps irregular, though there could be occasion for senior officers to 'guide' the investigators in accordance with the prevalent situation. To set minds at rest, the judge directed the police to place on record five similar letters issued in earlier contingencies. These were to be filed 'in a sealed cover within two days'.[57]

The submission of vital evidence in 'sealed covers' has been an increasing judicial recourse in recent years. Its implications for the demands of fair process and open justice remain, for some reason, unexamined.[58] In normal circumstances, the plea that the information came from 'intelligence input' is adequate to placate judicial anxieties about the irregularity of the process. In the instance of the Delhi riots, a similar strategy was in evidence. The cautionary letter issued from the top of the Delhi police hierarchy, counsel submitted, had been informed by 'an intelligence input...received through some agency'. This effort at obfuscation did not escape the attention of the court, which rebuffed the contention that the petition was 'mischievous' and deserved to be dismissed with a cost penalty. In defiance of the facts, counsel for the police then insisted that there was no effort to single out any particular community, since the circular pertained to all.[59]

Electoral Minorities and the Litigation Option

The story of India's democracy could be narrated as an effort at negotiating the tensions of an inherited social order and the traumas of colonial history, without frontally addressing them. The universal adult franchise made politics a competitive exercise in recruiting mass loyalties and also potentially an arena for an uncontrolled clash of group identities. This would have been a suicidal course for a nation born in the clash of religious identities, not fully placated in a bitter partition. There was also the unappeased resentment of an excluded segment, the Dalits and others consigned to a ritually inferior status under the religious tradition that, after Partition, sought to impose its identity on the Indian nation.

The Constitution assured all citizens of equality before the law, opportunity and freedom from discrimination. But no specific favour was extended to citizens of the Muslim faith, rendered leaderless and rudderless by a forced partition, yet also compelled to bear its stigma as a collective burden. As a salve to bruised sensitivities, the Muslim minority was given the assurance of identity, even if equality was not an immediate prospect. People of the Muslim faith were allowed to stay out of the proposal to reform personal laws in 1951, an effort led by Ambedkar that faltered over the opposition of Hindu orthodoxy.

Other token concessions were extended at regular intervals, giving the communal leadership just enough to retain the loyalty of the flock, which they could parlay into an assured vote for the ruling party of the time. But the processes of popular representation were always under pressure from the majoritarian impulse, impelling the Muslim community to seek redress through litigation. Rohit De argues that in the early years of India's independence, 'electoral minorities', i.e. communities of caste and religion that were unlikely to 'represent themselves through electoral democracy', were overrepresented in litigation invoking the writ jurisdiction of newly established constitutional courts. The Ayodhya petition claiming the restitution of a monument commandeered in the name of another faith was one such instance.[60]

Constitutional assurances and the fiercely asserted independence of the higher judiciary might have given hope at one time to those seeking fair treatment despite a drift towards majoritarianism. That expectation has gradually ebbed away. Prolonged inaction over Ayodhya was one among the factors contributing to the loss of faith. In 1986, when the locks on the structure were opened for worshipers to offer obeisance at the idols that had been surreptitiously introduced in the tortured aftermath of Partition, the judiciary did little. After the demolition of the structure, when called upon to definitively establish its writ over the disputed space and assert its commitment to the rule of law, it meekly gave in to a petition demanding the right to offer prayers at the makeshift shrine assembled after the vandalism.

Since then, the balance has gradually shifted. In 2010, the Lucknow bench of the Allahabad High Court, in a parody of Solomonic justice, ruled that the space occupied by two of the domes of the demolished structure should go to the Hindu faith, while the Muslim side could retain possession of one. This was set aside as 'perverse' on first sight by the Supreme Court, since neither of the petitioners had even remotely asked for a partition. But then the Supreme Court went ahead with its own rather muddled approach, delving into theological issues of territory and its centrality to the profession of faith. In 2018, while hearing a petition challenging the government's assumption of ownership over the territory of the Babri Masjid, the Supreme Court declined to intervene, since it was not competent to determine the 'comparative significance' of the land for various faiths. In this manner, while seeming to hold the scales even between all faiths, it placed the violent political campaign to reclaim the site on the same moral foundation as the fact of historical possession.

In November 2019, the Supreme Court delivered its final blow in a judgment that went without the signature of any one among the five judges on the Constitution Bench. Several pages into its long and digressive judgment on the Ayodhya title dispute, after many an excursus into the discipline of archaeology, the Supreme Court bench admitted that it had been embarked on an exercise in irrelevance. 'A finding of title', it pronounced, 'cannot be based…on…archaeological findings'. Likewise, after long expeditions to uncover textual records from history, the bench pleaded its inability to 'entertain claims that stem from the actions of the Mughal rulers against Hindu places of worship'. India's history, the Supreme Court wrote, is 'replete with actions that have been judged to be morally incorrect and are liable to trigger vociferous ideological debate'. But none of that could be dug up today for a settling of scores, since that 'watershed moment' when India adopted its republican constitution also brought liberation from the unappeased grievances of the past, both real and imagined. That was when 'we, the people of India'—as the resonant phrase in the Preamble put it—'departed from the determination of rights and liabilities on the basis of our ideology, our religion, the colour of our skin, or the century when our ancestors arrived at these lands'. It was when all Indian citizens 'submitted to the rule of law'.[61]

Heroic so far in squaring impossible circles, the Supreme Court then wandered into a deep moral quandary. Cutting through the mythology that has surrounded the act of trespass of 1949, the Supreme Court declared it a 'desecration of the mosque and the ouster of the Muslims otherwise than by the due process of law'. And then came the final act of destruction on 6 December 1992, when a monument with hoary references to India's history was effaced, in what the court recognized as 'an egregious violation of the rule of law'.[62]

The abiding mystery with the Supreme Court's ruling on Ayodhya, as the Indian Republic marches ahead, would be to negotiate the complicated routine through which the worst violators of the rule of law were awarded virtually undiluted title to the land. The victims of this cycle of physical and rhetorical violence were placated through the award of 5 acres in the near vicinity of Ayodhya, for the 2.77 acres lost. Evidently, the Supreme Court has decreed that the injuries to an entire religious community's sense of identity and belonging could be easily redressed through the seeming generosity of a land grant.

As the Constituent Assembly debated the issue of fundamental rights and heard representations from the diminishing and disempowered spokespersons of communities who argued for a charter of minority rights, Govind Ballabh Pant came up with a lofty response, rendered perhaps from his privileged perch as an upper-caste person. Pant's attitude and that of the Constituent Assembly in general has been likened by scholars such as Christophe Jaffrelot to a 'Jacobin' position, after the French revolutionary faction that insisted on the extinction of all intermediary loyalties between the citizen and the State, since in a republican order, none of these distinctions would have any reason to exist.[63]

Speaking in the Constituent Assembly, Pant deprecated the 'morbid tendency' to disregard the 'individual citizen who is really the backbone of the State, the pivot, the cardinal centre of all social activity, and whose happiness and satisfaction should be the goal of every social mechanism'. The citizen, Pant regretted, had been lost in the 'body known as the community' because of the 'degrading habit of thinking always in terms of communities and never in terms of citizens'.[64]

When the intrusion into the Ayodhya mosque took place under his watch as chief minister of Uttar Pradesh, Pant proved a little less mindful of the principle of equal citizenship. On 5 February 1950, Prime Minister Nehru wrote to Pant, asking that he be kept 'informed of the Ayodhya situation'. The matter was of 'great importance' because of 'its repercussions on all-India affairs and more especially Kashmir'.[65] Letters urging special attention to the dispute at Ayodhya were also written by Sardar Patel and other political leaders and social workers.

The Gandhian social worker Akshay Brahmachari placed the intrusion into the mosque in a wider context of hostile actions against the religious minority in Ayodhya. It would be short-sighted, he warned, to view the whole sequence of events as a simple 'Hindu–Muslim dispute'. There had been, as he recorded in a memorandum submitted to the state government and a succession of letters to Uttar Pradesh Home Minister Lal Bahadur Shastri, the desecration of several grave sites adjoining the mosque. The power of the state government, moreover, had been used in usurping commercial property that rightfully belonged to a person of the minority faith. A hotel in the town that belonged to a 'nationalist Muslim', he recorded, had been forcibly vacated by the district magistrate, who had then handed it over to a person of his choice. The allegation against the erstwhile proprietor was that he had rented out rooms to a number of co-religionists who came to the town heavily armed, with intent to cause violence. Police investigations, though, had revealed that all the men who had checked in at the hotel were unarmed and travelling for legitimate business purposes. Yet, the district magistrate had refused to undo the wrongful expropriation of Muslim property. For his pains in bringing to light these wrongful acts, Brahmachari recorded, he had suffered threats of violence and accusations of being indifferent to people of his own faith.⁶⁶

Little, however, was done on the ground. In a statement to the State Legislative Assembly on 14 September 1950, Chief Minister Pant addressed every one of these issues, testifying to the veracity of the information that Brahmachari had gathered. On the desecration of graves, he said that all possible action was being taken where the culprits could be identified. But on the Babri Masjid itself, he pleaded inability to do much, since the matter by then was sub judice.⁶⁷

Perhaps the entire saga may have vanished into the rabbit hole of history had not the course of Indian democracy exposed its assurances of republican equality as a thin cover for caste privilege. From being an unstated premise, sectarianism was officially reintroduced into India's electoral politics in the 1980s, when the foundations of upper-caste hegemony began to falter. The Ayodhya dispute was one among many manifestations of this moment of crisis. It was to play out with fateful consequences in the years that followed.

Notes

1   *Constituent Assembly Debates, Official Report, Volume X*, Lok Sabha Secretariat, Delhi, 2009, p. 979.
2   There is extensive literature available on Gandhi's epic fast of 1932, when he finally defeated Ambedkar's effort at gaining a separate electorate for the untouchables. See: Lelyveld, Joseph, *Great Soul: Mahatma Gandhi and His Struggle with India*, HarperCollins, New Delhi, 2016; Guha, Ramachandra, *Gandhi: The Years That Changed the World, 1914–48*, Penguin Random House, 2018, pp. 433–44. Ambedkar's own rather more acerbic observations were set down in the book *What Congress and Gandhi Have Done to the Untouchables* (Thacker, Bombay, 1946).

3   Ambedkar, B.R., 'Thoughts on Linguistic States', *Dr Babasaheb Ambedkar's Writings and Speeches*, Volume I, Vasant Moon (ed.), Education Deprtment, Government of Maharashtra, Mumbai, 1979, p. 167.
4   This was the case of Champakam Dorairajan versus State of Madras, decided in 1951. See: Galanter, Marc, *Competing Equalities: Law and the Backward Classes in India*, Oxford University Press, 1991.
5   Galanter, Marc, 'The Aborted Restoration of "Indigenous" Law in India', *Comparative Studies in Society and History*, vol. 14, no. 1, January 1972, p. 56; Singh, Tripurdaman, *Sixteen Stormy Days*, Penguin Random House, Delhi, 2020, pp. 1–2. Another irritant that cropped up in the early days of the Republic was with the Supreme Court invalidating significant land reforms and tenancy legislation on grounds that these violated the fundamental right to property.
6   The 'Congress for unity, Muslim League for Partition' account of modern Indian history has been dominant since Independence and Partition. For an account of how this fails to render justice to the complexity of the events, see Roy, Asim, 'The High Politics of India's Partition: The Revisionist Perspective', *Modern Asian Studies*, vol. 24, no. 2, May 1990, pp. 385–408.
7   The clause has had a varied career and, despite infirmities in interpretation, proved fairly robust when the judiciary was called upon to determine the constitutional validity of President Donald Trump's move, early in his term in 2017, to ban the entry of citizens from a number of Muslim-majority countries. It took three revisions of the hastily assembled executive order by a president who had made several statements of intent on the campaign trail before the US Supreme Court permitted the executive action, overruling a number of lower court decisions by the narrowest margin of one on a nine-judge bench. In doing so, the bench also chided Trump for his frequent public utterances suggesting that religious animus rather than security calculations lay behind the move.

8   'Article 25: Freedom of conscience and free profession, practice and propagation of religion', Constitution of India 1950, https://bit.ly/3JbVckz. Accessed on 6 April 2022.

9   The multiple layers and themes of the Constituent Assembly debates on religion are usefully presented in Bajpai, Rochana, *Debating Difference: Group Rights and Liberal Democracy in India*, Oxford University Press, New Delhi, 2011; Tejani, Shabnum, *Indian Secularism: A Social and Intellectual History 1890–1950*, Permanent Black, Delhi, 2007.

10 Bajpai, Rochana, *Debating Difference: Group Rights and Liberal Democracy in India*, Oxford University Press, New Delhi, 2011, pp. 52–53, p. 120, p. 122.

11 The theme is addressed in Bajpai, Rochana, 'Chapter 4', *Debating Difference: Group Rights and Liberal Democracy in India*, Oxford University Press, New Delhi, 2011; Tejani, Shabnum, *Indian Secularism: A Social and Intellectual History 1890–1950*, Permanent Black, Delhi, 2007, pp. 257–60. Jaffrelot Christophe in his book *Religion, Caste and Politics in India* (Hurst and Company, London, 2011, p. 7) describes the outcome of Constituent Assembly debate on the question as a 'Jacobin' rejection of communities, after the French revolutionary faction to which is ascribed the denial of any intermediary level of belonging between the citizen and the modern nation state.

12 In 2007, the National Commission for Religious and Linguistic Minorities, headed by former Chief Justice of India, Ranganath Mishra, in its's report (Ministry of Minority Affairs, Delhi, 2007, p. 4) observed that the words 'minority' and 'minorities' occur frequently in the Constitution, without ever being defined at any point. Under the National Commission on Minorities Act, passed in 1992, a 'minority' is any social group that is defined as such by the central government.

13 Jha, Krishna, and Dhirendra K. Jha, *Ayodhya, The Dark Night*, HarperCollins, New Delhi, 2012; Noorani, A.G., *The Babri Masjid Question: 'A Matter of National Honour'*, Volume I, Tulika Books,

Delhi, 2003. The reader can find an exceptionally detailed and vivid reconstruction of the events in the former, while the latter provides the documentary record.

14 On 24 September 1948, Nehru wrote to the minister of works and housing, reporting a conversation in which Maulana Abul Kalam Azad had informed Sardar Patel of some 15 mosques in Delhi, 'which had been converted into some kind of temples with an idol installed inside them'. That was seemingly the first that Nehru had heard about it, and he recorded how Patel was 'most anxious to remove these temple emblems', though preferably without using the police and in a 'cooperative' fashion. Nehru underlined the 'great significance' of the matter and urged that the matter be given 'some priority'. See: 'Letter to Mehr Chand Khanna,' *Selected Works of Jawaharlal Nehru*, Volume 7, S. Gopal (ed), Jawaharlal Nehru Memorial Fund, New Dlehi, 1988, p. 16.

15 Quoted in: Björkman, Lisa, and Jeffrey Witsoe, 'Money and Votes: Following Flows Through Mumbai and Bihar', *Costs of Democracy: Political Finance in India*, Devesh Kapur and Milan Vaishnava (eds), Oxford University Press, New Delhi, 2018, p. 155.

16 Ambedkar, B.R., 'Thoughts on Linguistic States', *Dr Babasaheb Ambedkar's Writings and Speeches*, Volume I, Vasant Moon (ed.), Education Deprtment, Government of Maharashtra, Mumbai, 1979, p. 167, p. 169.

17 Ibid.

18 'Narendra Modi's big play for Ayodhya could backfire', *The Indian Express*, 31 January 2019, https://bit.ly/3avtFPE. Accessed on 30 May 2022.

19 Pratt, David, 'The proposed new law threatening to tear India apart', *The National*, 22 December 2019, https://bit.ly/3LPzUet. Accessed on 8 April 2022.

20 Following the final passage of the Act in 2019, an appeal was filed in the Supreme Court challenging its constitutionality on these grounds. See: 'Criminalization of triple talaq challenged in Supreme

Court and Delhi High Court', *mint*, 3 August 2019, https://tinyurl.com/ycxp84am. Accessed 25 May 2022.

21. In the event, the bills were passed soon after the BJP won the general election: the Muslim Women (Protection of Rights on Marriage) Act was passed on 25 July 2019 and the Citizenship (Amendment) Act on 12 December 2019.

22. 'All should get benefit of govt schemes irrespective of caste, creed & other factors: PM Modi', *ThePrint*, 19 February 2019, https://tinyurl.com/y68cxmz5. Accessed on 27 April 2022; 'Narendra Modi says those mocking Vande Bharat Express should be "punished at the right time"', *Scroll.in* 19 February 2019, https://tinyurl.com/3vy6sa39. Accessed on 27 April 2022.

23. Galanter, Marc, *Competing Equalities, Law and the Backward Classes in India*, Oxford University Press, 1991, pp. 386–95. The definitive ruling on affirmative action remains the Supreme Court in the case of Indra Sawhney versus Union of India, AIR 1993 SC 477, 1992 Supp 2 SCR 454.

24. Parthasarathy, Suhrith, 'A test of law and justice', *The Hindu*, 4 December 2021, https://bit.ly/3JfZc3K. Accessed on 8 April 2022.

25. Ashraf, Ajaz, '"The Supreme Court has erred': Former Madras HC judge K Chandru on EWS and Maratha reservations', *The Caravan*, 20 July 2019, https://bit.ly/35SYegf. Accessed on 8 April 2022.

26. Ashley Tellis, an India-sympathetic person within the US strategic community, writing three weeks after the supposed airstrikes against terrorist-staging posts deep within Pakistan, had this rather ambiguous assessment to offer: '[T]he confusing welter of claims and counterclaims about the military action on both sides continues… Definitive answers appear elusive at the moment, despite insistent probing within South Asia and by the larger international community'. See: 'A Smoldering Volcano: Pakistan and Terrorism after Balakot', Carnegie Endowment for International Peace, 14 March 2019, https://tinyurl.com/yc88c3pd. Accessed on 23 June 2022.

27. Jha, Raj Kamal, and Ravish Tiwari, 'Prime Minister Narendra Modi

Interview to Indian Express: "Khan Market gang hasn't created my image, 45 years of tapasya has... you cannot dismantle it", *The Indian Express*, 13 May 2019, https://bit.ly/3xdN94n. Accessed on 8 April 2022.

28 Ibid.

29 Ibid. It is also pertinent to note here that Modi was not inclined to lay the blame for the disruptive agitations on the identified caste groups alone. To a question about why he had mentioned these three communities specifically, Modi warned against seeing the issue only through this limited 'prism'. 'The large number of NGOs that operate with support from foreign funds', he said, 'have also been involved in creating an unrest like this'. The identification of 'dominant castes' is from Ambedkar's, 'Thoughts on Linguistic States', in *Dr Babasaheb Ambedkar, Writings and Speeches* (Volume I, Vasant Moon (ed.), Education Deprtment, Government of Maharashtra, Mumbai, 1979, pp. 167-69). There will be more discussion later on these matters.

30 Translation by the author. The full address is available at the YouTube channel of Rajya Sabha TV, 2019, the public service broadcaster managed by the Upper House of the Indian parliament. See: https://www.youtube.com/watch?v=8XIqnmtowns. Accessed on 4 May 2022.

31 Hebbar, Nistula, 'End of Mandal era, says Bihar JD(U) chief Bashistha Narayan Singh', *The Hindu*, 29 May 2019, https://tinyurl.com/2k3dfhud. Accessed on 29 June 2022. Also see: Deshpande, Ashwini, 'Reiforcing caste hierarchies: on Maratha quota', *The Hindu*, 9 July 2019, https://bit.ly/39esMKx. Accessed on 27 April 2022.

32 Ashraf, Ajaz, 'Hindutva has done more for upper-caste politics than what was thought possible: Satish Deshpande', *The Caravan*, 27 July 2019, https://bit.ly/3y0O0G6. Accessed on 27 April 2022.

33 Tewari, Ruhi, and Pragya Kaushika, 'We analysed 1,000 BJP leaders & found the party remains a Brahmin-Baniya club', *ThePrint*, 1 August 2018, https://bit.ly/3vN5HpV. Accessed on 27 April 2022.

The 'general' category here refers to social classes that are not eligible for any form of affirmative action.

34 Jaffrelot, Christophe, and Gilles Verniers, 'Explained: In Hindi heartland, upper castes dominate new Lok Sabha', *The Indian Express*, 27 May 2019, https://bit.ly/3Mx4qdf. Accessed on 27 April 2022.

35 Ibid.

36 Ibid.

37 '"Historic" day as India outlaws "triple talaq" Islamic instant divorce', *The Guardian*, 31 July 2019, https://bit.ly/3vjF50C. Accessed on 27 April 2022.

38 Jain, Bharti, 'CAA a compassionate, limited Act, says MHA', *The Times of India*, 26 April 2022, https://bit.ly/3MvYMZ5. Accessed on 27 April 2022.

39 'India can't become world's refugee capital, Centre tells Supreme Court in Rohingya deportation case', *Scroll.in*, 31 January 2018, https://bit.ly/3rViw0m. Accessed on 27 April 2022.

40 The UN Convention on Refugees, agreed in 1951, prohibits the forced repatriation of refugees in situations where they would be exposed to danger. But India is not a signatory to the convention and can claim freedom from this principle of 'non-refoulement'. India is, however, a signatory to the UN Convention against Torture, which spells out a clear principle in Article 3 that no State party 'shall expel, return or extradite a person to another state where there are substantial grounds for believing that he would be in danger of being subjected to torture'. But India's signing of the convention in 1997, in what seemed a brief visitation of ethical responsibility under the I.K. Gujral government, was not followed by its ratification.

41 '"Hallmarks of genocide": ICC prosecutor seeks justice for Rohingya', *The Guardian*, 10 April 2018, https://bit.ly/3KhgGx3. Accessed on 27 April 2022.

42 'Amit Shah Calls Illegal Immigrants "Termites", Says BJP Will

Remove Them If Voted To Power In 2019', *HuffPost*, 23 September 2018, https://bit.ly/3ERpaKc. Accessed on 27 April 2022.

43 BJP 2019 Manifesto, *Sankalp Bharat, Sashakt Bharat*, p. 11, https://bit.ly/3vO7Xx3. Accessed on 27 April 2022.

44 Griffiths, James, and Manveena Suri, 'Outrage over BJP promise to "remove every single infiltrator" from India', CNN, 12 April 2019, https://cnn.it/3KiYCCL. Accessed on 27 April 2022.

45 FE Online, 'Nationwide NRC soon? Amit Shah promises to rid "every inch" of India from illegal immigrants', *Financial Express*, 17 July 2019, https://bit.ly/36Qgbwi. Accessed on 27 April 2022.

46 'Citizenship (Amendment) Bill: Amit Shah says Indian Muslims have nothing to fear', *The Economic Times*, 11 December 2019, https://bit.ly/3wWVZTz. Accessed on 30 May 2022.

47 Registrar General of India, Vital Statistics of India Based on the Civil Registration System, Ministry of Home Affairs, 2010, p. 28.

48 Ibid.

49 Ministry of Women and Child Development, Government of India, *Rapid Survey on Children, 2013–14, National Report*, https://tinyurl.com/527kzv67. Accessed on 30 May 2022.

50 'Citizenship Act: Protestors "creating violence can be identified by their clothes", claims Modi', *Scroll.in*, 15 December 2019, https://bit.ly/39oCH0j. Accessed on 28 April 2022.

51 'PM Modi counters what Amit Shah, BJP manifesto say on bringing all-India NRC', *India Today*, 22 December 2019, https://bit.ly/37NolpK. Accessed on 28 April 2022.

52 '"Shoot the Traitors": Discrimination Against Muslims under India's New Citizenship Policy', Human Rights Watch, 9 April 2020, https://tinyurl.com/yva6p9wk. Accessed on 28 April 2022.

53 Ibid.

54 Kapil Mishra, the BJP leader, spoke in the presence of a deputy commissioner of police. His statement was widely reported and led to a petition in the Delhi High Court, asking for his prosecution for inciting communal animus and violence. A video

recording of the day can be found here: https://www.youtube.com/watch?v=c64KynJC1X8. Accessed on 23 June 2022.

55 Delhi Minorities Commission, Government of NCT of Delhi, *Report of the DMC Fact-Finding Committee on North-east Delhi Riots of February 2020*, pp. 99, https://tinyurl.com/2yk8kvcv. Accessed on 29 June 2022. Also see: Khan, Aiman, and Arpita Jaya, 'Burkhas, All "Markers of Muslimness" Targeted, Report Details Women's Plight in Delhi Riots', *The Wire*, 19 July 2020, https://bit.ly/3wOU6as. Accessed on 30 May 2022.

56 Singh Manral, Mahender, 'Resentment in Hindus on arrests, take care: Special CP to probe teams', *The Indian Express*, 16 July 2020, https://bit.ly/3Kmp52b. Accessed on 28 April 2022.

57 'Delhi Riots: "Why Caution Probe Team Over Arrest of Hindu Accused?" HC Asks Police', *The Wire*, 2 August 2020, https://bit.ly/3xZxKVP. Accessed on 28 April 2022.

58 Bhatia, Gautam, 'The Troubling Legacy of Chief Justice Ranjan Gogoi', *The Wire*, 16 March 2019, https://bit.ly/3KvDHg4. Accessed on 28 April 2022.

59 Singh, Pritam Pal, 'On Delhi riot probe note, HC tells Special CP: Why the need, show 5 such letters', *The Indian Express*, 1 August 2020, https://bit.ly/39gUkip. Accessed on 28 April 2022.

60 De, Rohit, *A People's Constitution: The Everyday Life of Law in the Indian Republic,* Princeton University Press, Princeton, 2018.

61 Rajagopal, Krishnadas, 'Ayodhya verdict | Supreme Court not to entertain claims against actions of Mughals', *The Hindu*, 28 November 2021, https://bit.ly/3wVHxeM. Accessed on 30 May 2022.

62 Mustafa, Faizan, 'The Supreme Court has overlooked the gravity of the Delhi violence', *The Indian Express*, 28 February 2020, https://bit.ly/3vmpCwP. Accessed on 28 April 2022.

63 Jaffrelot, Christophe, *Religion, Caste and Politics in India*, Primus Books, Delhi, 2011, p 7.

64 Constituent Assembly Of India Debates (Proceedings) – Volume II, 24 January 1947, https://bit.ly/36Xts6q. Accessed on 28 April 2022.

65 Noorani, A.G., *The Babri Masjid Question: 'A Matter of National Honour'*, Volume I, Tulika Books, Delhi, 2003, p. 233.
66 Ibid. 238–44.
67 Ibid. 237–38.

3
VIOLENCE AND FORGETTING

One could look at the story of India's democracy as an effort at negotiating the contradictions Dr B.R. Ambedkar highlighted in the Constituent Assembly. Equality, opportunity and freedom from discrimination were rights the Constitution granted every citizen. Yet, these terms were never free of ambiguity and particularly prone to cause tensions in reconciling the assertion of rights by one individual or group with another's.

Ironically, these clauses within the Fundamental Rights chapter became the basis on which the Supreme Court overturned early measures targeted at egalitarian outcomes. This led to the first amendment, which introduced almost identical language into the articles on equality, non-discrimination and opportunity, enabling measures of special benefit for SEBCs. In judicial rulings that followed, these enabling clauses were read as contingent and transient exceptions to constitutional stipulations. In the 1970s, when the Supreme Court acquired greater intellectual heft and a more radical hue, these clauses were reinterpreted not as exceptions but as a stronger affirmation of the equality principle. Unequal treatment of those who had been denied basic dignity through long years of history did not vitiate the equality principle—it was little else than the removal of unseen disadvantages that persisted despite formal assurances of equality. So, from a formal conception of equality in the early years, the constitutional understanding could be said to have moved to a substantive definition.

Except for these preferences, the constitutional rights admitted no identity-based differences, though the immediate historical background of Partition compelled certain contingent adjustments. The Muslim community, scattered and, for the most part, leaderless, saw a possibility of an erosion of their identity in proposed changes in personal law. Jawaharlal Nehru offered his forbearance, extending an assurance, tacit rather than explicit, that they could choose a time to adapt to the common civil law. But he was insistent that the Hindu mainstream of the nation should accept a shared civil code to efface the multiple fractures within its social being.[1] For champions of the new politics of majority assertion, this was sufficient to brand Nehru an unprincipled appeaser, unfairly targeting the deeply held beliefs and convictions of the righteous faith.

A common law came for the majority faith after Ambedkar's initial failure, in piecemeal enactments that amended the existing statutes in relevant areas. Over time, identity became a trap, a ghetto of the mind that the majority was happy to let the minority faith wallow in. Political actors who could deliver safeguards of identity to the Muslim community consolidated their leadership positions while assuring the ruling party of a secure vote bank at the hustings. Identity, which the Congress leadership could ensure, became a substitute for equality, which it could not. Ironically, the supposed privilege the Muslim community enjoyed in preserving its systems of personal law became the foundation of a narrative that they were 'more equal' than other citizens and had gained undue favour as part of the Congress party's effort to lock in place an unshakeable electoral advantage.[2]

The partition rule, supposedly imposed upon the Indian nation by a recalcitrant Muslim League leadership, was that religion-determined national belonging. It was an inhuman and ungainly formula to implement because religious communities were mixed in a vast syncretic sprawl across the length and breadth of the subcontinent. Some part of that surgical excision was carried out by the civil servant Cyril Radcliffe, who came to India for the first time just on the eve of imperial Britain's infamous scuttle. Traumatized by the blazing hot summer of the subcontinent, his mind a clueless haze, Radcliffe wielded his knife and left Indian shores, vowing never to return.[3]

For years after Partition, the grim and barbaric violence of the act was submerged in the cycle of nationalist observances. There was deliberate intent there to foreground the greater event of freedom rather than its tragic accompaniment. Representations in popular culture, when they finally began to take shape after years of trauma, portrayed the sense of loss and longing with great sensitivity while acknowledging the human costs on both sides. As the Punjabi writer Krishna Sobti remarked, Partition 'was difficult to forget, but dangerous to remember'. There were some like Saadat Hasan Manto who wrote in rage at the unfolding cataclysm, but others such as Sobti, Bhisham Sahni, Intizar Hussain and Bapsi Sidhwa had to wait two decades or more to gather together their recollections into works of literature. Ritwik Ghatak's trilogy of Partition films, made over a decade after the events, elaborated on the themes of 'migration, dispossession, and the experience of being refugees in familiar yet unfamiliar lands'.[4]

On 14 August 2021, while launching a series of observances to mark India's entry into its 75th year in freedom, Prime Minister Narendra Modi signalled a significant abridgement of the popular conventions on Partition. The day before India's Independence anniversary, which incidentally is when Pakistan celebrates its freedom every year, would henceforth be marked, he proclaimed, as Partition Horrors Remembrance Day.[5] Modi was being true to form, since his prime ministership has been marked by radical departures from convention. But it is appropriate to ask what manner of new solidarities are being fashioned in the new day of remembrance.

Episodes of violence are not usually featured in nationalist calendars unless they involve an unequivocal identification of guilt. An example would be Holocaust remembrance in the West, a collective crime for which modern Europe cannot possibly atone in full. Victories in war are also celebrated, as with modern Russia commemorating 9 May as the day of victory over Germany in 1945, or France's celebration of Armistice Day and Victory Day, marking the end of the two world wars of the twentieth century. The storming of the Bastille is commemorated in France as the moment of a revolutionary break with the past, though the events that followed—notably the Jacobin takeover, the Reign of Terror of 1793 and the Napoleonic coup d'etat—were equally consequential in the creation of modern France. Yet, neither the days of terror nor Napoleon's coup is part of any cycle of nationalist observances. Certain episodes in history can be studied in academia and portrayed in the creative arts and literature, but not made a part of the rituals of national identity except at risk of discord.

The Radcliffe Line, drawn rudely across the Indian map, caused enormous disruption in the lives of millions but carried the collateral benefit, once all the bloodshed had abated, that the two sides had no option but to submit to them. The vast swathes of territory where native princes reigned under a doctrine of paramountcy posed another set of problems, especially the three states unwilling to submit to the new political sovereign of the Indian nation.

India sorted out the three—Jammu and Kashmir (J&K), Junagadh and Hyderabad—on principles that were rather inconsistent. In Junagadh, India imposed a blockade, followed by limited use of force and a referendum to bind the popular will to the nation. In Hyderabad, military force was the only arbiter. And in J&K, the consent of the ruler was obtained in a situation of duress, when the state seemed under attack from across the border. Accession was followed by the first of many wars that the two nation states born out of the British Raj were to wage, and a tenuous peace based upon a shared understanding that the will of the people would be ascertained before final status determination.

India's evolving nationalist ideology was not seriously ruffled by the inconsistency in the standards applied across the states. There was perhaps an unstated premise at work: that India as an incipient republic and democracy, safeguarding the sovereignty of the individual citizen rather than the feudal overlord, had a superior claim to popular allegiance. That proposition was left to be proven in the future of modernity and prosperity the Indian nation state promised. The process of bringing the three states in line, though, involved episodes of violence that left deep scars.

Mahatma Gandhi was one person who acknowledged the violence and saw with some clarity that the reckoning could not be indefinitely postponed. And typically for Gandhi, that religious rite of atonement assumed the guise of clear-sighted political commentary. At a prayer meeting on 27 November 1947, after the accession of Junagadh and J&K had been secured, Gandhi spoke of his concern at reports that there had been 'considerable excesses by the Hindus' in the Jammu region.[6] He had also received representations from Junagadh (or Kathiawar, as he preferred to call the province of his birth) that people of the Muslim faith feared they would never again 'live in peace'. Incidents in the Jammu region, he said, had 'not been fully reported in the newspapers', and the situation in Kathiawar would not have come to his notice except for personal messages and news reports published by *Dawn* in Karachi. It was open to all to disregard the Karachi newspaper's reporting, said Gandhi, but that would really be quite pointless, since that option could just as well be exercised by the other side, making dialogue impossible.[7]

Acknowledging the Shame, Ascribing Blame

Gandhi was disturbed by the reported culpability in the Jammu violence of the Dogra Maharaja of the state and his top officials but reassured that Sheikh Mohammad Abdullah, leader of the independence movement against the Dogra Dynasty, had gained the confidence of all:

> I do not know if what happened in Jammu was at the instance of the Maharaja or his new Premier. But these things happened and it is a matter of great shame for us... Still Sheikh Abdullah did not lose his balance and the Hindus in Jammu fully supported him.[8]

There was no need to tell Sheikh Abdullah anything by way of counsel, but Gandhi worried that he was 'still to convince Kashmir and the entire India that the only way for Hindus, Muslims and Sikhs is to live together in amity and to trust one another'.[9]

Turning to Junagadh, Gandhi was partially reassured by Sardar Patel's visit to the province but worried that the situation had since deteriorated. This was for him 'unbearable', since he still retained his bonds to Kathiawar and knew 'all the princes and thousands of people there'. His nephew, Shamaldas Gandhi, who had emerged as head of the provisional government of Junagadh, was 'like a son', but there was no use in him holding any position if 'innocent Muslims are killed' and people 'take the law into their own hands'.[10]

The developments in Jammu that deeply agitated Gandhi were part of a cycle of events that could be traced back—depending upon the purpose of the inquiry—to the uprising in Kashmir against the Maharaja in 1931, or to the growing disaffection that exploded in insurrectionary conditions in Jammu in 1947, just on the eve of Partition. India's freedom struggle went through several cycles through this time, but for the people of J&K, these were a distant reality. The history of greater consequence for the collective identity of the people of J&K was the rebellion against the Dogra Dynasty that simmered for long years before erupting on 13 July 1931. That day, when 22 protesters agitating for an end to discriminatory practices against the Muslim majority were shot dead, has for long years since Kashmir's accession to India been commemorated as Martyrs' Day.[11]

In 2017, after wedging itself into the communal divide between the Jammu region and Kashmir and creating a situation in which it had to be accommodated in the state government, the BJP declared its very loud opposition to this commemoration. As a Hindu ruler, the Dogra Maharaja, in the BJP estimation, had every right to crack down on rebellious subjects.[12] In September that year, the son of the ruler who was responsible for that crackdown, Karan Singh, issued a public statement deploring the failure of the state government to declare his father's birthday a public holiday.[13]

These different strains within the composite known as Indian nationalism have coexisted for long. But how strong is the factual foundation on which they rest? At the time of Independence, which was the moment for that vital decision, the subjects of J&K, despite their shared opposition to the Dogra despotism, were disagreed on the best way forward. Pakistan had a constituency, built up particularly in Jammu region, where soldiers demobilized from active duty in the British cause in the Second World War had launched a tax boycott. A flood of Muslim refugees from adjacent areas of Punjab caused further aggravation, leading to near insurrectionary conditions. The Dogra dynasty responded with harsh repression, switching to a strategy that would, in today's vocabulary, be called 'ethnic cleansing'.[14] There were reliable estimates, made concurrent with the events or perhaps soon afterwards, that 'half a million Muslims were displaced, and 200,000 were either killed or died of epidemics or exposure as refugees'.[15]

Subsequent work, involving an excavation of the archives and the oral history record, has concluded that the story—even if it was briefly the official narrative of an adversarial state—has a kernel of truth. In August and September 1947, the maharaja's army, as Christopher Snedden records, 'fired on crowds, burned houses and villages indiscriminately, plundered, arrested people, and imposed local martial law'.[16] A resistance movement emerged, which soon had most of the Poonch jagir, except its main urban centre, under its control. The Maharaja blamed Pakistan for fomenting the trouble because he had no one else to blame. Though evidence of support from organized sources across the Radcliffe Line is scant, there likely was ample assistance rendered by Muslim communities from Punjab and the North-West Frontier Province, 'with whom Jammu Muslims had close ethnic, familial, cultural, geographical and economic links.'[17]

Resistance was local until some Poonchi Muslims with military experience organized an army, known as the Azad Force. From this event in August, the terrain of conflict spread, rapidly engulfing Kashmir. The October invasion by Pashtun tribes, which is where India officially begins its narrative of the Kashmir dispute, was linked in many ways to the Poonch uprising.[18] Early September, the media based in Srinagar, Jammu and Lahore began reporting the state of armed insurgency and large-scale loss of life in Jammu. But once the Pashtun invasion happened, drawing in an active engagement by the Indian Army, these reports ceased. The story then was about the war between two newly independent States. Having signed the instrument of accession to India, the Maharaja faded from the scene.

Resurrected Memories

India had an obvious interest in allowing events preceding the Pashtun raid to fade from historical memory. Yet, the events of

Jammu remain on the official record. A 1949 report by the United Nations Commission for India and Pakistan (UNCIP) mentions that 'many of the Muslim refugees have lively recollections of the Jammu massacres'. And it records the eyewitness testimony of a revenue official who saw the Maharaja personally 'shooting two or three' of his subjects while issuing orders 'that Muslims were to be exterminated'.[19]

While Kashmir was erupting in warfare, Hyderabad continued to simmer as the Nizam held out against the compulsions of accession. The state's forced incorporation into India through the military operation codenamed 'Polo', took place within six days of Mohammad Ali Jinnah's death. In received nationalist lore, it was a painless operation, celebrated to this day in the city of Hyderabad and the contiguous districts of Maharashtra and Karnataka as Liberation Day. As remembered in the official historiography, Hyderabad state forces surrendered meekly as the Indian Army moved in with clear intent and purpose, and the Nizam quickly signed the instrument of accession in return for a few token honorifics. This mythology is part of the erasure of memories contrary to dominant national ideology.

Wounds of history can be easily assuaged as part of the nationalist compact. But some varieties of nationalist ideology are sustained on keeping the wounds fresh. The story of Hyderabad's accession remains in a limbo between the two.

In 2012, a book written by Mohammad Hyder, a long-serving civil servant in the Nizam's court, emerged in print. Written in the time he spent in prison after Operation Polo, the notes remained unpublished for years after he was released unconditionally. Hyder expected to be rehabilitated in the bureaucracy of the Indian government in recognition of his years of service, but that day never came. He was instead, in what he believed a denial of fair process, dismissed from service in 1956, with retroactive effect from 1948. It took a while for Hyder to recognize that seeking a fair deal was futile, following which he chose exile. In 1972, he was coaxed into revisiting his manuscript and working it into a concise narrative. His son helped in the process, and Hyder reviewed the manuscript a year before he died, aged 58, in 1973. His memoir, titled *October Coup: A Memoir of the Struggle for Hyderabad*, emerged in print close to four decades later, a delay caused in part because of his son's professional commitments.

Hyderabad was a battle the Indian Army won with little effort. But did it win the peace? Hyder recounts that the Indian Army had been 'preoccupied with fears of an anti-Hindu uprising' in the city of Hyderabad and failed, in the bargain, to prepare for eruptions of violence in other parts of the state. 'I have no desire to exaggerate the horrors that followed Police Action but these tragic occurrences were largely preventable', he writes:

> Instead of just smashing through, the victorious army could have taken greater care to either restore local administration, or set up its own military administration. It did neither. Thugs quickly filled the vacuum...The anarchy lasted weeks. Mobs broke into prisons and set convicts free. There was murder, loot and arson...Thousands of families were broken up, children separated from their parents and wives, from their husbands. Women and girls were hunted down and raped...I cannot bring myself to write about them even now.[20]

The Indian nation is yet to reckon with this troublesome legacy, though scholars who have focused their attention on the matter have been calling out for some gesture of recognition. In 1998, the British travel writer and historian William Dalrymple set down his impressions from a visit to Hyderabad when he met with several of the descendants of the old aristocracy. He found vivid memories of the old days as too a growing sense of grievance at the modern city's manifest disregard of its historical grandeur. Particularly hurtful were the persistent traumas of the

1948 massacre and the denial that had become a part of official nationalist narrative.[21]

A.G. Noorani took up the theme in 2001, referring to a report on the aftermath of Operation Polo, that a deeply troubled Prime Minister Nehru had commissioned. Three senior Congress members—Pandit Sundarlal, Kazi Mohammad Abdul Ghaffar and Maulana Abdulla Misri—were involved in the inquiry. The typewritten report of the inquiry was suppressed soon after submission and subsequently destroyed in most part. 'Suppression of records is not only unethical but futile', Noorani commented. 'More often than not, the foreign scholar will unearth it from archives in London or Washington, or in India itself.'[22]

In a book on Hyderabad over the four decades before its accession, published in 2000 in English translation, the German scholar Margrit Pernau did just that. She found that while 'the occupation by the Indian army had been quick and had caused only relatively few casualties, the following communal carnage was all the more terrible.'[23]

The weeks before Operation Polo were suffused in the nationalist narrative with stories of the horrors the Razakars were inflicting, though Hyder insists that every action the militia undertook was only an effort at containing and perhaps retaliating against provocations by volunteers of the Rashtriya Swayamsevak Sangh (RSS) and the Arya Samaj operating with impunity from districts bordering the state.[24] As Pernau describes the aftermath of Operation Polo: 'The Razakars had sown [the] wind and reaped not only a storm but a hurricane which in a few days cost the lives of one-tenth to one-fifth of the male Muslim population primarily in the countryside and provincial towns.'[25]

In her study on the integration of Hyderabad state, Taylor C. Sherman concluded, 'Conservative estimates suggest that 50,000 Muslims were killed. Others claim several hundred thousand died. Indian troops in some places remained aloof from these activities, in others, they were implicated in them.'[26]

When apprised of the findings of the Pandit Sundarlal Committee, Sardar Patel chose not to worry about factual veracity but to angrily question the credentials of the inquiry team and attack their focus on the aftermath of Operation Polo while glossing over Razakar atrocities. This, obviously, was a weak defence, since the report on Hyderabad was carried out at Nehru's explicit request, conveyed in a letter to Pandit Sundarlal in November 1948. The Prime Minister's information was that even if the army had generally 'functioned well', there were a 'very large number of outbreaks...in the small towns and villages resulting in the massacre of possibly some thousands of Muslims by Hindus, as well as a great deal of looting, etc'. It was imperative to ascertain the truth, he said, 'or else we shall be caught saying things which are proved false later'.[27]

Patel's rather overwrought reaction was misplaced for more than this reason. Far from glossing over the Razakar atrocities, the Sundarlal Committee had specific observations about their incidence and intensity. Importantly, the committee concluded from wide-ranging interviews that these atrocities were part of a cycle that began in the immediate aftermath of India's independence, when the movement for responsible government that Hyderabad had witnessed over the preceding decade and a half gained a new spirit of aggression. Hyderabad, in short, was trapped in a spiral of violence that bred communalism. Religious and social reform bodies from the Muslim side assumed an aggressive political aspect because they saw the demand for responsible government as a thin veil for the imposition of the politics of the Hindu raj. The Razakars, as the 'military wing' of this movement, came, in the Muslim mind, to represent 'an effective barrier' against this threatening prospect. That was the reality on the ground. Yet, for all that, Razakar atrocities had been portrayed 'in a section of the Indian and foreign press in an exaggerated form'.[28]

Though suppressed, the truth continued to fester under the make-believe that became the official Indian practice of secularism, a term the Sundarlal Committee had been anxious to expound upon at numerous meetings in Hyderabad. As recorded in its report, the committee repeatedly urged all who appeared before it, 'to forget the past and to work unremittingly for the establishment of peace and harmony'. The Indian Union, in which Hyderabad had been forcibly incorporated, was committed to the 'establishment of a secular government', a system in which all would 'enjoy equal freedom and civil rights and... equal opportunities for development and progress'. That was an assurance that the Indian Union would extend to all citizens, 'irrespective of religion, caste, or creed'.[29]

Noorani in a later work titled *The Destruction of Hyderabad*, looked back on a time gone by, when Hyderabad represented a rare synthesis of cultures. Following the trauma of Partition, the prolonged stalemate over the status of Hyderabad was part of the story of how a delicate situation was aggravated by the continuing 'bankruptcy of statesmanship'. With even the 'tallest leaders' proving susceptible to these deviations, the consequences of those baneful years, Noorani concludes, 'are still with us'.[30]

History in Service of Nationalist Ideology

These retrievals of history are free of ideological debris and a reading of Partition within the teleology of the modern nation. But Partition had multiple and complex causes and it was not driven by any ultimate purpose. Two case studies in formative violence, remarkable in that they were both far removed from arenas where the politics of Partition was fiercely contested, are the contiguous and princely states of Alwar and Bharatpur. These states involved the Meo Muslims, a community that drew heavily from the traditional lore of the Brindavan region and venerated a heterodox pantheon of gods and practised ways of life resistant to the competitive proselytization that sought political strength in numbers. A comfortably settled agrarian community, the Meos were ecumenical in their identity and practice, and indifferent to the faith-based game of numbers.[31]

As the communal schism deepened during India's freedom struggle, the Alwar–Bharatpur region became a focal point of the Congress 'Muslim mass contact' programme.[32] Nehru and his close associates within the left wing of the Congress sought a strategy to deal with the embitterment between faiths by creating identities of shared material interests between peasants and workers. Numerous other demands, long suppressed under the surface of dynastic autocracy, surfaced in this atmosphere of ferment, including better representation for the Meo in the administration, equity in land ownership and decentralized governance that would take the reins of power away from the court and its vassals.

Though far from the epicentre of Partition tensions, the Meo region boiled with communal animosities on account of this intense political competition. Partition was a moment in history when the choices of subject populations were limited to the strictly defined binary of faith. To seek a third way by transcending this binary in a politics that challenged the authority of the old order was a mortal threat to an orderly transition. The result of the political ferment was, as Shail Mayaram points out, a 'mass extermination campaign'.[33]

The 'frenzy and holocaust of 1947' are absent from contemporary press reports and historical records. Where the ruling dispensation was compelled to take note, the violence was coded with terms such as 'communal strife' and 'disturbances', subsumed within the wider narrative, and morally neutered by the large-scale context of violence on the frontiers, where Hindu and Muslim were equally victim and perpetrator. In the Meo region, though, the violence was decidedly one-sided, and soon enough, it was a vehicle for the assertion of mundane interests, like taking over the lands of the Meo as they fled.[34]

Alwar and Bharatpur witnessed intense armed fighting as the Meos resisted. Outnumbered by the combined forces of Alwar, Bharatpur and Patiala, they suffered massive losses. Victor's justice was then imposed, involving the extinction of the identity of those who survived, in the *shuddhi* or purification ritual that ostensibly removed all traces of their faith. The statistics about these campaigns of extermination have long since sunk into the memory hole. Mayaram makes an effort at retrieval and finds numbers that are staggering, though the greater significance, she argues, is in the suppression of the events themselves.[35]

Ian Copland's inquiries bring to light an oral history archive that has N.B. Khare, prime minister of Alwar at the time, claiming to have made his state free of the Muslim presence. He obviously exaggerated, Copland concludes, but not by much. A diligent dig into the census figures over the relevant years reveals, in Copland's words, that in 1941, 'Muslims made up 27 per cent of Alwar's population and 19 per cent of Bharatpur's'. A decade later, 'they comprised in the order of 6 per cent. This represented a net loss of 115,000 Muslims—more allowing for some small natural increase between 1948 and 1951. Here we have, not just a "communal" episode, but something arguably far worse: a case of systematic "ethnic cleansing"'.[36]

Violence can be studied as pathological or instrumental, but here was a chapter in India's history when the 'making and remaking of social order' was premised on 'violence organized by the state'. The ensuing silence had to become embedded as a 'truth claim' within nationalist ideology, which requires a sense of 'sociability' among all or a pretence that life can go on despite all that has happened. After violence on the scale that the Meo region witnessed, the restoration of sociability required 'silences from the victim'.[37]

Memory and amnesia, to recall Ernest Renan again, are both key in the construction of modern national identities. History can unite when agreement exists on how amnesia should be applied but becomes an active agent of national disintegration when traumas are recalled with a sense of grief on one side and exultation on the other. Hyderabad, J&K and the Meo belt near Delhi, were stories of unrequited violence in the formation of the Indian nation. Amnesia is a possible antidote. Modernization and economic growth, which invite all into its putatively benign embrace, could make an ill-remembered past irrelevant to how nations construct their future, except, that is, when modernization fails to deliver on its promises.

When is it possible to conclude that the promise has failed? An early symptom would be when several decades into a nation's modernization project, injustices from a recent past are celebrated, indeed portrayed as rightful restitution for the sufferings inflicted in a more distant time. Remedies within the constitutional order—the final underpinning of the shared sense of belonging together—fail at the time. A perfect illustration, though by no means the only one, was the ruling by the Supreme Court in November 2019 that there could be no restitution for the egregious crimes of intrusion into a Muslim place of worship in Ayodhya in 1949 and its demolition in 1992.[38]

The triumphalism that surrounds the event makes amnesia impossible, since the nation has to live in the continuing sense of humiliation of a section of its citizens. Sardar Patel's visit to Junagadh soon after the state's accession, which Gandhi found comforting in a moment of moral turmoil, was equal parts reassurance and triumphalism. Accompanying him was the Union Minister for public works, N.V. Gadgil, who recorded in a later memoir how the decision on the reconstruction of the Somnath shore temple was made. 'One morning, while walking on the beach, the idea of the restoration occurred to me and I mentioned it to Vallabhbhai', he wrote. Patel apparently approved of the project, and Gadgil subsequently made an announcement of the intention to 'restore the ancient glory that Somnath once was'. Gadgil had in mind a project his department would execute, though he soon ran into a snag:

> Earlier it had been decided to undertake the work through the central government. Nehru did not approve. On Gandhi's advice it was decided to entrust the work to a Trust which would have one representative of the central government.[39]

The Temple and the State

Sardar Patel had died by the time the reconstruction of the Somnath temple was completed, but in one of the first instances of conflict between independent India's heads of state and the government, Nehru firmly set his face against any manner of official patronage of the inaugural. President Rajendra Prasad, nonetheless, went, ostensibly in his 'personal capacity', delivering on the occasion an anodyne speech celebrating the richness of India's cultural heritage.[40] Nehru felt compelled, nonetheless, to write to all chief ministers explaining why he thought governments should maintain a clear distance from religious activity:

> While it is easy to understand a certain measure of public support to this venture, we have to remember that we must not do anything which comes in the way of our state being secular. That is the basis of our Constitution and governments, therefore, should refrain from associating themselves with anything which tends to affect the secular character of our state.[41]

Nehru's tussle with the President was an early assertion of his determination to keep religion out of State policy. Aside from his reservations about an official embrace of religion, another of the many reasons Nehru opposed government patronage to the temple reconstruction was the possibility that it would be seen as unseemly triumphalism. In the telling by K.M. Munshi and others with a pronounced revivalist streak, the vandalization of Somnath temple in the early years of the second millennium was a dark and deplorable chapter, a milestone in the decline of the Hindu religion and, by implication, the Indian nation. Its reconstruction as an act of nationalist commitment in the first rosy flush of Independence was symbolic of the restoration of ancient India's glories.[42]

The commandeering of places of worship and their plunder was part of politics as the second millennium began. But could it remain an element in politics towards the end of the millennium? Did India's constitution as a republic with sworn values of liberty, equality and fraternity, mean nothing at all? Nehru had quite decisive views on the matter. And among the reasons he had for setting his face quite firmly against vandalization of Muslim heritage sites and their reclamation as patrimony of the eternal Hindu nation was the potentially fatal blow that would render India's standing in Kashmir.[43]

A month after his urgent letter of 5 February 1950 to Gobind Ballabh Pant, Nehru wrote to all chief ministers, sharply calling out the Hindu Mahasabha and other communal organizations as 'fatal for India', with their demand that Muslims prove their loyalty at every turn. 'Loyalty', he warned, 'is not produced to order or by fear', and the constant 'criticism and cavilling at minorities' did not help one bit in the process. A few years later, in September 1953, Nehru drew attention to the deterioration in the 'position relating to minority groups in India'. A constitution that promised equality seemed unable to combat the subtle prejudices of everyday life. That was the occasion for Nehru to issue a wider warning about a narrow form of nationalism growing within the country. As he then wrote:

> The feeling of nationalism is an enlarging and widening experience for the individual or the nation. But, a stage arrives when it might well have a narrowing influence. Sometimes, as in Europe, it becomes aggressive and chauvinistic and wants to impose itself on other countries and other people... [A] more insidious form of nationalism is the narrowness of mind that it develops within a country, when a majority thinks itself as the entire nation and in its attempt to absorb the minority actually separates them even more.[44]

Continuing his tradition of regular correspondence with the chief ministers, Nehru wrote in 1954, upholding secularism as a vital value in public life. It was a word that did not acclimatize very well in the Indian political milieu but conveyed a profound meaning, little less indeed than 'social and political equality'. A 'caste-ridden society is not properly secular', said Nehru, and though averse to intervening in anybody's personal beliefs, he was concerned that caste distinctions could become 'petrified' and 'affect the social structure of the state'.[45]

If the systemic violence in which a nation is born is not fully rooted out, there could, alternately, be the collective amnesia that comes from participation in the processes of modernity. But modernity is often a contentious process, involving dislocations, disruptions and competition over the rewards of economic progress. Creating a peaceful ambience in which modernization acts as a solvent for animosities of the past requires strong institutional processes and cohesive social structures. In this perspective, violence is not an exceptional circumstance in democracy and modernization but a feature of its weakly institutionalized or de-institutionalized variants. In a volume dealing with this theme, Amrita Basu and Srirupa Roy go further to argue that democracy can often nurture virulent pathologies. Rather than being an exceptional circumstance, violence may well have 'significant points of convergence' with democratic practice.[46]

Was there an effort to root out the systemic violence that had been part of the foundation of the nation? For the first decade and a half since Independence, violence seemed submerged. Nehru's constant admonitions, and perhaps also the aura of optimism he created over India's 'tryst with destiny'—its delayed but inevitable emergence on the world stage as a nation of knowledge and influence—may have been key in subduing the violent strains. The pact of memory and forgetting was honoured in certain years but frayed visibly in others. Social violence, in its incidence, frequency and spread, could be used as a barometer—in the reverse sense—for the soundness of the nationalist compact. In junctures when violence is minimal, the compact could be deemed to hold. And it is not violence in all its variants that is relevant but only those connected directly to the identity—social, cultural, religious or any other—of perpetrators and victims.

Equality before the law implies that redress should be available to all victims, and perpetrators of violence should have penalties imposed, irrespective of identity. Because of historical circumstances, India introduced protection based on identity for certain categories of citizens: the SCs and STs. As a first step, the crime of untouchability was abolished by Article 17 of the Constitution. In further affirmation of this intent, the Protection of Civil Rights Act was legislated in 1955, with very narrow application to those rights 'accruing to a person by reason of the abolition of untouchability'. The purpose was not to deny civil rights to others but to signal that certain classes of citizens were under greater threat of a denial of rights. Identity-based violence, though, has not abated significantly with all the legal protections available. A long-period analysis of the incidence of violence is not easy because of changing definitions and data sources. The National Crime Records Bureau is a source for data on crimes against the SC and ST population because these are officially notified identity categories. Monitoring the other variant of identity-based violence across religious lines, more especially the Hindu–Muslim divide, poses a different challenge.

It is necessary, before a deeper dive into this question, to address a basic question: how do caste and religion compare as identity-based triggers of social violence? It is a matter that has for long been debated, though perhaps caste-based violence has not attracted similar scholarly attention as the other. In 1984, in a symposium organized by Asghar Ali Engineer, most committed among independent India's researchers and activists in matters of intercommunity relations, the political scientist Imtiaz Ahmed argued in favour of treating them alike. And his reasons were clearly set out:

> Once I was able to think about violence in comparative terms, it became clear to me that a consideration of all kinds of social group violence, including violence between Hindus and Muslims, irrespective of the identities of the social groups involved, was more likely to lead to an understanding of the social, economic and political factors which generate social group tensions, the contexts and situations within which these occur, and the aims they are designed to serve...[47]

This is a lucid rationale if the object is the study of violence *qua* violence. The aim here being different, i.e. to study violence as an elaboration of nationalist ideology, the religious divide in India has a special significance. For one, religion as a marker of social differentiation is baked into India's nationalist ideology by virtue of the theology about Partition every child is taught in school. Beyond that, the religious distinction pervades all national life, whereas a caste grouping, construed strictly in the sense of the endogamous *jati grouping,* is localized. Inter-religious strife could be contagious, and the demographics of Muslim settlement in India—their relatively higher concentration in urban centres—creates greater potential of transmission.

Nehru's personal example and his constant admonitions may have quelled the flames for some time in a nation born in communal antagonism. In 1961, independent India registered its first communal riot, a term that has been its unique contribution to the political science vocabulary, combining the benign ambience of community with the malevolent intent of a riot. Riots could be triggered by purely local factors and contained by responsible law enforcement procedures. Just as well, rioting could be caused by wider political determinants.

Jabalpur in 1961 seemed to belong to the former category, an affray that has entered the history books because it was the first sign of the Nehruvian peace unravelling. Historian Ramachandra Guha traces the origins of the violence to the suicide of a young girl of the Hindu faith, an incident that was 'given lurid publicity' by a local newspaper aligned with the Hindutva political cause.[48]

The scholar and social reformer Asghar Ali Engineer, who has personally investigated most incidents of communal violence that occurred during his lifetime and arrived at interesting typologies of how and why they occur, puts down the Jabalpur riots to the 'economic competition between a Hindu and a Muslim *bidi* manufacturer'. Its proximity to Partition led to every manner of baseless allegation gaining traction, including the supposed role of Pakistani spies in organizing the riots, and the 'instructions' being imparted to local Muslims through a 'hidden transmitter from Pakistan'.[49]

Violence in Action-Reaction Sequence

The suggestion that violence between people of different faiths was locally determined was rudely punctured in 1964, in a cycle of events that began in action-reaction sequence in Kashmir. The state of J&K was in the process of a political transition: Bakshi Ghulam Mohammad, who had served India's cause well, had been induced to step down from the premiership of the state under a plan devised by K. Kamaraj, Nehru's confidant and president of the Congress, for the revitalization of the party apparatus. It was not an orderly transition of power. Bakshi had enjoyed the patronage of New Delhi since 1953, when he toppled Sheikh Abdullah and assumed power. Though none too popular in the Kashmir Valley and no real match for Sheikh Abdullah, who continued to be in incarceration, Bakshi was afforded the luxury of choosing his successor, and from the perspective of the national leadership, made a manifestly bad choice.

On 27 December 1963, a sacred relic from the Hazratbal Masjid in Srinagar was reported missing. Political leaders rushed to the venue to quieten the unrest that threatened. But by the following day, the city was astir. Efforts by the political establishment to pacify matters were met with a serious backlash, and dissidents who raised inconvenient questions about the accession of the state were beginning to regain an audience among the public. Then, as Balraj Puri, a veteran civil rights activist from the state records it, the 'holy relic was recovered as mysteriously as it was lost'. India's security and intelligence agencies claimed credit for swiftly settling the matter, but scepticism about their claims was rife. There were serious questions, particularly about the genuineness of the article recovered.[50]

Puri remembers meeting with Gulzari Lal Nanda, the home minister at the time, who, in turn, was in close consultation with his top officials. The head of India's Intelligence Bureau, B.N. Mullick, was duly summoned, and presented a picture of extreme insouciance. The article in question had been recovered and would be restored to its rightful place, he asserted. Nanda worried that when the relic was placed on public display, anybody with the inclination to challenge its authenticity could set off an explosion. Mullick was unfazed, insisting that all possible doubts would be properly assuaged. Puri was irate: it was 'neither bravery nor wisdom to first create an explosion and then try to face it', he said.⁵¹

Unrest within Kashmir continued for a month, during which time Nehru sent a trusted Cabinet colleague, Lal Bahadur Shastri, to Srinagar to participate in the first public display of the relic after its recovery, when empowered religious authorities certified its authenticity. Matters seemed to settle down in Kashmir, only for trouble to erupt with a terrible virulence in faraway places of the map.

As the annual report of the Ministry of Home Affairs (MHA) for 1964–65 puts it, there were 'communal disturbances' in East Pakistan in the early part of January 1964. A backlash was soon witnessed in West Bengal, particularly in Calcutta, 24 Parganas and Nadia districts. 'These incidents included cases of stabbing, arson, looting, and other forms of lawlessness'. Interventions by the administration and the political leadership contained the violence, but there was another outbreak in March in the states of Bihar, Madhya Pradesh and Orissa. 'The industrial areas of Rourkela and Jamshedpur were seriously affected', observed the MHA.⁵²

From contemporary press reports, the story that emerges is of violence breaking out in Khulna and Jessore districts of East Pakistan within a week of the disappearance of the sacred relic from Srinagar. Panic set in as minorities from East Pakistan streamed across the border into India. Trouble began in Calcutta almost simultaneously, triggered apparently by the thousands of persons displaced by Partition still awaiting resettlement. But there soon was common cause between them and the 'large criminal element in the population'. The situation stabilized within a couple of weeks but then flared up yet again two months later. Meanwhile, the conflict was widening in expanse. The cycle of violence triggered in partitioned Bengal by events in distant Kashmir convinced state and central authorities that resettlement of Partition refugees was a matter that had far too long lain in neglect. An accelerated resettlement programme in the forested plains of central India was agreed, and the core area of resettlement, corresponding to the Bastar region of present-day Chhattisgarh, expanded to include neighbouring districts from Maharashtra, Andhra Pradesh and Orissa. Local sentiments were inflamed as trains transited through these areas, carrying refugees towards their new homes. Attacks on Muslim properties began along the routes the trains took, with old and new steel towns of Jamshedpur, Rourkela and Raigarh being among the most seriously affected. A statement by Home Minister Nanda on 8 April put the number of victims at 346 killed and 458 injured in the three towns. Violence elsewhere claimed more lives.[53]

Nehru was, from the very first glimmers of the crisis, in an infirm state. He suffered a stroke while on a visit to Orissa and, according to press reporting, was being shielded from news about the violence. Once back and abreast of all that happened, he moved with a certain sense of purpose. After a long absence from public view, he was first heard over the airwaves on 26 March, when he broadcast an appeal for peace and announced that Pakistan had agreed to talks in India, with the object of containing the rampage of communal violence.[54] Soon afterwards, Sheikh Abdullah was released from his long incarceration and encouraged to resume consultations within J&K and also authorized to visit Pakistan for discussions with the political leadership there.

Seeking Reconciliation

Sheikh Abdullah was himself in no hurry to visit Delhi, taking a leisurely road trip from Jammu to Srinagar, with multiple stops en route, where he spoke to large crowds, asserting the need for India and Pakistan to honour the wishes of the people of the state after long years of denial.[55] His triumphal procession created anxieties in India, where the right-wing opposition saw a possible surfacing of a secessionist tendency. Closure, they argued, had been secured in the general elections held to the J&K Assembly in 1957 and 1962, and the participation of the people of the state was also implicit endorsement of the accession to India.

One person who did not buy the fiction was Jayaprakash Narayan or JP, as he was popularly known, the socialist radical once seen as Nehru's heir but functioning, since the late 1950s, outside the political realm in an effort at building a moral force. JP deployed an unanswerable rhetorical trope, after first deprecating the facility with which the freedom fighters of 'yesterday' had begun to speak the language of imperialists. If India was so certain about the underlying popular sentiment in J&K, he wrote in a newspaper column, why should it be hesitant about 'giving them another opportunity to reiterate it'?[56]

C. Rajagopalachari, the conservative former Congressman from Madras state, now alienated by what he saw as Nehru's unseemly swing towards state-led policies of economic growth, stepped up with his endorsement, urging a fundamental rethink to deal with the crisis. He asked:

> Are we to yield to the fanatical emotions of our anti-Pakistan groups? Is there any hope for India or for Pakistan, if we go on hating each other, suspecting each other, borrowing and building our armaments against each other...? We shall be making all hopes of prosperity in the future a mere mirage if we continue this arms race based on an ancient grudge and the fears and suspicions flowing from it.[57]

There was dissent from the left wing. Romesh Thapar wrote in the *Economic & Political Weekly* of JP's supposedly 'peurile' attitude. Early optimism that Sheikh Abdullah would herald a change for the better in the national conversation around Kashmir had been punctured by his 'adventurist outpourings'. His base in India had splintered, 'causing even those who would conciliate him to panic'. Nehru's Kashmir policy, which was to 'have been one of the pillars of India's secularity', Thapar fretted, now threatened to become its 'main corrosive agent'.[58]

In a following newspaper column, JP observed wryly that his earlier observations had 'provoked a rather fierce controversy'. This was good to a point, he wrote: it was much to be desired that the people of the subcontinent think through a problem that had plagued them since Independence. Yet, little would be achieved by those 'who thought it necessary to preach angry sermons' and 'refused to look squarely at the truths'. The 'ballyhoo', he said, spoke of a 'vast, organised attempt to work up a state of mind which was hysterical and closed to reason and intolerant to a violent degree of all dissent'. Somehow, the mood, to him, seemed reminiscent of the days when the 'father of the Nation was sacrificed at the altar of a similar synthetic hysteria'.[59]

The attempt to settle had some traction for as long as Nehru remained at the helm, and he seemed intent on forcing a major reckoning, a seeming gestalt switch, upon both party and government. At a meeting of his party's highest decision-making forum, the All India Congress Committee (AICC), on 16 May 1964, Nehru delivered a most unpopular account of the violence that had gutted large parts of India. He spoke very briefly, a mere six minutes, in English and then just so long as needed to render the same sense in Hindi. Prior speakers had dwelt at length on the horrors inflicted upon Hindus in Pakistan and the forbearance shown the Muslims in India. Nehru had a different story to tell. The violence inflicted upon citizens of the Muslim faith in the eastern parts of India, he declared, was simply 'horrible'. The meeting hall in Bombay reportedly fell into a sullen silence at this admonition. Nehru then commended Sheikh Abdullah for the possibilities of peace he represented. If Abdullah could bring about 'closer and more intimate relations' between the people of India and Kashmir, Nehru told his deeply uneasy audience, it would be good for the entire region.⁶⁰

Nehru died within 11 days of the AICC session. Sheikh Abdullah, then in Pakistan, hurried back attend his funeral. Despite falling out with Nehru in 1953 and the subsequent very partial reconciliation, his death was a deep personal loss for Abdullah. And with it, he seemingly saw chances of the larger reconciliation on the subcontinent vapourizing. He remained in India and was arrested and imprisoned afresh on the generalized charge of undermining the nation.

The year following Nehru's death was relatively equable. However, in September 1965, border skirmishes with Pakistan and civil unrest in Kashmir, following Sheikh Abdullah's arrest, flared up in outright hostilities. Economic stresses were building up concurrently. Alongside a rather poor monsoon, which deeply scarred agricultural production through the year, there was loss of export earnings. Though industrial capacity had expanded, there was a shortage of foreign exchange for the import of components and raw material. The hostilities with Pakistan had caused a 'pause in foreign aid from some countries', which added to the 'disturbance of the economy'.⁶¹

Civic peace, though, was maintained. The home ministry's annual report spoke of the 'general communal situation' remaining 'satisfactory', and 'peace and harmony' prevailing despite stresses, particularly in the border states of Assam, West Bengal, Rajasthan and Gujarat. Governments in states worst affected by the 1964 violence, the home ministry noted, had allocated generous budgets for the 'relief and rehabilitation of the riot-affected persons'.⁶²

This was also a time when the infirmities of conviction within the Congress began surfacing. Nehru, as prime minister and also the Congress president for long years, had kept ideological deviances within a measure of control. His successor as prime minister, Lal Bahadur Shastri, had a rather brief tenure, and when Nehru's daughter, Indira Gandhi, assumed the position with the blessings of the party's old guard, she took a while to find her footing. A movement for a ban on cow slaughter began in October 1966, a mere nine months into Indira Gandhi's tenure, triggering acts of violence in various parts of the country.[63]

The Cabinet discussed the matter, and Home Minister Nanda recommended that all states introduce a cow-slaughter ban on their own initiative. Nanda's unseemly proximity with the Bharat Sadhu Samaj (BSS), a newly formed organization of militant monks, was now an open secret. Early in November 1966, a violent BSS mob marched to Parliament and vandalized its interiors. It then went on a rampage through neighbouring streets, setting fire, among other things, to the residence of Congress party president K. Kamaraj. By that evening, 'the army was patrolling the streets, for the first time since the dark days of 1947.'[64]

Unlike the violent ruptures of 1964, which had roots going back to Partition, the gathering storm of 1966 was about a new ideological ambience in domestic politics. The Congress monopoly on power was weakening, and novel social coalitions were being constructed. The Congress old guard was responding with strategic and tactical choices at complete variance with the Nehruvian ethos. Members of the so-called Congress syndicate—an informal grouping of powerful regional leaders—did not seem greatly averse to seeking political mileage from stoking the fires of communal animosity.

In a comment in January 1967, the *Economic & Political Weekly* made note of some ironies in the agitation over cow slaughter. 'The Prime Minister may say that the agitation for a ban on cow-slaughter is not an issue', it observed with some irony, though Congress strongman and syndicate member S.K. Patil expressed himself otherwise at a press conference in Bombay:

> [He] left no one in any doubt that as a protector of the cow he yielded to none... It deserved to be noted that for the first time perhaps Patil has found it necessary to

call a press conference to propagate his candidacy for the
Lok Sabha from the South Bombay constituency, which has
been considered as his pocket borough...But what was most
significant were the views he aired at the press conference.
They seem to have been entirely aimed at projecting himself
as a champion of the cow, a good Hindu and a staunch
Maharashtrian.[65]

Patil's opponent in the election just ahead was the fiery socialist
and trade unionist George Fernandes, a Christian from Mangalore.
In the event, Patil's appeal to the true spirit of the Maharashtrian
Hindu did him little good. He was one among several party
stalwarts defeated in 1967, as the Congress coalition fragmented
and fell apart.

In the months that followed, violence against the religious
minority escalated. In June 1968, a working paper circulated by
the MHA spoke rather ruefully of having missed all cues. Conflict
had broken out with Pakistan in 1965, but contrary to early fears,
there had only been sporadic incidents of violence against religious
minorities, mostly unrelated to the conflict. A sharp deterioration
occurred the year after. In a state of alarm, the home ministry put
down the number of 'communal incidents' as 'relatively high'. The
states of Andhra Pradesh and Maharashtra 'suffered from persistent
tension'. And 'another disturbing development' through 1967 was
the 'extension of communal tension to Kashmir'.[66]

The Spectre of Violence Revives

What factors could possibly have precipitated the upsurge in
violence between 1967 and 1970? Explanations could be found
in both the larger and the smaller contexts. The larger picture was
of an economic crisis that began with successive monsoon failures
in 1965 and 1966. The promise of material improvement for all,
irrespective of identity, now stood threatened by the enveloping

situation of scarcity. In the smaller context, differences in perception on official language policy and cow protection acquired an extra charge of communal animus. Following the battle on the streets of Delhi in November 1966 and the general elections of 1967, loose and inherently fractious coalitions came to power in the two pivotal northern states of Uttar Pradesh and Bihar. Anti-Congress sentiment was a cement, but one of limited durability. Post the elections, the opposition parties that had loosely coordinated election strategies to avoid a split in the anti-Congress vote had to seek a deeper unity in running governments.

One such incongruous partnership in Bihar was led by a politician who had broken off from the Congress and created an alliance with the right-wing Jana Sangh. A socialist group, led by the redoubtable backward-class leader Karpoori Thakur, completed that implausible political troika. It was an ideologically disparate grouping, which sought, in the days after the election result, to hammer out a programme of work and, in the haste of it all, came up with a portmanteau stuffed with irreconcilable promises. One such promise the socialists managed to include, despite Jana Sangh opposition, was the formal recognition of Urdu as second official language in Bihar.

As the Raghubar Dayal Commission inquiry into the recurrent incidents of violence observed, there was no formal notification of policy nor any manner of a decision by the state cabinet. However, a 'circular appears to have been issued by the Deputy Chief Minister, Shri Karpoori Thakur', directing government offices, within the limits of feasibility, to receive written communication and to furnish responses in Urdu. Moreover, advice was rendered that important official publications should, where possible, 'be translated into Urdu' and government signboards 'written in Urdu besides Hindi'.[67] Without the imprimatur of the state cabinet or a reference to the Legislative Assembly, Thakur seemingly intended this circular as a request seeking best endeavour from government agencies.

The issue lay dormant for a while. Socialists within the governing coalition and communists of all stripes outside it remained committed to the change, while the Jana Sangh was unrelenting in its opposition. The Congress was typically divided but also keen to use the issue to drive a wedge into the unlikely coalition. In July 1967, a Congress member moved a bill in the Legislative Assembly, seeking formal recognition of Urdu as a second official language of the state. As a private member's bill, it was far from assured of consideration, let alone passage. Yet, in the fraught atmosphere of the time, it triggered an escalating cycle of protests. As documented by the Commission, the protests involved members of the Jana Sangh as well as the Congress. Soon after the bill was introduced, protesters from the two parties forced their way into the Assembly chamber, shouting abuse.[68]

A statewide agitation began on 12 August, drawing in interest groups arguing both sides of the case. On 22 August, a spark was lit in the industrial town of Ranchi, after the participants in a student march against Urdu began dispersing. It was a familiar routine: stones hurled at demonstrators drawing retaliation, and then an explosion with a characteristic pattern of tit-for-tat violence.

The Raghubar Dayal Commission examined witnesses in large numbers and, with great effort, reconstructed the entire sequence of events. The proximate causes were easily enough identified, though the Commission struggled to put its finger on the underlying determinants. Like in other parts of the country that witnessed the ravages of Partition, memories of trauma lingered and were aggravated by the war with Pakistan. Whispered accusations about the divided loyalties of people of the Muslim faith were common; yet, personal bonds and cooperative relationships had been forged over the years, and the reality was not, by any means, one of unbridgeable antagonisms. As in several towns with changing economic landscapes, there were parallel systems of business, with their own mechanisms of enforcement. Civic bonds that sustained the peace had to continually contend with these parallel systems, themselves held together by kinship ties. And intensifying competition in a context of shrinking opportunities conceivably triggered violence in an overtly communal form.[69]

Was there a pattern there, some common attributes in locations of the worst violence? At a time when the government was invested in the sustenance of peace and harmony, the MHA, in an analytical mode, found some clues to the roots of the problem. Its annual report of the year 1967–68 records a letter issued to all chief ministers urging them to be especially mindful of the need to 'maintain vigilance in industrial communities'.[70] In its report the following year, while taking note of 'an increase in the number of communal incidents', the ministry recorded the decisions taken at a conference of chief ministers in May 1968: 'full use' was to be made of the provisions of the law, particularly those dealing with provocative words, written or spoken. Further, 'all possible efforts' were to be made to 'step up the recruitment of the members of the minority community in services subject to the observance of the relevant constitutional provisions'.[71]

Modernity involves the acceptance of the rule of law, and the principles of equality and fairness. It also involves the transformation of spaces, with urban centres becoming locations of modernity. Nehruvian modernity had chosen certain focal points, where the new temples of India—a term originally used for the Bhakra Nangal Dam but soon applied to steel, electricity and machine tools plants—were placed. Why were these exact focal points of modernity being torn apart by ancient animosities of religion? Were certain jealousies being unleashed by competition for living spaces? Was a fair distributive bargain built into these development programmes to assure every participant that they had nothing to fear from the transformations and possible dislocations of modernization?

In years of economic stability or buoyancy, it is perhaps easy keeping up an appearance of fairness. Besieged by conflicting demands through the years of crisis following the death of two prime ministers, the Congress had lost its way. The nation, as sovereign represented in the State, was faltering in its promise to deliver fair opportunity to all, and as its authority diminished, the street took over. After the outbreak of 1967, the graph of violence stayed persistently in the higher reaches, with Ahmedabad in 1969 and Bhiwandi in 1970 being centres of especially brutal outbreaks.

By 1969, the novice Prime Minister Indira Gandhi had acquired sufficient political acuity and tactical sense to turf out the power brokers within her party and establish a quite distinct claim to legitimacy in slaying the demon of poverty. The call to the universal ideal of abolishing poverty from a land stricken with deprivations at multiple levels did not immediately render a quietus to the surge in communal violence. But following a landslide win in the 1971 general elections, Indira Gandhi seemed to have reconstituted the hegemony of the Congress.

Yet, the demon of poverty proved persistent. The sweeping electoral triumph in 1971 was no magic ticket towards undoing the oppressive structures that kept India poor. Deeply embedded social relations were resistant to the effort at legislating them out of existence, much more than Indira Gandhi imagined. Her effort at sustaining the populist appeal through successive economic catastrophes—monsoon failures and then, most lethally, the global oil price shock of 1973—created greater unrest on the street.

In the desperation of her struggle against the recalcitrant enemy, Indira Gandhi banished freedom itself.[72] The basic raison d'etre of the nation state, the freedom of its citizens, was discarded because Indira Gandhi alone embodied the greater glory of the nation. All who thought otherwise would simply be locked away till realization dawned. That outbreak of megalomania was quashed in 1977. A government came to power with explicit claims to undo the institutional damage, but soon afterwards, had to cope with the return to the political arena of the holy cow.

In April 1979, a Gandhian with a great sense of moral righteousness but little subtlety went on a fast unto death in the cause of securing a ban on cow slaughter.[73] This set off a crisis of sufficient gravity to compel the prime minister of the time, Morarji Desai, one of the few survivors from the clique that Indira Gandhi had dislodged in 1969, to promise his special attention to the cow.

Perhaps it was only tenuously connected to the reappearance of the gentle ruminant animal on the political stage, but another cycle of communal violence began from 1979 on. The MHA annual report for the year recorded sectarian affrays involving loss of life in states across the length and breadth of the country.[74] Some of these were sparked by the cow, others by seemingly trivial local disputes involving competition over space, the perceived dishonouring of religious symbols and alleged offences against feminine dignity.

In its annual report the following year, the MHA returned to its analytical, social-scientific mode. Disturbances in the communal situation, it observed 'are the flash-points of some deep-rooted factors linked with socio-economic, educational and other aspects.' Governments in the states that had a more troubled record of communal relations had been advised to carry out studies from 'socio-economic, educational and historical angles and formulate time-bound programmes for implementation.'[75]

Kinship, Community and the Anxieties of Modernity

Asghar Ali Engineer has assembled an extensive catalogue of incidents of communal violence in independent India. Political alliances at the local level, he has found, have a bearing on the prospects of sustaining harmony as also migration patterns into urban centres, community demographics, economic competition and the rival dynamics of cooperation.[76] Each urban centre is unique, but the pattern of violence through the 1960s and 1970s suggests certain common elements. The early observation that industrial towns needed close observation and monitoring was seemingly underlined by the experience of 1969 and 1970, when Ahmedabad and then Bhiwandi were gutted by riots. Rourkela, Ranchi and Jamshedpur, sites of serious violence in preceding years, were all focuses of the heavy industry-based strategy of economic growth inaugurated by Nehru. They had received large doses of industrial investment and were seen, in the eastern region, as centres of growth and magnets for immigrants.

Ahmedabad and Bhiwandi were textile towns but otherwise very different. Ahmedabad was an early pioneer that had evolved towards a highly diversified industrial base but was, by the late 1960s, in the early stages of decline. It had attracted migrants in large numbers both from other parts of Gujarat and from the states of Maharashtra, Uttar Pradesh, Rajasthan and Madhya Pradesh. The declining industrial fortunes of the city meant that it was not as hospitable towards immigrants as before.[77]

In the vacuum created by the decline of the organized textile industry, power-loom towns like Bhiwandi, Malegaon, Surat and Ichalkaranji stepped in, all growing rapidly through the 1960s. For reasons related to the importance of kinship and community ties, Bhiwandi attracted a large number of Muslim artisanal weavers as it grew.

A snapshot of the changing religious demography of these cities is available from the decennial census enumerations. All the urban centres identified as especially vulnerable through the decades of the 1960s and 1970s had significant concentrations of the Muslim community in 1961, ranging from a low of 14.11 per cent of the population in the case of Jamshedpur to a high of 55.23 per cent in Bhiwandi. By 1971, the proportion of Muslims to the total population had declined in both Jamshedpur and Ranchi—appreciably in the former case and marginally in the latter. The proportion in Bhiwandi, in contrast, had increased significantly. By 1981, however, the proportion had fallen for all these urban centres. In the case of Ahmedabad, which was a different case study because of its older vintage as an industrial city, the Muslim population, in proportion to the total, diminished steadily through the 1960s and the 1970s.[78]

These trends are offered as part of a hypothesis that modernization involves a competitive dynamic between individuals working from within their kinship and community networks. This competition is often reflected as a contest for urban spaces, where opportunities are seen to be expanding. The pursuit of opportunity, though, could be affected by a perceived deficit of physical security. When workers and their families contemplate migration options for employment, an urban milieu with a recent history of communal violence is unlikely to be a viable option. The deterrent effect is likely to be stronger for the minority faith that invariably comes out much the worse off in conflict outbreaks.

Ernest Gellner, among others, has proposed that nationalism is a form of politics uniquely created by the industrial revolution. Yet, industrialization does not create a seamless and internally undifferentiated entity called the nation. It is a milieu rife with fractures and dislocations, with multiple processes of fission and fusion occurring almost continuously. How stable would the national political order be through these processes of modernization? How far can the nation state, with its claim to acting in the general interest, keep the peace as modernization proceeds with all its dislocations? And when the State fails to hold the peace, how does violence come to be an instrumental means of politics?[79]

The story could be told in the Indian context by tracing the trajectory of the Congress from its authoritarian interlude to its first stint in the Opposition. These were educative moments for a party that had, at least in its more lucid moments, actively championed a nation built on the republican values. The party had hedged and equivocated right through its years of unchallenged power, rhetorically opposing the power brokers in civil society while actively accommodating them in political practice. The loss of power in 1977 perhaps taught the Congress that an egalitarian democracy was a quixotic pursuit. Sectarian sentiment, rather than republican values, offered greater reward. Stoking religious and linguistic and every other manner of sectarian loyalty across the entire spectrum was a way of staying afloat as a viable political entity. Nationalism was not about shared values. Rather, it was about a political sovereign holding together an assemblage of distinct interest groups—by pandering today to one and tomorrow to the other.

It was a shift in political strategy presaged by Indira Gandhi's assumption of office in 1980, after the Janata Party experiment at governing through an amalgam of all non-Congress forces went down in flames. In 1966 and all subsequent occasions till 1971, Indira Gandhi had taken her oath of office with the 'solemn affirmation' of her commitment to the Indian constitution. In 1980, she took her oath 'in the name of god', picked an astrologically propitious time and performed a slew of rituals to placate newly discovered overseers of her destiny.[80]

Indira Gandhi remained quiescent through the shameful record of communal violence since her return to power in 1980. When the veteran Congressman Shahnawaz Khan warned her of a programme of civil disobedience, Indira Gandhi's reply was telling and won her the instant approval of the RSS: 'We must remember', she said, 'that no minority can survive if their neighbours of the majority are irritated'.[81]

In the June 1983 elections to the J&K Assembly, Indira Gandhi put her strategy of competitive communalism to test in what seemed the perfect laboratory. In the Kashmir Valley, she projected the aura of champion of rapprochement with Pakistan, while in Jammu, she was the Hindu saviour. In October 1983, she inaugurated the Bharat Mata Mandir built by the Vishwa Hindu Parishad (VHP) at Haridwar. Faced with public criticism, her trusted lieutenant C.M. Stephen sprang to the defence, proclaiming that the Congress was on the 'same wavelength' as Hindu culture.[82]

How has violence shaped the politics of the nation since then? After briefly reappearing on the political scene with Vinoba Bhave's fast in 1979, the cow soon lost its status as a symbol around which sectarian mobilization could be organized. In the mid-1980s, a new symbol presented itself in a plot of land in Ayodhya, where a medieval mosque stood allegedly in defilement of a revered god-king of Hindu mythology.

Changing political attitudes at the time were reflected in a certain casualness in official reporting. Numbers collated by the MHA showed a steady rise in the casualties of communal violence, both dead and injured, through the years 1981 to 1984, but in contrast with the official narrative of 1980, the MHA seemed to hedge and finally dismiss the growing menace. Of 1981, the MHA observed that there had been a 'reduction both in the number of communal incidents and in the number of casualties'[83], which was factually true, though not by much. Of the year following, it observed that the situation was 'by and large... under control', despite some 'outbursts of violence'.[84] Of 1983, it noted that 'fatalities resulting from communal clashes have been less during the year when compared to previous years'[85], while finding a way of classifying the ghastly Nellie massacre of literally thousands in Assam under a different rubric. And of 1984, it had the perfectly bland and partly self-congratulatory observation that the situation 'remained comparatively peaceful...on account of concerted efforts made by the Government'.[86]

New Political Compacts Sealed in Violence

In the years that followed, as the movement over the Babri Masjid at Ayodhya gathered virulence, culminating in the demolition of the mosque in 1992, the graph steadily rose. So, too, did official indifference and an effort at transforming the violence in society into an instrumental means of securing State power.

Asghar Ali Engineer's inquiries into the riots in Meerut in 1987, the first serious outbreak triggered by the Ayodhya campaign, uncovered certain political calculations preceding the actual violence. Administrative failure had been blamed by the official inquiry, but this reading, he concluded, was seriously askew. Either because of its sloppy procedure or its failure to 'muster enough political courage to pinpoint the events which led to the real conflagration', the inquiry had failed to see that 'it was political design much more than administrative failure' that caused the violence.[87]

Through the Ayodhya campaign and its aftermath in the 1990s, the dividends that could be harvested through instrumental violence were a key driver of political competition. Perhaps the most vivid display occurred in Gujarat in 2002. A study on the spatial patterns of violence in Gujarat reveals much about the political calculations that went into it. Raheel Dhattiwala and Michael Bigg have gathered all relevant media reports from the time and sought to correlate the sites where violence occurred to various political factors. The relative strength of the BJP is assessed from the party's performance in preceding rounds of elections. The 1995 election, which brought the BJP to power for the first time in the state—only to be followed by early elections in 1998 after the party was torn by internal dissidence—form the background to their study. Despite the discord, the BJP retained power in 1998 on the back of strong public sentiment against 'traitors' within the ranks. Dhattiwala and Bigg take the 1998

Assembly results as a marker of the areas where the BJP had reason, going forward, to be worried about an erosion of votes. Their conclusions are clear:

> Violence was a product of political calculation and economic deprivation. Killings were low where the…BJP…was weak, but were also low where the BJP was strong; it peaked where the BJP faced the greatest electoral competition. Killings increased with greater economic deprivation, measured by underemployment and youth unemployment…[88]

Beyond the theories that have been spun about the spontaneous occurrence of riots and the futility of administrative action in such situations, studies carried out over the years have shown how they reflect a definite political design. Secularism in India has been about confining cultural identities to a sphere deemed private, but competitive democracy became, in reality, an arena for sharpening these. In the absence of a solid civil society consensus against violence, the fiercely competitive impulses unleashed by electoral politics became a factor aggravating the clash of identities.

Paul Brass has written about the riot as purposive and politically directed activity. Ashutosh Varshney offers a different diagnosis, since he begins from the other end of the spectrum, seeking conditions in which communal peace and amity are sustained.[89] Steven Wilkinson carries some of these insights forward and seeks to place collective violence within the context of political competition. Riots, he argues, 'are best thought of as a solution to the problem of how to change the salience of ethnic issues and identities among the electorate in order to build a winning political coalition'. In situations of competitive democracy based on universal franchise, minorities usually enjoy protection, since it would be in the 'government's electoral interest'.[90] Security for minorities would particularly be the outcome where they are a constituency that ruling parties or coalitions depend upon for gaining an electoral plurality, or when competition at the hustings is intense enough to invest their votes with a strategic value.

Electoral contests since the 1990s have cast the minorities in varying political roles. In the days of Ayodhya, people of the Islamic faith were portrayed as legatees to various indignities inflicted in the past on India's primordial national identity. Later, with all their supposedly outdated beliefs and practices, they were portrayed as an impediment to the glittering promises of modernity that lay ahead as India strode confidently to take its appointed place in global councils. Terrorism, portrayed in the dominant political narrative as a virtual monopoly of fundamentalist Islam, was the weapon deployed to thwart India's march towards global prestige and modernity.

From the Mandal moment of 1990, when communities stigmatized under the ritual hierarchy of caste Hinduism were given the assurance that they could be participants in the administrative process, Indian politics, in Christophe Jaffrelot's words, underwent a process of 'plebeianisation'. Social groups that had little influence ascended to positions of leadership, in political configurations of elaborate complexity. An important countervailing (or in Jaffrelot's words, 'dialectical') influence was also at work in the majoritarian mobilization, which purported to restore Indian nationhood to an imagined primordial foundation of Hindutva. This introduced facets of 'ethnodemocracy' into Indian politics, reducing certain religious minorities to 'the status of second-class citizens'. The under-representation of Indian Muslims in the Lok Sabha, the directly elected house of India's parliament, became 'more and more evident' as this variety of politics came insidiously to influence the entire spectrum.[91]

Muslim representation in the Lok Sabha reached its peak in the early to mid-1980s. Jaffrelot's figures indicate that in 1980, there were 49 candidates of the Muslim faith who were elected to the Lok Sabha out of 131 who contested from the various parties.

This put their representation in the Lower House at 9 per cent of the total—less than their share in total population but not by much—and their success rate in relation to the number of contenders at 37 per cent. The gap has since grown. In the 2009 general elections, just 30 candidates of the Muslim faith were elected to the Lok Sabha out of 832 who contested. Persons of the Muslim faith, in other words, had a mere 5.5 per cent of the seats in the Lok Sabha, and just over 3 per cent of their candidates actually won. And in an early foretelling of the Modi strategy, of the 89 seats the BJP won in the 1989 Lok Sabha elections, 47 were in constituencies directly affected by the riots of the Ayodhya mobilization.[92]

Jaffrelot's statewise survey showed that Gujarat, Jharkhand, Karnataka, Rajasthan and Maharashtra had, for years together, failed to elect a person of the Muslim faith to the Lok Sabha.[93] The diminishing Muslim presence in legislative bodies and their disappearance from violence-prone urban milieus are testament to the success of the Hindutva political agenda. Uttar Pradesh, the epicentre of the Ayodhya mobilization, affords one picture of the course followed by the politics of riots. With over 18 per cent of its population being of the Muslim faith, it is a state where the community could potentially play a significant role in politics. In 1989, when preparations for the conquest of Ayodhya were beginning to gather momentum, Muslims won 41 out of the 425 seats in the Uttar Pradesh Legislative Assembly. In the next round of elections, when the BJP won power for the first time in the state, minority representation was decimated, the number of successful candidates of the Muslim faith falling to 21.[94]

Following the climactic act of destruction at Ayodhya in December 1992, the BJP seemed set to sweep the elections held after the lapse of a year. But an unprecedented coalition of the 'plebeian' political formations—the Samajwadi Party (SP) and the Bahujan Samaj Party (BSP)—checkmated these ambitions. From then, the number of candidates from the Muslim faith winning election to the state legislature went steadily up. In the 2012 Assembly elections, they won 66 seats, or over 16 per cent in a legislature of 403 members, perhaps for the first time almost matching their share within the total population of the state.[95] Tactical voting and alliances of varying configurations, between Dalits and Muslims—a smattering of the higher castes in one conjuncture—and between substantial sections of the backward classes were keeping the Hindutva brand of nationalist assertion at bay.

All that was set at naught in 2014 and the years that followed. Muslim representation in the Lok Sabha in 2014 fell to its lowest-ever figure of 23. Of these, a mere six were from Uttar Pradesh. In elections to the Uttar Pradesh Legislative Assembly that followed in 2017, Muslim representation fell back to the levels of the early 1990s: from its highest-ever figure of 66 in 2012 to a mere 24. In the 2019 Lok Sabha elections, Muslim representation went up marginally by three, principally because the two quarrelling parties in Uttar Pradesh, the SP and BSP, managed to stitch their alliance back together and avoid the fragmentation of votes in constituencies where the community had significant strength in numbers. Yet, the numbers did little justice to their presence within the wider electorate and failed to slow the pace of the ghettoization.

The resurgence of Muslim representation in the Uttar Pradesh State Assembly for roughly a quarter century following the Ayodhya demolition and the relative peace that prevailed on the inter-communal front through those years seem to bear out Wilkinson's finding that 'high levels of party competition combined with strong backward-caste movements that regard Muslims as acceptable and valuable coalition partners puts Muslims in an extremely good position to demand security as the price of their votes.'[96] The difficulty with this model, though, is that it omits the specific character of the parties contending for power, particularly the fact that one among them has by design written away any chance of gaining votes from an entire category of citizens, defined by faith. By ideological persuasion and strategic intent, the BJP has sought to build its electoral fortunes on majoritarian sentiment constructed purely by negative association with the religious minorities. Given the single-member, simple-plurality system in place in India, voters whose collective strength numbers well below 20 per cent of the total electorate in most of the country could be isolated and their votes made inconsequential.

Hindutva, with its claims to being the singular fount of Indian nationalism, could not win without sinking deep roots in civil society. Political scientists Sudha Pai and Sajjan Kumar have through extensive field research shown how an ambience of 'everyday communalism' could be fostered, camouflaged under slogans such as 'development', to stigmatize an entire religious minority, virtually neutralizing the strategic value of its collective vote.[97] The seeds for this assertion of a narrow nationalism, quite contrary to the inclusive spirit that India embraced at its freedom moment, run deep. Recognizing this reality is about travelling back those decades and into the recesses of history where the origins of Indian nationalism can be found.

Notes

1. On the Hindu Code Bill and its aborted passage, see Guha, Ramachandra, *India After Gandhi: The History of the World's Largest Democracy*, Pan Macmillan, New Delhi, 2017, pp. 228–43.
2. On the identity anxieties, see Prime Minister's High Level Committee, Cabinet Secretariat, Government of India, *Social, Economic and Education Status of the Muslim Community of India: A Report*, November 2006, pp. 32–34, https://bit.ly/39bKz58. Accessed on 12 May 2022; on problems of political representation, see Jaffrelot,

Christophe, 'A De Facto Ethnic Democracy', *Majoritarian State: How Hindu Nationalism Is Changing India,* Angana P. Chatterji, et al. (eds), HarperCollins, Noida, 2019, pp. 41–68.
3. W.H. Auden's portrayal in poetry of the Radcliffe mission remains a great historical document. For more, see: 'W.H. Auden's unsparing poem on the partition of India', *Scroll.in,* 15 August 2014, https://bit.ly/39iGagV. Accessed on 12 May 2022.
4. Rai, Haimanti, *The Partition of India*, Oxford university Press, 2018, pp. 137–39.
5. 'Narendra Modi picks August 14 to recall Partition trauma', *The Hindu*, 14 August 2021, https://bit.ly/3NggC2F. Accessed on 13 May 2022.
6. 'Speech at Prayer Meeting', 27 November 1947, *Collected Works of Mahatma Gandhi*, Volume 90, Navajivan Trust, Ahmedabad, pp. 114–19; also, *Collected Works of Mahatma Gandhi,* (Online) Volume 97, pp. 401–7, https://bit.ly/3Mx7NSd. Accessed on 15 May 2022.
7. Ibid.
8. Ibid.
9. Ibid.
10. Ibid.
11. Khan, Ghulam Hassan, *Freedom Movement in Kashmir (1931–40)*, Light and Life Publishers, New Delhi, 1980.
12. 'Dogras heckle J&K Dy CM in Jammu', *DNA*, 24 September 2017, https://bit.ly/3yUogMj. Accessed on 15 May 2022.
13. 'Declare birth anniversary of Hari Singh public holiday: Karan Singh to J-K Guv', *The Economic Times*, 20 September 2019, https://bit.ly/3LegPlp. Accessed on 15 May 2022.
14. Kaul, Suvir, 'An' you will fight, till the death of it: Past and Present in the Challenge of Jammu and Kashmir', *Social Research*, vol. 78, no. 1, Spring 2011, pp. 187–88.
15. Ibid.
16. Snedden, Christopher, *Kashmir: The Unwritten History*, HarperCollins, Noida, 2013, p. 42.

17 Ibid. 45.
18 Ibid.
19 Ibid. 50–51.
20 Hyder, Mohammad, *October Coup: A Memoir of the Struggle for Hyderabad*, Masood Hyder (ed.), Roli Books, Delhi, 2012, p. 79.
21 Dalrymple, William, 'Under the Char Minar', *The Age of Kali*, Penguin India, 1998.
22 Noorani, A.G., 'Of a massacre untold', *Frontline*, 16 March 2001, https://bit.ly/3PzDJav. Accessed on 15 May 2022.
23 Quoted in: Ibid.
24 Hyder, Mohammad, *October Coup: A Memoir of the Struggle for Hyderabad*, Masood Hyder (ed.), Roli Books, Delhi, 2012, p. 64.
25 Quoted in: Noorani, A.G., 'Of a massacre untold', *Frontline*, 16 March 2001, https://bit.ly/3PzDJav. Accessed on 15 May 2022.
26 Sherman, Taylor C., 'The Integration of the princely state of Hyderabad and the making of the postcolonial state in India', *Indian Economic and Social History Review*, December 2007, p. 497.
27 Quoted in: Noorani, A.G., 'Of a massacre untold', *Frontline*, 16 March 2001, https://bit.ly/3PzDJav. Accessed on 15 May 2022.
28 *Pandit Sundarlal Committee Report On The Massacres in Hyderabad (1948)*, p. 28, https://tinyurl.com/2p84ssu6. Accessed on 5 June 2022. The Sundarlal Committee report remained a classified document till 2013, when a typewritten copy with several handwritten amendments was made accessible at the Nehru Memorial Museum and Library in New Delhi. The quotes are sourced in accordance with the manually numbered pages. The report otherwise has some discontinuities and repetitions, which make the original page numbering at the top of each page somewhat unreliable. For all the problems with the sole copy that has survived the years, there have been few questions raised about the authenticity of the document. It has since been scanned and widely circulated over the internet.
29 Ibid. 1–2.
30 Noorani, A.G., *The Destruction of Hyderabad*, Tulika Books, New

Delhi, 2013, p. xiv.
31 Mayaram, Shail, *Resisting Regimes: Myth, Memory and the Shaping of a Muslim Identity*, Oxford University Press, Delhi, 1997, pp. 51–63.
32 Ibid.
33 Ibid. 183.
34 Ibid. 185, 193.
35 Ibid.
36 Copland, Ian, 'The Further Shores of Partition: Ethnic Cleansing in Rajasthan, 1947', *Past & Present*, no. 160, August 1998, p. 216.
37 Mayaram, Shail, *Resisting Regimes: Myth, Memory and the Shaping of a Muslim Identity*, Oxford University Press, Delhi, 1997, p. 172.
38 In the Supreme Court of India, Civil Appellate Jurisdiction, Civil Appeal Nos 10866–10867 of 2010, M. Siddiq Thr Lrs v Mahant Suresh Das, decided 9 November 2019. Attention may particularly be focused on Section P, titled 'Analysis on Title', and paragraphs XVI and XVII, where the Supreme Court, in summing up the act of trespass of December 1949, expresses itself thus: 'This led to the desecration of the mosque and the ouster of the Muslims otherwise than by the due process of law'. And then, in December 1992 came the final act of vandalism, when 'the structure of the mosque was brought down and the mosque was destroyed. The destruction of the mosque took place in breach of the order of status quo and an assurance given to this Court. The destruction of the mosque and the obliteration of the Islamic structure was an egregious violation of the rule of law'.
Yet, despite these clear-cut observations of right and wrong, the Supreme Court proved unable to live up to the principles of lawful restitution and to deliver appropriate punitive sanctions against the wrongdoers. The matter is also dealt with in chapter 2.
39 Quoted in: Noorani, A.G., *The Babri Masjid Question: 'A Matter of National Honour'*, Volume I, Tulika Books, Delhi, 2003, pp. 11–15.
40 Guha, Ramachandra, *India After Gandhi: The History of the World's Largest Democracy*, Pan Macmillan, New Delhi, 2017, p. 132.

41 Quoted in: Noorani, A.G., *The Babri Masjid Question: 'A Matter of National Honour'*, Volume I, Tulika Books, Delhi, 2003, p. 15.

42 For all the attention lavished upon the event and the mythology that has surrounded it, the raid by Mahmud of Ghazni on Somnath at the beginning of the second millennium was one among several instances from a time when warfare—the pursuit of politics by other means—focused obsessively upon religious sites. Indeed, as Richard Eaton records in his recent work, a veritable tour de force of Indian history through the eight centuries that followed, Mahmud's expedition south from what is now a town of eastern Afghanistan, occurred three years after Rajendra I began his military excursion north from the Chola capital of Thanjavur, marching in force along the eastern Indian coast to subdue rival kingdoms and bring back the treasures of their temples as war booty. Among the trophies carried back by the Chola conquest were richly bejewelled images of Siva, Bharava, Bharavi and Kali from the Bengal and Kalinga dynasties. This was the accepted code of the time (Eaton, Richard, *India in the Persianate Age, 1000–1765*, Allen Lane, Delhi, 2019, p. 19).

43 See chapter 2.

44 The letters were written on 1 March 1950 and 20 September 1953, respectively, and can be accessed from the relevant volume of the *Selected Works*. They were extracted and published by a news website on Nehru's birth anniversary in 2018, and can be viewed here: 'My Dear Chief Minister…Three Letters Nehru Wrote That Indians Today Need to Read', *The Wire*, 14 November 2018, https://bit.ly/39nAC4u. Accessed on 15 May 2022.

45 'Nehru to the presidents of state Congress party units', August 5, *Selected Works of Jawaharlal Nehru*, Volume 26, Oxford University Press, 2000, pp. 200–1.

46 Basu, Amrita, and Srirupa Roy (eds), *Violence and Democracy in India*, Seagull Books, Kolkata, 2007, p. 7.

47 Ahmed, Imtiaz, 'Perspectives on Communal Problems', *Communal*

Riots in Post-Independence India, Asghar Ali Engineer (ed.), Sangam Books, New Delhi, 1984, p. 7.

48 Guha, Ramachandra, *India After Gandhi: The History of the World's Largest Democracy*, Pan Macmillan, New Delhi, 2017, p. 324–25.

49 Engineer, Asghar Ali, 'Communal violence in India', *The Hindu*, 12 January 2000, https://bit.ly/3PmOlcv. Accessed on 15 May 2022.

50 Puri, Balraj, 'Theft of Holy Relic in Kashmir', *J.P. on Jammu and Kashmir*, Balraj Puri (ed.), Gyan Publishing House, New Delhi, 2005, pp. 43–46.

51 Ibid. 44.

52 Ministry of Home Affairs, *Report 1964–65*, pp. 22–23, https://bit.ly/3G2Y9Et. Accessed on 16 May 2022.

53 This account is drawn from the excellent monthly digest of global events that used to be assembled by Keesing's Contemporary Archives, begun in 1931 as an effort to collate all the authoritative reporting available on global events of economic, and political and social significance. The Archives ceased by 1987 but for the period of relevance here, can be regarded as reliable. See: Keesing's Contemporary Archives, 1963–64, Volume 14, pp. 20185–56.

54 'PAKISTAN AGREES TO TALK IN INDIA; Nehru in Broadcast Appeals for End of Sects' Strife', *The New York Times*, 27 March 1964, https://nyti.ms/3LgBt4r. Accessed on 16 May 2022.

55 Guha, Ramachandra, *India After Gandhi: The History of the World's Largest Democracy*, Pan Macmillan, New Delhi, 2017, p. 350.

56 Ibid.

57 Ibid. 351.

58 Thapar, Romesh, 'The Corrosion of Secularity', *Economic & Political Weekly*, vol. 16, no. 17-18, pp. 754–55.

59 Puri, Balraj, 'Theft of Holy Relic in Kashmir', *J.P. on Jammu and Kashmir*, Balraj Puri (ed.), Gyan Publishing House, New Delhi, 2005, p. 50.

60 'Nehru Deplores Hindu Violence Against Moslems; Party Reaction Is Cool', *The New York Times*, 17 May 1964, https://

nyti.ms/3syGNcQ. Accessed on 16 May 2022.
61 Ministry of Finance, Government of India, *Economic Survey, 1965–66*, p. 1.
62 Ministry of Home Affairs, Government of India, *Report 1965–66*, pp. 21–22, https://tinyurl.com/42h8nzew. Accessed on 16 May 2022.
63 Ministry of Home Affairs, Government of India, *Report 1966–67*, p. 51, https://tinyurl.com/mu9hschf. Accessed on 16 May 2022.
64 Guha, Ramachandra, *India After Gandhi: The History of the World's Largest Democracy*, Pan Macmillan, New Delhi, 2017, p. 414.
65 'Cow-based Politics', Letter from Maharashtra, *Economic & Political Weekly*, vol. 2, no. 1, 14 January 1967, https://bit.ly/3NknvjA. Accessed on 16 May 2022.
66 Keesing's Contemporary Archive, Volume 16, 1967–68, pp. 20185A, 22831–32.
67 Ministry of Home Affairs, Government of India, *Report of the Commission of Inquiry on Communal Disturbances Ranchi-Hatia*, 22–29 August 1967, p. 10.
68 Ibid.
69 Ibid. 69–80.
70 Ministry of Home Affairs, Government of India, *Report 1967–68*, p. 41, https://bit.ly/3wfOqaf. Accessed on 16 May 2022.
71 Ministry of Home Affairs, Government of India, *Report 1968–69*, pp. 71–72, https://bit.ly/3sDJU3k. Accessed on 16 May 2022.
72 The Emergency, as this 19-month suspension of civil liberties under the Constitution was called, has generated voluminous literature. For a brief account of what it meant, written on the 25-year anniversary of its declaration, see Muralidharan, Sukumar, 'The Legacy of the Emergency', *Frontline*, 8 July 2000, https://bit.ly/39y5sry. Accessed on 17 May 2022.
73 For a scholarly dissection of the issues raised by Vinoba Bhave's fast unto death for cow protection, see Raj, K.N., 'Demand for Total Ban on Cow Slaughter in Kerala and West Bengal, Some Observations', *Economic & Political Weekly*, vol. 14, no. 18, 5 May

1979, https://bit.ly/3wrRgbc. Accessed on 17 May 2022.

74 Ministry of Home Affairs, Government of India, *Report 1979–80*, pp. 5–9, https://tinyurl.com/2ae93fz5. Accessed on 23 June 2022. The unprecedented five pages devoted to the communal situation is an index of the serious view that the Ministry took of the deteriorating climate.

75 Ministry of Home Affairs, Government of India, *Report 1980–81*, 5–6, https://bit.ly/38vO4Dv. Accessed on 17 May 2022

76 Engineer, Asghar Ali, *Communalism and Communal Riots in India: An Analytical Approach to Hindu-Muslim Conflict*, Ajanta Publications, New Delhi, 1989.

77 Shah, Ghanshyam, 'Communal Riots in Gujarat–Report of a Preliminary Investigation', *Economic & Political Weekly*, vol. 5, no. 3-4-5, January 1970, pp. 187–200.

78 The demographic information is abstracted from census volumes. See Census Commissioner and Registrar General of India: Census of India, 1961; District Census Handbooks (various); Census of India, 1971, Series I, Part VI-A, Town Directory; Census of India, 1981, Paper 4 of 1984; the following articles by this writer (S.M. Menon) have presented the detailed figures: 'Raising the Stakes, Communalism and Worldly Interests', *Frontline*, 8 November 1991, pp. 123–26; and 'Hindu Upsurge in Perspective', *Mainstream*, vol. XXIX, no. 29, 11 May, pp. 17–25.

79 Gellner, Ernest, *Nations and Nationalism*, Kindle Edition, Cornell, 2009, Location 755. 'Industrial society', he argues, 'is the only society to ever live by and reply on sustained and perpetual growth, on an expected and continuous improvement. Its favoured mode of social control is universal Danegeld, buying off social aggression with material enhancement; its greatest weakness is its inability to survive any temporary reduction of the social bribery fund, and to weather the loss of legitimacy which befalls it if the cornucopia becomes temporarily jammed and the flow falters.'

80 Ghose, Sagarika, *Indira: India's Most Powerful Prime Minister*,

Juggernaut, New Delhi, 2017.
81. Muralidharan, Sukumar, 'The legacy of the Emergency', *Frontline*, 8 July 2000, https://bit.ly/3zjeJyd. Accessed on 6 June 2022.
82. This story has been recounted in a variety of sources. See Muralidharan, Sukumar, 'The Many Faces of Indira Gandhi', *Economic & Political Weekly*, vol. 53, no. 3, 20 January 2018, https://bit.ly/3wzI3gW. Accessed on 17 May 2022.
83. Ministry of Home Affairs, Government of India, *Report 1981–82*, pp. 3–4, https://bit.ly/3MnDc9v. Accessed on 17 May 2022.
84. Ministry of Home Affairs, Government of India, *Report 1982–83*, p. 3, https://bit.ly/3PnWAVN. Accessed on 17 May 2022.
85. Ministry of Home Affairs, Government of India, *Report 1983–84*, p. 3, https://bit.ly/3LzjPct. Accessed on 17 May 2022.
86. Ministry of Home Affairs, Government of India, *Report 1984–85*, p. 2, https://bit.ly/3yBKjqO. Accessed on 17 May 2022.
87. Engineer, Asghar Ali, 'Gian Prakash Committee Report on Meerut Riots', *Economic & Political Weekly*, vol. 23, no. 1/2, January 1988, https://bit.ly/3Q33xM5. Accessed on 6 June 2022.
88. Dhattiwala, Raheel, and Michael Bigg, 'Spatial Variation in Hindu-Muslim Violence in Gujarat, 2002', Working Paper Number 2011-06, Oxford University, Department of Sociology, 2011; See also: Dhattiwala, Raheel, 'Deliberateness and Spontaneity in Violence', *The Hindu,* 31 December 2013, https://bit.ly/3yEXuHx. Accessed on 17 May 2022.
89. These works have been extensively analysed. For a basic summary of their main points, see Muralidharan, Sukumar, 'Modi, Mulayam and Muzaffarnagar: The Communal Riot and the Electoral Politics of the Ghetto', *Economic & Political Weekly,* 15 February 2014, vol. 49, no. 7, February 2014, https://bit.ly/3wlbfcM. Accessed on 17 May 2022.
90. Wilkinson, Steven, *Votes and Violence, Electoral Competition and Communal Violence in India*, Cambridge University Press, Cambridge, 2014, p. 1, p. 6.

91 Jaffrelot, Christophe, *Religion, Caste and Politics in India*, Hurst and Company, London, 2011, pp. xx–xxx.
92 Ibid. xxiv, 179.
93 Ibid. xxv.
94 The figures are abstracted from the detailed results of every election as published on the website of the Election Commission of India. The candidates of the Muslim faith are identified by their names.
95 Calculated by name identification in results as presented on the Election Commission website.
96 Wilkinson, Steven, *Votes and Violence, Electoral Competition and Communal Violence in India*, Cambridge University Press, Cambridge, 2014, p. 203.
97 Pai, Sudha, and Sajjan Kumar, *Everyday Communalism: Riots in Contemporary Uttar Pradesh*, Oxford University Press, New Delhi, 2018, pp. 296ff.

4

THE MANY PERCEPTIONS OF INDIA

Late in the year 1909, Mahatma Gandhi set sail from England to South Africa after concluding an unrewarding political mission in the mother country. With little to divert him, Gandhi turned his attention to India, a country he had visited only in brief and sporadic intervals over two decades. Writing at a furious pace, he completed *Hind Swaraj* during the voyage, setting out the terms of his political engagement with Indian nationalism.

Organized as a dialogue with an unidentified interlocutor, *Hind Swaraj* was a book that Gandhi insisted till his last days represented the clearest distillate of his political philosophy. An early biography holds that the interlocutor Gandhi engaged with was Vinayak Damodar Savarkar, the political agitator then living in London, shortly afterwards brought to trial by the British Raj for crimes of sedition and convicted to life in the desolation of the Andamans penal colony.

Gandhi and Savarkar had, just weeks before, shared a platform at a Dussehra gathering of the Indian community in London. As a guest of honour, Gandhi had in his remarks revelled in the generosity and kindness of Lord Ram, a figure from the Hindu pantheon who he saw as an intimate companion and retained as a source of inspiration to his last days. If all creeds and races in India were to unite behind the banner of Ram, evil would soon be banished from the land, he declared.[1]

Speaking shortly afterwards, Savarkar held forth on the cultural richness of India, which was only enhanced by its many-coloured diversity:

> Hindus are the heart of Hindustan. Nevertheless, just as the beauty of the rainbow is not impaired but enhanced by its varied hues, so also Hindustan will appear all the more beautiful across the sky of the future by assimilating all that is best in the Muslim, Parsi, Jewish and other civilisations.[2]

He went on to echo all that Gandhi had said about Ram before pointedly referring to the celebration over the nine days preceding Dussehra, of the cult of Durga, who embodied the attributes of anger and retribution.[3]

That was the fateful first encounter when the seeds of a momentous political divergence in later years were sown. An Indian nation then seemed a prospect greatly to be desired, though one subject to extreme differences in interpretation. Closure in some respects was applied four decades later when Savarkar went on trial for Gandhi's assassination and secured an acquittal because of infirmities in the legal process and his own clever and evasive testimony.[4]

The South African backstory of the legend of Mahatma Gandhi has mostly been told in the glow of reverence that envelops his struggles in India. Effective as nationalist iconography, this obscures the complexity of the Gandhian persona and its evolution. In a 2015 book, two South African scholars used in most part their subject's own locutions to develop a picture that did some justice to his many complexities.[5] Far from a resolute adversary, Gandhi was, for much of his time in South Africa, a loyal subject, anxious to gain for his narrowly constructed community the privilege of equal citizenship within the British Empire. Native Africans, though, remained rather remote from his perceptions, and Gandhi stayed steadfastly clear of advocating on behalf of their rights.

Gandhi served the British imperial cause against the Boer when hostilities broke out between the two settler populations in South Africa. Yet, this did him little good when the British and the Boer ceased their hostilities to create a new union based on white supremacy and shared plunder of the land. It was in this interlude of bitter disappointment that Gandhi wrote *Hind Swaraj*, originally in Gujarati, later translated under his own hand into English and variously republished.

Since returning to India to a tumultuous welcome in 1915, Gandhi had been propelled, within a matter of three years, to the forefront of the Indian nationalist movement. And what he offered as a prognosis for the movement was very simple. *Hind Swaraj* had fallen into neglect, he wrote, since the 'only part of the programme which is now being carried out in its entirety is that of non-violence'.[6] Unlike Rabindranath Tagore, who he was yet to personally encounter, he had little reserve about embracing nationalism as an organizing principle of political action. And unlike Tagore again, he was willing to give the Congress ample credit as the principal vehicle of the Indian nationalist project then. For all its failings, the Congress, said Gandhi, had imbued all of India with the spirit of nationalism.[7]

The juncture at which Gandhi enters the nationalist fray is crucial. The last decades of the Mughal Empire had witnessed a feeble effort at the transition from doctrines of sacred kingship to something approaching an impersonal system, governed by the rule of law.[8] That was an incomplete transition. Monarchical regimes functioned on a notion of legality and moral rectitude that the supreme sovereign alone had the power to specify. The rule of law required every monarchical decision to measure up to a universally applicable standard, independent of any claims of a divine mandate. But with the country divided between competing satraps, there was little chance the principle would be implemented with any consistency.

British colonialism began formulating a legal code for the administration of the Raj early in the nineteenth century but with a perspective clouded by a vision of pre-industrial society—stratified and segmented. Part of the job of co-opting every segment of a complex society into the colonial project was about instituting a notion of autonomy, giving each social class a sense of self-governance. Colonialism created its own segmentation and stratification, imposed over the patterns imagined by the rulers and their local intermediaries.

The code of laws inscribed by the Raj dispensed with the principles of liberty and equality, even in the nominal sense. India acquired some among the systems of governance of the nation state in the second half of the nineteenth century, after the uprising of 1857 had been crushed and the British Crown had assumed authority over the subcontinent. A basic requirement for the system of administration was sorting the population into legible categories. India's first census took place in 1872, and from 1881, settled into a regular decennial cycle. Social identities now acquired a political dimension, with numbers seen to decide collective strength. Ecumenical definitions of identity now had to yield to the choice every subject could make between various 'official' categories.[9]

The Ripon viceroyalty, beginning in 1880 following Lord Lytton's ruinous term of famine and military adventurism, was a period of accommodation between the imperial rulers and the rising class of Indians who thought themselves deserving of political autonomy. The Ilbert Bill, establishing equality before the law in the nominal sense between the British settler and the native, came to a sticky end. But Ripon's 1882 resolution promising local bodies to be filled in some part through elections fared a little better. The political space available to the Indian subject showed promise of expansion, and the competitive game of numbers, played within categories introduced by the Raj, was key to securing influence within that space.[10]

Identity and Political Representation

The Indian Councils Act of 1892 is significant in recognizing, not so much in words as in practice, the principle of separate representation by religious categories. Commenting upon this constitutional innovation, Dr B.R. Ambedkar, in 1942, observed: 'It is a mystery as to who was responsible for its introduction. This scheme of separate representation was not the result of any demand put forth by any organised Muslim association'.[11] Separate representation was perhaps a scheme hit upon by Viceroy Dufferin, who was convinced that mass politics in India could not be determined in accordance with stratifications of class and property as in Britain but needed to necessarily provide for social identities, as tabulated under the decennial census.

Universal franchise was an idea whose time was yet to come. And it seemed then, within a society segmented and stratified by the categories of governance, that separate representation was a means of ensuring some measure of equity. The North-Western Provinces and Oudh Municipalities Act, 1883, introduced stringent property and income qualifications in the system of representation in the United Provinces as a precondition for the franchise right. Candidates were required to have five times the threshold level, both in property and income, at which voters were admitted. The consequence of the restricted franchise was that Muslims who had been resistant to the new systems of commerce and administration were grossly underrepresented in relation to their number within the population of the province.[12]

There was a similar experience in Punjab as well. A considerable accentuation of inter-communal tensions followed the introduction of elected municipalities in the province. And the provincial government sought a remedy in separate and assured representation for the Muslim community, as early as 1886.[13]

A privilege once granted is never voluntarily surrendered. In the following years, inter-communal relations in the northern region remained tense on account of two controversies—cow protection and the contention for official status between the Urdu and Nagari scripts.[14] Aligarh in the United Provinces became the centre of Muslim consolidation towards the end of the nineteenth century. It was here that the Urdu Defence Association was formed in 1900 as a reaction to the notification of the Nagari script as the official medium of written transactions. It was here, again, that the Mohammadan Anglo-Oriental Defence Association was formed to mobilize the community against the cow-protection movement.[15]

Hindu Identity

Ideologically, the construction of the Hindu identity had begun through the recreation of an imagined past. Bal Gangadhar Tilak is a key figure here, the quintessential theorist of a new praxis of Hindutva, with its elaborate symbolism of the Ganpati festival and celebration of the medieval warrior king Shivaji. Tilak was convinced that 'religion is an element in nationality', and his reading of India's subjugation harked back strongly to a mythical golden age. 'Vedic religion was the religion of the Aryans from a very early time', he wrote, 'During Vedic times, India was a self-contained country. It was united as a great nation. That unity has disappeared bringing on us great degradation and it becomes the duty of the leaders to revive that union'.[16]

Tilak's reading of history taught him that India's greatness existed only in those periods when Hindu hegemony was secure. He equated those years when Hindu ideology was at a low ebb—for part of which Buddhism flourished as a powerful secular ideology of social equality—with the dark days under British colonialism:

For some two hundred years India was in the same condition as it is today. Buddhism flourished and attacks were made on the Hindu religion by Buddhists and Jains. After 600 years of chaos arose one great leader, Shankaracharya, and he brought together all the common philosophical elements of our religion and proved and preached them in such a way that Buddhism was swept away from the land.[17]

Along with the restoration of the pristine religious identity of the nation, Tilak championed the cause of a common language for India. In this advocacy, too, he chose to adopt a principle of exclusion, arising yet again from a reading of history that saw an Indian nation in perfect harmony in dimly remembered times but thrown into disarray by later developments: 'The contest between the Aryans and the non-Aryans in ancient India, and between the Mohammedans and the Hindus in later years have destroyed the linguistic harmony of the country.'[18]

The situation had to be set right in its proper temporal order. Since the prior tension between the Aryan and non-Aryan remained unresolved, primacy had to be given to this task before the Islamic cultural influence was brought into the reckoning. As he then wrote:

> There are two great important elements which we have to harmonise and bring together before we venture to go to the Mohammedan or Persian characters. I have already said that though a common language for India is the ultimate step we have in view, we have to begin with the lowest step of the ladder, I mean, a common character for Hindus.[19]

The fellow feeling of nationalist sentiment also involved, for Tilak, a clearly articulated opposite. The Ganapati revival was, at the local level, Tilak's exploration of new symbols of political mobilization. Unsurprisingly, Hindu distinctness, rather than the capacious cultural inheritance of India, was the theme propelled to the foreground in this revival. Since it coincided in the early years with the Muharram observance, the nationalist identity could be conveniently defined in terms of what it was not. The songs rendered at the Ganapati mela capture some of the flavours of the occasions. One asked of participants: 'What boon has Allah conferred upon you, that you have become Mussalmans today? Do not be friendly to a religion which is alien, do not give up your religion and be fallen.' Another was a straightforward exhortation to action: 'Disturbances have taken place in several places, and Hindus have been beaten. Let all of us with one accord exert ourselves to demand justice.'[20]

Reform and Revival

Late in the nineteenth century, the political terrain in India was dominated by two schools of thought—the greater Hindu nationalists and the genteel anglophiles of the Indian National Congress. Islamic revival was a minimal strain then, torn between the traditionalism that had been brutally put down in 1857 and the new synthesis Syed Ahmad Khan was seeking. On the margins, though increasingly voluble, were the vehicles of lower-caste political assertion, as represented typically by Jyotirao Phule in Maharashtra. It was in recognition of these aspirations of the lower orders of a rigidly hierarchical society that the annual sessions of the Indian National Congress were always held in conjunction with an Indian Social Reforms Conference. In 1895, the Hindu nationalists led by Tilak, heady from their victory in the Age of Consent Bill agitation, effectively wrecked this convention. Rather than risk a split in the ranks, the more liberal elements of the Congress agreed to remove social reforms entirely from their agenda of action.[21] Recounting the event in a later year, Ambedkar observed:

> The opposition to the Social Conference was led by no other person than the late Mr Tilak, who was one of those social

tories and political radicals with whom India abounds... The rebellion succeeded largely because the pro-Social Reform Party in the Congress was not prepared to fight its opponents. This rebellion had one effect. It settled that the Congress was not to entertain any question of social reform, no matter how urgent.²²

Tilak's contemporaries in the pantheon of Hindu nationalism, primarily those who emerged from the ideological ambience of the Arya Samaj, were more favourably disposed towards social reform. But like Lala Lajpat Rai, the man who earned the sobriquet of 'Lion of Punjab', they were prepared to view the matter entirely within the perimeters of Hindu scripture. 'Reform is revival and revival is reform', said Lajpat Rai. While national consolidation was undoubtedly important, it was a mission to be pursued on rational foundations. And nothing, said Lajpat Rai, could 'be either national or rational which is against the spirit of the Vedas'.²³

The resonances of the European experience in nation-building are evident in the effort to create by an act of will the same conditions in India. And the means of doing so is a reimagination of history. In a debate with an ideological opponent of his time, Lajpat Rai asked if Hinduism was 'entirely devoid of any basal principles on which the foundations of a church could be laid'. And he was emphatic in refuting that premise, since there were 'substantial reasons to maintain that Hinduism is at least as much a religious nationality as its sister faiths, Christianity or Islam'.²⁴

These beliefs were based less on an understanding of the culture and material life of the mass of the Indian people than upon supernatural faith, a feature of Lajpat Rai's thought that emerges when he confesses—with great candour—that his comprehension of the Hindu scripture is limited. 'The fact is that the best and the most glorious period of Aryan supremacy is yet a closed chapter to us', he wrote. And yet, the magic quality of the inscrutable Vedic texts was such that Lajpat Rai was prepared to suspend credulity and assert that the Hindus, 'directly or indirectly, profess to accept the Vedas as their religious scripture', and believe that these are the 'words of God' and 'infallible'.[25]

In his memoir written after retirement from active politics, the Bengali nationalist Bipin Chandra Pal identified two major influences upon the development of Hindu nationalism: the Theosophical Society of Colonel Olcott and Madame Blavatsky, and the German philological school best represented by Max Mueller.[26] The Aryan theory of race, developed by German philologists around the middle of the nineteenth century, had a profound effect in this regard. Purporting to show a common ancestry for the people of Europe, Persia and the northern Indian subcontinent, the Aryan theory of race carried connotations of racial equality that the rising Indian middle classes deeply appreciated.

In the hands of Tilak, the Aryan theory of race became a manifesto of Hindu revivalism. In the first of his efforts at Vedic interpretation, *Orion,* Tilak argued that amongst the Aryan peoples, only those in India had preserved the great traditions of the race, 'with a super-religious fidelity and scrupulousness'.[27] In his later work, *The Arctic Home in the Vedas,* Tilak went even further, celebrating the 'vitality and superiority of the Aryan races, as disclosed by their conquest, by extermination or assimilation, or the non-Aryan races, with whom they came in contact'.[28]

Lajpat Rai, too, was deeply committed to the Aryan theory of race as a basis for defining Indian nationhood. 'Arya', he pointed out, is the first known appellation used for the people of India. He conceded a certain difficulty proceeding from here to a definition of nationality, since Arya was, in his perception, no more than a racial description. But no matter, Lajpat Rai found sufficient traces of the spirit of nationality 'in the passages in which the Rishi ordained all *Aryas* to combine against the attacks of *Dasyus, Chandalas* and *Mlecchas.*'[29]

Both Tilak and Lajpat Rai are comfortable with the recognition that the Aryan cultural incursion into India involved an element of conquest, a proposition that left them vulnerable to withering counter-attack. The Aryan theory was a two-edged sword, and an anticipatory rejoinder had indeed been prepared by the Marathi visionary and social reformer Jyotiba Phule, at least two decades ahead of Tilak's Vedic excursus.[30]

Phule's discovery of Indian tradition followed a course diametrically opposed to that of the Hindu nationalists. The word 'Hindu' is notable for its rarity within Phule's discourse and the word 'Aryan' is used consistently in a negative sense. In *Ghulamgiri*, Phule fired his first salvo against the effort to reinterpret Indian history in terms of the glories of the Aryan civilization. The Aryans, he said, 'appear to have been a race imbued with very high notions of self, extremely cunning, arrogant and bigoted'. The self-important epithets they use with reference to themselves, 'confirm us in our opinion of their primitive character, which they have preserved up to the present time, with perhaps, little change for the better'.[31]

A Civic Definition

Alongside these identity-based claims of nationality, another perspective was emerging, professing to see political rights as reward for civic merit, an attitude showcased by early presidential addresses delivered from the platform of the Indian National Congress. There was, to begin with, the effort to demystify the element of identity in the characterization of the nation in favour of a functional or pragmatic definition. As Pherozeshah Mehta puts it in his presidential address to the 1890 session of the Congress, the force that brought the gathering together was a 'common nationality'. And this arose simply from being 'citizens of one country, subjects of one power, amenable to one code of laws, taxed by one authority, influenced for weal or woe by one system of administration, urged by like impulses to secure like rights and to be relieved of like burdens.'[32]

Mehta's successor, P. Ananda Charlu struck up a similar theme in his 1891 address. Deprecating the 'desultory controversy' that had arisen over the word 'nationality', Charlu asserted that it was neither a common language nor a common religion nor even a provable common extraction that defined the nation. These could undoubtedly be circumstances reinforcing the sense of mutual belonging, but in its essence, the word nationality 'should be taken to have the same meaning as the Sanskrit *prajah*, which is the correlative term of *Rajah*—the ruling power'.[33]

Citizens living under the same sovereign were not to be differentiated in terms of rights. Representation in the decisions of the sovereign was foremost among the rights that the Congress chose to assert in its early years, though not for all. In his 1895 presidential address to the Congress, Surendranath Bannerjee was anxious to avoid what seemed an impossible demand. It was nobody's case, he said, that the benefit of political representation should be granted to women or to the mass of Indian people. Rather, the Congress would be satisfied if it managed to obtain 'representative institutions of a modified character for the educated community who, by reason of their culture and enlightenment... might be presumed to be qualified for such a boon.'[34]

There was an unstated identity assertion here, since the caste differentiation that began with modernization was being deepened through administrative processes of the Raj. Every citizen had to belong to one or the other of the categories invented to suit the governance imperatives of the Raj. And there was generalized consent, even among the rising class of Indian nationalists, that hierarchies could not be disturbed.

Nationalist doctrine was comfortable with this inconsistency. Securing equality in rights was desirable but not feasible, given the cultural lags between different strata of Indians. Numbers were immaterial, since this was a doctrine sustained by the moral imperative of governance in accordance with the best values of western civilization. On the other hand, the identity-based nationalist consolidation was crucially dependent on numbers. It drew its sustenance from the ability to bring masses out on the streets, making the case for recognizing an identity construct as the foundation of self-government.

Years later, Jawaharlal Nehru reflected in his autobiography on those early years of nationalist consolidation, recording how the project remained dormant all through this period of stalemate between the radicals and the moderates. The moderates controlled the Congress, but they were not up to the challenge in tactical terms. Motilal Nehru—then and for long an important political influence upon his son—found himself ideologically in tune with the moderate position but somewhat averse to their poverty of tactics. And though he found much to commend in the tactics advocated by the radicals under Tilak's leadership, he hesitated before committing to that brand of politics. 'Often he used to say', Jawaharlal recounted about his father, 'that moderate tactics were no good, but nothing could be done till some solution for the Hindu-Muslim question was found'.[35]

There was an early recognition of the problem, but none of the remedies imagined could overcome the perception that an individual's civic existence was derived from religion. The 1916 Congress session is recalled in history texts for the simple reason that the Muslim League was an active participant in the person of Mohammad Ali Jinnah. And he forged with Tilak the compact under which the Muslim and Hindu would accept a system of popular representation premised upon distinct and, by implication, irreconcilable identities. Tilak's concession to the principle of separateness was opposed by others in the ranks of Hindu nationalism, principally Madan Mohan Malaviya and Lala

Lajpat Rai. The latter remained hostile to the practice for much longer and, in later writings, denounced separate electorates as a 'denial of the principle of nationality' and a 'partition of India'.[36] From quite a different perspective, Jawaharlal Nehru, too, opposed separate electorates as a 'political barrier' around the Muslim community, 'isolating them from the rest of India and reversing the unifying and amalgamating process' underway for centuries.[37]

Awakening of Hindu Nationalism

The Hindu–Muslim entente cordiale formalized in Lucknow survived very briefly. It collapsed following the withdrawal of the Khilafat agitation in 1921. In this time, Hindu nationalism came up frontally against another major fault line: the alienation of the non-caste population. E.A. Gait was merely one of many obscure British officials who administered the British Raj. But as a statistician who directed the census operations in 1911, he may have played an unwitting, though still unacknowledged, role in the Hindu consolidation. As he saw it, his mission was to provide an accurate count and a sorting of the population that served the cause of administration. With that purpose, he issued a circular to all provincial census supervisors 'to report as to the criteria which might be taken to determine whether or not a man is a genuine Hindu in the popular acceptation of the term'. The responses he received covered 'an extraordinary diversity of opinion', which convinced him of the 'extreme complexity of the question and the indefiniteness of the word's connotations'.[38]

Gait listed beliefs and ritual practices considered in some degree integral to Hinduism. In different provinces, though, census enumerators found that no single criterion was satisfied in full and most others in varying degree. In the Central Provinces and Berar, Gait's explanatory memorandum in the budget volume reported that:

> A quarter of the persons classed as Hindus deny the supremacy of the Brahmans and the authority of the Vedas, more than half do not receive the *mantra* from a recognised Hindu *guru*; a quarter do not worship the great Hindu gods and are not served by good Brahman priests; a third are denied access to temples, a quarter caused pollution by touch; a seventh always bury their dead, while a half do not regard cremation as obligatory; and two-fifths eat beef.[39]

The picture from other provinces was equally mixed. While abandoning the method of classification under pressure from Hindu nationalism, Gait did observe that the 'Hindu' category included several who were denied entry into places of worship and also various low castes, whom many census enumerators in northern India 'hesitated' to describe as Hindu. There were also several who did not consider themselves as Hindus but nevertheless came into the fold under the census enumeration, and many who actually 'objected to being so classed'.[40]

While it seemed likely to influence census categorization of people by religion, the Gait circular caused enormous consternation within Hindu nationalist ranks. As Lajpat Rai noted with some asperity in a history of the Arya Samaj written in 1915:

> One fine morning the learned pandits of Kashi rose to learn that their orthodoxy stood the chance of losing the allegiance of six crores of human beings who, the Government and its advisors were told, were not Hindus, in so far as other Hindus would not acknowledge them as such, and would not even touch them.[41]

Hindu nationalism came, from then on, to regard the lower-caste population as a political resource: useful in boosting numbers and bolstering claims to political representation but not yet deserving of a full measure of autonomy. 'Enumerated communities' is the term of art devised by political scientists to describe how official processes of administration, notably the modern census, impact social identities.[42] When the census exercise began in India, colonial officials expected to find clear patterns of religious practice but were 'confronted by and irritated by, Indian conceptual non-conformity'.[43] Hinduism remained a category of enumeration in the first census of 1872 and every subsequent one, though 'without a formal definition'. Prior to the 1881 census, the British parliament was informed that an effort at refining conceptual categories was underway but had not made much headway because of the difficulty of drawing a line 'between Hindooism (sic) and the rude religions of some tribes'.[44] Despite the untidiness of the classificatory scheme, a committee looking at the format of the 1881 census decided that Hinduism should remain the residual category, i.e. all who did not specifically claim another religious allegiance should be categorized as Hindu.[45]

In 1909, with competition over political representation intensifying, one U.N. Mukherji, in a brief flirtation with immortality, wrote a book that presaged an existential struggle for survival: *Hindus, A Dying Race*.[46] The book was serialized in a magazine and republished in 1910. Mukherji followed up with *Hindus and the Coming Census*, a clear call to use the census enumeration as a strategic opportunity. Even amidst the clamour, there was scepticism over the supposed decrease in Hindu numbers, but as Pradip Kumar Datta points out, these were 'dispelled' by 'bigger fears'. Among these larger anxieties was a petition placed before the Raj authorities by the London branch of the All-India Muslim League that called for detaching 'the lower castes as a bloc from the Hindu category'. There were also escalating demands from the 'so-called backward castes for autonomous and preferential consideration'.[47]

Hindu nationalism deployed a number of strategies to dampen this political assertion and to wrap the excluded classes into its embrace. Prior to Gandhi's arrival on the political scene, the

Arya Samaj-approach held the field, with an emphasis on shuddhi or purification. Swami Shraddhanand was its most ardent votary, having met Mukherji soon after he sounded the alarm over the imminent demise of Hindus.[48] Facing down opposition, often violent, from caste Hindu ranks, Shraddhanand worked energetically to bring the untouchable, particularly the sanitation labour castes, into the body of Hinduism. There was a vast sprawl of castes that performed the most menial of tasks in the partially modernized ambience of colonial India. Shraddhanand was convinced that they had to be brought out of that liminal space between Islam and Hinduism. '[I]f the untouchable castes become Muslims', he warned, 'then the Muslim party will become equal to that of the Hindus'.[49]

Shuddhi, as practised by the Arya Samaj, involved the admission of the untouchable castes into the ritual observances of mainstream Hinduism. The abandonment of contrary practices such as the burial of the dead and the consumption of beef was sought through moral suasion. The Arya Samaj also propagated a new identity appellation for the sanitation labour castes, tracing their myth of origin to Valmiki, creator of the Ramayana epic. Prior to the creation of this myth of origin, and even afterwards, these castes were known to venerate the cult of Lal Beg, which had uncomfortable affinities with Islamic practice.[50]

This strategic awakening of Hindu nationalism was precarious in its timing. The lower castes were, by then, already alive to political prospects outside the Hindu fold. In 1917, the Depressed Classes Association, under the chairmanship of Justice Narayan Chandavarkar, met in Bombay and resolved that negotiations underway on a new constitutional order should guarantee them the 'right to elect their own representatives…in proportion to their numbers.'[51]

As he looked back many years later, Ambedkar drew a direct causal link between this political awakening and the greater willingness the Congress leadership then began showing in the inclusion of the depressed classes. Ambedkar refers to this awakening as a 'strange event' because it did not seem to reflect any manner of real concern with the values of human dignity or equality but was rather about buttressing Congress claims to representing the seamless whole of the Indian nation.[52]

Gandhi was, by this time, established as the dominant voice within the nationalist movement. If he was quick to recognize the power of nationalism—as a slogan and a concept—for mobilizing the people against British colonialism, he disdained the implied coercion of political mobilization. He remained indifferent, when not actively hostile, to the Arya Samaj's shuddhi programme and to countervailing movements from the Muslim side. Neither numbers nor electoral competition had a place in his imagination of the Indian nation.

Nationalism as conceived by the early thinkers involved a relationship between citizens and sovereign. For Gandhi, it was almost akin to a relationship between the individual and a benign Creator. The civic bonds between one citizen and another were a way of realizing a higher divine purpose. Humanity was being led astray by the conceit that the political State could replace the sole power that demanded loyalty. Gandhi's imagined interlocutor in *Hind Swaraj* expressed this conceit in his vision of the Indian nation. 'We must have our own navy, our army, and we must have our own splendour, and then will India's voice ring through the world', says the 'reader', intent on challenging the most deeply held beliefs of Gandhi, who speaks through the medium of the 'editor'. Gandhi is equal to the challenge, though not quite able to descend to the same level of banality. In his guise as the editor, he gently chides the reader: 'You have drawn the picture well. In effect, it means that we want English rule without the Englishman. You want the tiger's nature, but not the tiger; that is to say, you would make India English...This is not the Swaraj that I want.'[53]

These are powerful formulations, yet strange and paradoxical. Gandhi titles a pamphlet after 'Indian Home Rule', but then proceeds to denounce 'Indian rule' as a form of tyranny. There are echoes here of Tagore, who was then in the process of recoil from the Swadeshi movement and preparing an explicit critique of nationalism. He had been an early and enthusiastic propagandist for the Swadeshi movement in Bengal. But in 1907, with little explanation to his close associates, Tagore 'resigned his membership of every committee, severed the connection with every organisation—all in the course of a single day—and fled to (Shantiniketan) from where he could not be dragged out for several years'.[54]

The Nation as Oppression

Tagore emerged from this reflective cocoon many years later with *Ghare Baire*, a novel that in its time failed to spark the kind of interest that later years would invest in it. In the contention between the novel's main characters—Sandip and Nikhil—Tagore articulated all the unresolved ethical tensions of the nationalist project, known then by its most visible manifestation in the Swadeshi movement. Nikhil is more or less Tagore's alter-ego, the man who responds to his wife's complaints about his lack of sympathy for the spirit of Swadeshi with a gentle reproach, when he says, 'I am willing to serve my country, but my worship I reserve for Right, which is far greater than my country. To worship my country as a God is to bring a curse upon it.' With fewer scruples, Sandip, the politician, is convinced that 'in the immense cauldron where vast political developments are simmering, untruths are the main ingredient', and 'man's goal is not truth but success'.[55]

Nikhil similarly sees no way that the 'nation'—so alien to the popular sensibility—could be internalized within the Indian mind as a focus of mass mobilization. The cause of forging solidarities between vastly disparate people could not be served by creating 'illusions', he chides his friend. But Sandip is unapologetic: 'Illusions are necessary for lesser minds'.[56]

Tagore also serves up a subtle characterization of the growing sectarian attitude within the two major communities, as the nationalist project was changing from an elite pursuit into a mass phenomenon. Communal antagonism was not, in Tagore's portrayal, an accidental intrusion into the Swadeshi movement but integral to its ideology. He has Nikhil asking Sandip why 'Mussalmans' should not be an integral part of the nation. Sandip responds with ill-concealed disdain: 'Quite so. But we must know their place and keep them there. Otherwise they will constantly be giving trouble.'[57]

Free of the subtleties of fiction, Tagore articulated his political sensibilities in a series of later reflections on all that was wrong with the nationalist project. Confidently swimming against the dominant current, which viewed the nation as a platform of collective salvation, Tagore declared in a series of talks in Japan and the US, in 1916, that it 'is that aspect which a whole population assumes when organised for a mechanical purpose'. 'When this organisation of politics and commerce', he wrote, 'becomes all powerful at the cost of the harmony of the higher social life, then it is an evil day for humanity'.[58]

Tagore makes no distinction between the 'Nation' and the 'State', but he does speak in places of 'government by the Nation' as one of the most oppressive features of nationalism. This form of government, he suggests, is 'like an applied science and therefore more or less similar in its principles wherever it is used'. India could be governed by the British or by the Dutch, or French or Portuguese, but the 'essential features' would remain 'much the same as they are'.[59]

For Gandhi, the State was entirely dispensable since he saw

India as a country in intrinsic harmony. 'We have no system of life-corroding competition', wrote Gandhi in *Hind Swaraj*, 'Each followed his own occupation or trade and charged a regulation wage'.[60] Nationalism was, for Gandhi, a compact between men within the benevolent embrace of shared piety.

The Swadeshi movement and the agitation against the partition of Bengal had seen the emergence of a strain of nationalism tethered strongly to Hindu revivalism. Their differences apart, the leaders who came to prominence then as also the older nationalist lions—Lala Lajpat Rai, Aurobindo Ghosh, Bal Gangadhar Tilak and Bipin Chandra Pal—held the Congress in a fair amount of disdain and were firmly wedded to national salvation through Hindu revival. Tagore, indeed, earned the displeasure of this influential group of leaders very early on for his lack of enthusiasm for the revivalist agenda.[61]

Gandhi, in *Hind Swaraj*, welcomed the forging of a strategy other than the mendicancy that the Congress practised. 'Hitherto we have considered that for redress of grievances we must approach the throne', he wrote, 'and if we get no redress we must sit still, except that we may still petition'. But after the partition of Bengal, 'people saw that petitions must be backed up by force, and that they must be capable of suffering'.[62] The force referred to here, of course, is of the moral rather than physical variety.

Though faith was his most stable anchor, Gandhi had little patience for institutionalized religion. Hindutva was then an incipient doctrine awaiting its full articulation in the works of Savarkar and M.S. Golwalkar. But Gandhi's critique was already laid out in *Hind Swaraj*, where he elaborated his perception of religion as a set of personal rules of conduct rather than a criterion of identity fixation or political mobilization:

> In reality, there are as many religions as there are individuals, but those who are conscious of the spirit of nationality do not interfere with one another's religion…In no part of

the world are one nationality and one religion synonymous terms; nor has it ever been so in India.⁶³

There is a radical notion of individual liberty in these locutions, born in the disavowal of the authority of both the State and the institutions of religion. It was that sense of individual liberty that was to be affirmed through the withdrawal of consent to an oppressive State. The maintenance of order would then call forth State coercion. Violence, even in self-defence—and especially in retaliation—was explicitly proscribed for participants in the nationwide mobilization. The purpose of Gandhi's first nationwide movement of non-cooperation was to transfer the locus of control from the government to the people.

Non-cooperation was withdrawn following the Moplah uprising in Malabar and the disturbances in Chauri Chaura. Writing shortly afterwards, Gandhi offered a sober stocktaking:

> [F]or the time being progress has been arrested in Malabar and the government has had its way...Malabar has demonstrated that we non-cooperators have not yet gained full control... There is only one way in which we can gain such control, and that is through non-violence.⁶⁴

The movement would supplant the government without itself becoming one. And the movement would maintain order in society because non-violence would be its most deeply internalized virtue.

Non-cooperation provided the context for a celebrated debate between Gandhi and Tagore, who was both exhilarated and alarmed at the massive national upheaval, unprecedented in his memory. The moment, to him, seemed to prove that 'the frail man of spirit', with none of the apparatuses of coercion, would prove that 'the meek would inherit the earth'. This glowing preamble aside, Tagore proceeded to ask the hard questions. 'What is *Swaraj*?' he asked, before deflating the concept itself with his answer: 'It is *maya*, it is like a mist that will vanish leaving no stain on the radiance of the Eternal. However we may delude ourselves with the phrases learnt from the West, swaraj is not our objective.'[65]

Gandhi's struggle for Swaraj seemed rather too mundane for Tagore, since he perceived the fight as little less than 'a spiritual fight' to release 'Man' from the 'National Egoism' he was 'enmeshed' in. The task before the 'famished, ragged ragamuffins' who Gandhi had roused from their slumber was to 'win freedom for all Humanity'. The 'Nation' was an alien concept for all Indians—and here Tagore returned to the theme of universal humanism that he remained faithful to all his life: 'We have no word for Nation in our language. When we borrow this word from other people, it never fits us.'[66]

Tagore plainly felt that Gandhi had isolated himself from the world to an unacceptable degree by casting his political project within the framework of the 'Nation'. This insularity was exacting a price that the politicians were not willing to recognize. Non-cooperation meant 'political asceticism', said Tagore, but the country's students, motivated by nationalism, were seeking not a 'fuller education' but a 'non-education.'[67]

The turbulence of non-cooperation, for Tagore, was uncomfortably reminiscent of the anarchy, as he remembered it, of the Swadeshi movement. And by seeming to repudiate all things western, Gandhi had unwittingly fallen into a trap of cultural insularity and set himself on a pathway towards the embitterment just seen in the World War. Cultural rejection pained him, since he was prepared, with 'unalloyed gladness', to accept all the 'great glories of man' as his own. There was no doubt in Tagore's mind that the 'West had misunderstood the East', leading to much disharmony. But he was unconvinced that matters would be rendered any better by the East, in its turn, misunderstanding the West.[68]

Gandhi responded soon, repudiating the accusation of cultural insularity in justly famous words:

> I do not want my house to be walled in on all sides and my windows to be stuffed. I want the cultures of all lands to be blown about my house as freely as possible. But I refuse to be blown off my feet by any.[69]

The purpose of the movement, he assured Tagore, was not to 'erect a Chinese wall between India and the West'. Rather, it was to 'pave the way to real, honourable and voluntary cooperation based on mutual respect and trust'. The coercive power of the colonial State was the target of the mobilization, and the object was to 'end the armed imposition of modern methods of exploitation, masquerading under the name of civilisation'. Non-cooperation was not, as Tagore feared, all about 'saying no'. It had an affirmative component too in the revival of vernacular traditions so that every Indian could 'think (and) express the best of thoughts in his or her own vernacular'.[70]

The Nation in Consent and Coercion

British historian E.P. Thompson observes in his introduction to a 1991 edition of *Nationalism* that Tagore was 'a founder of 'anti-politics'. His aloofness from politics, Thompson notes, arose from the clarity of his conception, which he had ahead of any other thinker of his time, of 'civil society, as something distinct from and of stronger and more personal texture than political or economic structures.'[71]

Clearly, the observation applies with almost equal force to Gandhi. The political strategies that Gandhi crafted since his return to India revolved around a notion of the relationship of the individual to civil society and, in turn, to the State. The objectives of his agitational work included the dismantling of the coercive powers of the State and the recovery of individual autonomy and freedom within a framework of civil society. The animating force of the struggle was, in his terminology, satyagraha or the pursuit of truth, and this was a brand of politics that was completely under the thrall of his religious beliefs. The distinction to him was entirely artificial, since politics and religion were just two different terms for the same process—of mediating an individual's relationship with society. As he said in a 1925 speech, 'The seemingly different activities are complementary and produce the sweet harmony of life. Politics separated from religion stinks, religion detached from politics is meaningless.'[72]

Unfortunately, in the competitive political model that was being introduced in India, religion was becoming syndicated. It was the primary form of political identity the rising middle classes asserted as they prepared incrementally to occupy spaces in governance being vacated by the colonial power. Gandhi's remedy for the ills of competitive politics looked towards tradition and, rather idiosyncratically, read hidden harmonies in the *varnashrama* and the institution of caste. As he put it after a contentious tour of the south of the country, where he was constantly pressured to explain himself, '*varnashrama* is, in my opinion, inherent in human nature, and Hinduism has simply reduced it to a science'.[73] There was, however, no sanction for the evil of untouchability in the varnashrama nor for one occupational group claiming higher privileges than another.

As an adherent of the *sanatana dharma*, Gandhi believed in the holy writ of the Vedas and all texts from the Hindu scripture. But he did not insist on their exclusive claims to divinity.[74] In fact, he could claim, with little seeming contradiction, that being an adherent of the sanatana dharma, he could be a Hindu, a Muslim and a Christian at the same time.

The times were turbulent, filled with practical challenges. With the withdrawal of non-cooperation, the short-lived amity between Hindus and Muslims had fallen away in fierce tit-for-tat violence. With communal violence raging through the mid-1920s despite all his entreaties, Gandhi chose withdrawal, often giving expression to an overwhelming sense of despair. Through these years of relative isolation and despair, Gandhi remained anchored in his conception of politics as a process of intensive self-purification, of achieving a harmony between the individual and society. He showed little inclination to engage with the realities of the bureaucracy and the law, or to attend to the mundane tasks of framing terms or agreements that would govern a transfer of power to Indian hands.

Motilal Nehru and Chittaranjan Das took issue with this attitude in 1924, when the question of contesting elections to Legislative Councils arose. Was the principle of 'non-cooperation' as endorsed by the Congress 'more a matter of mental attitude' than the 'application of a living principle to the existing facts'? If so, the principle was one worth sacrificing, they insisted, since the nationalist agenda required an engagement with the 'bureaucratic Government' that ruled Indian lives.[75]

In later years, Gandhi remained aloof from the nationwide agitation over the Simon Commission. Writing in February 1928, he disavowed any desire to 'interfere with the...evolution of the national movement, except through occasional writings'. Despite his personal regard for Motilal Nehru, Gandhi could not, later that year, summon up very great enthusiasm over the report of the All-Parties Conference he chaired. The Nehru Report of 1928 is recognized today as the first effort to give independent India a constitution. But Gandhi remained focused on human essences rather than the forms and outward trappings of political structures. As he put it in a communication to Motilal: 'I feel that we shall make nothing of a constitution, be it ever so good, if the men to work it are not good enough'.[76] A few days before, writing in *Young India*, Gandhi had lauded the unanimity that had been displayed by all parties in the Nehru report, which he said, took the country one step closer to 'constitutional Swaraj'. But he still sought to make a distinction between this political state and what he called 'organic Swaraj'.[77]

Radicalized by his first-hand observations of the global capitalist crisis of the 1920s and the experiences of the Soviet Union, Jawaharlal Nehru was pressing for a declaration of independence by the Congress and a future for the Indian nation in the socialistic mould. The Nehru Report had fallen short of his ambitions by opting for the more moderate demand of dominion status rather than independence. Gandhi urged a shift of focus from the terminology to the essence. 'Dominion status can easily become more than independence, if we have the sanction to back it', he said, and 'independence can easily become a farce, if it lacks sanction'.[78] The sanction, as a term in Gandhi's terminology, clearly meant the popular will. Given sufficient robustness there, it did not matter whether Swaraj, his preferred term, was spelt dominion status or independence.

Nehru reflected some of the impatience of the popular mood in his aloofness from the constitutional scheme devised by his father. But he pressed, with Subhas Chandra Bose and other radical elements, for a one-year deadline between the adoption of the Nehru Report and a formal commitment to the goal of independence. Gandhi introduced the resolution, setting out a one-year ultimatum for the colonial government at the Calcutta Congress of 1928. As the year ran its course and the Lahore Congress of 1929 approached, he rebuffed the unanimous opinion within the provincial units that he should take over as Congress president and instead nominated Jawaharlal Nehru to the post.[79] The independence resolution was adopted at the Lahore session, but the Congress remained unclear about the tactical means it should adopt. It looked once again to Gandhi.

The Dandi March followed and a series of meetings with Viceroy Lord Irwin. Nehru was disappointed at the outcome and saw little in the Gandhi–Irwin pact that served the cause of India's independence. He remained in deference to Gandhi, who, for his part, began the process of shifting his model of pacifist anarchism towards the socialistic paradigm favoured by Nehru. The outcome was the resolution on fundamental rights, adopted at the Karachi Congress in 1931, drafted perhaps by Nehru, with Gandhi fronting for him. An unseen influence here was the young revolutionary Bhagat Singh, who had, through his personal example and courage, unleashed a wave of excitement among the youth of India and been executed just days before.[80]

The Karachi Congress firmly committed the future state of independent India to the philosophy of welfare and economic equality. The State would, moreover, be obliged to protect the working class and the poor from the predatory tendencies of unbridled capitalism and maintain 'neutrality between all religions'. Speaking to the Karachi Congress on the fundamental rights resolution, Gandhi described 'religious neutrality' as an 'important provision'. But as usual, he remained focused on essences. 'Swaraj will favour Hinduism no more than Islam, nor Islam more than Hinduism', he said: 'But in order that we may have a State based on religious neutrality, let us from now adopt the principle in our daily affairs.'[81] The term 'secularism' would enter Gandhi's discourse only many years later. But the foundations had been laid by 1931.

The 1920s and 1930s were a period of sprouting and multiplying social identities. Gandhi's epic nationwide mobilizations of 1919–22 and 1930–32 had much to do with the entry into the nationalist stream of several sections that till then had remained isolated. But Gandhi could not dictate the terms on which these new entrants would engage with the nationalist project or the range of political interests and aspirations they would bring to the table when negotiating the contours of the future Indian State. It was a process of bargaining that went from local politics, with all its mundane concerns over the control of municipal revenues and urban spaces, to larger questions of identity, law and constitutional governance.

Rising social conflict was inherent in the situation, with different groups staking a claim to the powers that colonialism was reluctantly ceding. Many of these demands, when not represented at the high table of constitutional negotiations, had the potential to trigger conflict at the street level. It took the Congress three decades since Gandhi's entry into the nationalist domain to achieve a manifestly imperfect job of composing these proliferating movements and identities into a semblance of political consensus. Without the frequent political interventions of Mahatma Gandhi, in forms that oscillated between moral seduction and coercion, this reconciliation may perhaps have been impossible. Independence was accompanied by partition along the most pronounced fault line of the Indian polity in the colonial period. But several other schisms were repaired by Gandhi's constructive work through the 1920s and 1930s, perhaps not fully but adequately for an effective salvage operation under the rules of the Nehruvian democratic polity.

For a person who believed deeply in religious differences and caste ascriptions, Gandhi saw India's freedom, or *swaraj*, not as a mission of capturing State power but of establishing a harmony within a complex social whole. Speaking to two petitioners from the untouchable castes who visited him in the early 1920s for an exchange of views and advice, he said:

> There is not a shred of doubt in my mind that so long as we have not cleansed our hearts of this evil [of untouchability] and have not accepted the path of non-violence, so long as Hindus and Muslims have not become sincerely united, we shall not be free.[82]

Yet, there was a fundamental asymmetry between the Mahatma's approach towards the Muslim and the untouchable populations.[83] In an exchange with two members of the depressed classes in the early 1920s, for instance, he asked if the untouchables would 'ascend to heaven' once the caste Hindus 'washed off their sins'.

Clearly not, he said in answer, since it required corresponding effort from the side of the untouchables:

> They should give up drinking, refuse to eat leftovers, stop eating meat and, though for the sake of service, engaged in the most uncleanly work, remain clean and worship God. All this is for them to attend to. Others cannot do it for them.[84]

Does this attitude amount to the easy option of blaming the victim, available only to those fortunate not to have experienced the worst of life's vicissitudes? Certainly, Ambedkar, the leader of the Indian untouchables' movement, thought so. Looking back in 1945 at the Gandhian efforts at addressing the untouchability issue, Ambedkar refers to the formation of the Harijan Sewak Samaj and his prolonged correspondence with the Gandhian body over the best strategy it could adopt. With abundant enthusiasm, Ambedkar wrote to the principal trustee of the Samaj in November 1932, identifying two possible approaches to the issue, based on quite different social philosophies. One would focus on the individual and seek to foster 'temperance, gymnasium, cooperation, libraries, schools, etc.', on the premise that personal effort is all it takes. The other would look at the larger context, taking account of the fact that 'if an individual is suffering from want and misery, it is because the environment is not propitious'. The first of these approaches could work, but only in the case of a 'few stray individuals'. The second approach, Ambedkar was convinced, was 'the more correct', since the emphasis should be on 'raising the whole class [of Untouchables] to a higher level'.[85] The project of eradicating untouchability, in turn, required the active agency of communities that had the most to gain. This meant, essentially, that the workers of the Samaj should be drawn from the ranks of the depressed classes, for whom the mission would be a 'labour of love.'[86]

Ambedkar's letter addressed to the trustees of the Samaj,

who included the industrial magnate Ghanshyam Das Birla and Amritlal V. Thakkar, remained unacknowledged. Looking back on this in 1945, Ambedkar thought the whole cycle of events entirely characteristic of Gandhi's approach. He recalled a rude rebuff in 1932, when a deputation from untouchable communities 'waited on Gandhiji' with the request for representation in the Harijan Sewak Samaj. Gandhi allegedly told the delegation that the Samaj was 'meant to help Harijans' but it was 'not a Harijan organisation'.[87] The aim, in Ambedkar's reading, was to make untouchable uplift a social object while denying those who bore the brunt of the evil an active agency. They were to be cast in the role of inert matter, to be moulded into shape by the caste Hindu elite.

Gandhi's attitude towards untouchability was to assume the burden of guilt for untouchability and seek deliverance from the scourge through his own messianic efforts. In preparation for his epic struggle against Ambedkar over the political representation of the untouchables, he wrote to the young newspaper reporter William L. Shirer, explaining his opposition to granting them a distinct status: 'You must not be startled by my presuming to know the interests of the depressed classes more than its leaders... Though I am not untouchable by birth, for the past fifty years I have been untouchable by choice.'[88]

Ambedkar drove a hard bargain for separate and assured representation for the untouchables when constitutional reforms were under negotiation. His demand for separate representation was conceded by the British colonial government in the Communal Award of 1932, a scheme of political representation premised upon identity, since equality in the Indian milieu seemed an impossible ideal. Gandhi declared, in words that have resounded through the ages, that he would rather lose his life than allow a 'vivisection of Hinduism'. Nehru and Bose were mystified by the obduracy but were unable to rouse themselves to anger against the patriarch of their political family. Left alone to bear the burden of guilt from the possible death of the man who had begun to exert a mystic influence, Ambedkar caved in.

An account of a meeting between the two in Poona's Yeravda Central Jail has Ambedkar protesting at 'Mahatmaji's' unfair treatment of him. Gandhi shrugged off the plaint. It may be his lot to 'appear to be unfair', but he could not 'stand the idea that your community should either in theory or practice be separated from me'. Repeating his theme that as 'an untouchable by adoption' he had as much authority as anybody else to represent their political cause, he urged that caste Hindus and the untouchables should be 'one and indivisible'.[89]

Gandhi's tone of forbearance was reserved for Ambedkar. In dealing with others from the untouchable segments, he showed considerably greater asperity. In 1946, he received a letter from a self-described Mehtar, a person from the sanitation labour caste, questioning his approach to political representation. What essentially was Gandhi's objection to the Mehtars representing themselves democratically, asked the correspondent, since even the lowest of the ritually ostracized segments of India could, if given the opportunity, 'discharge their duty of citizenship and pick up their legitimate share in the future constitution of Free India'.[90]

After reproducing the letter in full, Gandhi poured scorn on its language: it was 'not of English English nor yet of Indian English'. Rather his Mehtar correspondent was writing in 'bookish English which (he) probably half understands'. Rebuffing all his professions of 'love' for the Mehtar or Bhangi, Gandhi brushed aside the 'discontented graduate' who was setting either 'no example or a bad example' to others of his caste.[91]

Separate representation for the untouchable was abandoned in favour of assured representation under the Poona Pact between Ambedkar and Gandhi. Despite this brief concord, relations between the two became progressively embittered. Ambedkar was soon assailed by the thought that the system of assured representation did little to safeguard the political autonomy of the lower castes. Methods of co-opting them into the Congress-dominated system were rife, fatally impairing their prospects of social liberation. Little wonder then that after cataloguing a few more instances of Gandhi's patronizing attitude towards those at the bottom of the ascriptive social hierarchy, Ambedkar concludes with an agonized and rather agitated question, 'Is there any wonder if the Untouchables look upon the Harijan Sewak Samaj as an abomination, the object of which is to kill them by kindness?'[92]

In a 1936 address, printed for mass circulation at his own cost after the organizers of a caste reform event in Lahore banished it from their platform, Ambedkar frontally challenged what he regarded as Gandhi's unseemly superstitions. The rationalization of caste as another name for the division of labour—a necessary feature of every settled society—was flagrantly off the mark. Caste, said Ambedkar, was the 'division of labourers' into 'unnatural' and 'water-tight compartments'. The 'stratification of occupations' was 'positively pernicious' because industry is 'never static [and]... undergoes rapid and abrupt changes'. This made it imperative that 'an individual must be free to change his occupation' according to available opportunities.[93] A 'biological trench' had been dug with the argument that caste helped preserve cultural purity. Claims that the division of labour prescribed under the system enhanced economic efficiency were pure fiction. Ultimately, 'by preventing common activity', caste 'has prevented the Hindus from becoming a society with a unified life and a consciousness of its own being.'[94]

An exegesis of the Hindu scriptures revealed to Ambedkar that despite their inherent illogic, they had the common unifying theme of opposition to individual liberty and social progress. A true social reform process needed to 'apply the dynamite' of critical thinking to 'the *Vedas* and the *Shastras*, which deny any part to reason [and] which deny any part to morality'. Achieving political liberation in this sense meant the destruction of 'the religion of the *Shrutis* and the *Smritis*', which would not represent a loss to society, since religion truly constructed could only be about principles, not a rigid set of rules. What was called Hinduism, said Ambedkar, was really speaking 'legalised class-ethics' or a 'code of ordinances' that did not merit the title of 'religion'. Even in rejecting these constructs, Ambedkar was anxious to uphold an alternative conception of a 'religion of principles' built on values of freedom and social advancement. This required that the scriptures venerated by the faithful be reduced to a single acceptable text, consistent with modern values of liberty and progress. The religious priesthood as a social institution would be an immovable obstacle that simply had to be abolished. Though tricky in terms of its practicalities, it was a task that could be tackled akin to the European experiences in secularization through the separation of State and Church. Priests, he recommended, should qualify for their status through an examination prescribed by the State. They would function as servants of the State, subject to its disciplinary jurisdiction.[95]

It is little wonder that the Jat-Pat-Todak Mandal of Lahore, which had invited Ambedkar to deliver its annual keynote speech in 1936, should have summarily withdrawn its hospitality in sharp recoil from these pronouncements. Gandhi, for his part, was deeply offended by the discourtesy shown to Ambedkar and chided the Mandal for depriving 'the public of an opportunity of listening to the original views of a man who has carved out for himself a unique position in society'. It was commendable, nonetheless, said Gandhi, that Ambedkar had published the address at his own expense, though perhaps the price at which it was sold could be halved since the message deserved wider dissemination. 'No reformer can ignore the address', wrote Gandhi, which was not to say that it was 'not open to objection'.[96]

With that said, Gandhi's effort to address the points made by Ambedkar suggested evasion rather than engagement. Hindu scriptures, he said, had attracted vast accretions over the years, some authentic some not quite so. To merit reverence, the scriptures needed to be concerned solely 'with eternal verities' that would 'appeal to any conscience'. Nothing could be accepted 'as the word of God' unless it could 'be tested by reason'.[97]

Ambedkar pulled back from these exchanges after another cycle of robust polemic, but as the years wore on, he was drawn towards harsher rhetoric. In a 1939 address titled 'Federation versus Freedom', he castigated Gandhi for dragging India back into an imagined past:

> To my mind there is no doubt that this Gandhi age is the dark age of India. It is an age in which people instead of looking for their ideals in the future are returning to antiquity. It is an age in which people have ceased to think for themselves and…ceased to read and examine the facts of their lives. The fate of an ignorant democracy which refuses to follow the way shown by learning and experience and chooses to grope in the dark paths of the mystics and the megalomaniacs is a sad thing to contemplate.[98]

Gandhi recognized neither past nor present, and remained focused on what he regarded as the eternal virtues invested in mankind through intimate contact with divinity. To take one consequence of this attitude, Gandhi in his riposte to Ambedkar firmly discounted the notion that caste has anything to do with religion. Neither did it have anything to do with the institutions of varna and ashrama. The origins of caste were irrelevant. He knew nothing about it, and neither did he need to for the 'satisfaction' of his 'spiritual hunger'.[99]

Prisoners of History

Ambedkar had a powerful argument to back up his belief that the untouchables were distinct from Hindu society. Even if they had similar customs and venerated a common pantheon, their 'cycle of observances' and patterns of social reproduction were entirely different.[100] There was no 'concomitance' between religion and nationality, said Ambedkar—there were indeed any number of cases where 'there is no separation though religions are separate'. There were also multiple cases 'where separation exists in spite of a common religion.' Worse still were the cases where 'separation exists because religion prescribes it.'[101]

Could these distinct trajectories of history be fused into a common sense of belonging? Could the burdens of the past be shed in an endeavour to forge a shared sense of nationhood? Ambedkar believed in these possibilities, though under circumstances he sought to define. He was aware that government could be a 'unifying force', since 'there are many instances where diverse people have become unified...by reason of their being subjected to a single Government'. In practice, though, the obstacles to such unification in India were immense. 'The limits to Government working as a unifying force are set by the possibilities of fusion among the people...In a country where race, language and religion put an effective bar against fusion, Government can have no effect as a unifying force.'[102]

Ambedkar drew a contrast between the pious hopes of unity and the record of intercommunity relations, which he had witnessed from close quarters, reproducing, in graphic detail, some of the worst incidents of communal violence over the years after 1920. He concluded with a grim summation: 'It would not be much exaggeration to say that it is a record of twenty years of civil war between the Hindus and the Muslims in India, interrupted by brief intervals of armed peace.'[103] Gandhi himself had recognized this reality, he suggested, when he abandoned communal unity in a spirit of despair, acknowledging that the 'mirage' he had seen was 'out of sight and also out of mind'.[104]

The characteristic Gandhian theme of civic concord being key to swaraj is striking in its contrast with Ambedkar's conviction that the State, rather than society, should be the locus of control. With his relentless focus on issues of practical politics, Ambedkar found that there was 'no distinction of a fundamental character between a State and a society'. It was true that 'the plenary powers of the State operate through the sanction of law', while 'society depends upon religious and social sanctions'. But this was not yet a fundamental difference: people made up society and also constituted the State. The power of coercion was held by both State and society.[105] Escapist minds were making out the alibi that the British were responsible for divisions within India and for the constitutional deadlock. Yet, it was evident to the plainest intelligence that the failure to obtain independence was a consequence of the 'defects of (the) social system', which, in turn, had engendered 'the communal problem and stood in the way of India getting political power'.[106]

If Ambedkar believed that the objective of self-rule could be achieved through institutional politics, Gandhi did not. If Gandhi tended to view the coercive power of the State as an unhappy recourse under all circumstances, Ambedkar thought it an essential means of achieving undeniable social purposes. As he said during his address on Ranade:

> Many people do not realise that society can practise tyranny and oppression against an individual in a far greater degree than a Government can. The means and scope that are open to society for oppression are far more extensive than those that are open to Government…[107]

Ambedkar's indictment resonates powerfully to this day through Dalit political movements. But Gandhian politics was always evolving, and even if he chose not to explain himself, Gandhi broke new ground even in the years after these exchanges. He had no use for rationalizing the iniquities he saw around and busied himself with banishing them. His attitude towards tradition was nostalgic and uncritical but forged in a conscious act of rebellion against the competitive politics that he saw as corrosive of individual autonomy and social harmony.

For people of deep religious faith, the doctrine of theodicy, which justified a benevolent God in the face of all the evils and iniquities of the world, has been a source of sustenance. Mankind lost its opportunities for perfection by succumbing to temptation in the earthly paradise it was placed in by divinity. In Hinduism, *karma*—with all its interpretations—is the equivalent of the doctrine of theodicy.

Lower-caste liberation movements transformed the dogma of theodicy into a narrative of primordial belonging. In the hands of the great liberator Jyotiba Phule, the Hindu scripture was interpreted as a morally obtuse inversion of good and evil, motivated by the political intent of justifying the invasion of the earthly paradise that was India. When not claiming the mantle of being original settlers, the lower castes also fell back upon myths of origin, springing invariably from a pivotal figure of history or myth, and a hypothetical golden age of perfect equality and harmony. This utopian state of well-being, in this narration, is vitiated by some act of treachery that established a hierarchical social order.[108]

European modernity, beginning in Thomas Hobbes's political theory, represented man as inherently violent in his acquisitive urge, a being who could not be kept in check except through coercion. To allow free play to all human urges was to open the door to a 'war of all against all', which meant that social order required that absolute sovereignty, including the undiluted right to own and dispose of property, remained a monopoly of the

State. The 'Commonwealth', as the State is termed in Hobbes's work, would then assign power and property to those in society it saw as meriting that trust.[109]

Later variants of the doctrine, in a context of settled bourgeois society, saw the human being as a naturally peaceable character who only needed the protection of the State to beat back the depredations of the wilfully evil. There were two logical lacunae in this doctrine. It failed convincingly to explain how the perfect harmony that man enjoyed in his natural state come to be vitiated by the impulse to encroach on another's freedom and property. And it also failed to explain, in a logically consistent way, how inequalities in material possessions arose. If all humanity was created equal by a wise and benevolent God, society, in its actual existence, bore witness rather to a whimsical Creator, with marked preferences and partialities.

European modernity had no answer but to unthinkingly fall back upon a notion of inherent good and evil. Gandhian modernity worked on a principle of man as necessarily peaceful, since the alternative would be a war of all against all. The inspiration for this worldview was distinctly religious. No religion, in the Gandhian reading, could condone violence while being true to its basic precepts. Where civil society failed to institute these principles, the State needed to step in, though only temporarily. Harmony finally required not the indefinite sustenance of the coercive power of the State but the fostering of consent within society.

Gandhi remained a sceptic about the State, while Tagore, to his last days, could not accept the nation. Both believed in a notion of individual liberation through civil society. Ambedkar. in sharp contrast, viewed the inherent and subtle coercion of civil society to be a considerably greater evil, which required that social life should submit to coercive law as applied by the State. Ambedkar posed a powerful critique of the sanctions imposed by religion and civil society: coercion could not be eliminated within society, he believed, except through the overarching authority of the State.

Ambedkar had been in conspicuous and outspoken dissent from mainstream Indian nationalism for at least two decades before the Constitution came into existence. In 1945, in a famous polemic against Gandhi and the Congress, he rebuffed the slur that the 'untouchable' constituency he spoke for was opposed to freedom from British rule. The reason that untouchables remained detached from the freedom struggle was not the 'puerile one suggested by the Congress'. Far from it, the untouchables insisted not just on securing freedom from British rule but in making free India 'safe for democracy'. Starting with this aim, the untouchables argued that 'on account of the peculiar social formation in India there are minority communities pitted against a Hindu Communal Majority, that if no provisions are made in the constitution to cut the fangs of the Hindu Communal Majority, India will not be safe for democracy.'[110]

Ambedkar was ambiguous then and in subsequent writings about how the 'Hindu Communal Majority', as he put it, capitalizing each term to underline its reality, is constituted. In the context of his later work, it is reasonable to read the term figuratively: Ambedkar was in all probability referring to a minority acquiring majoritarian power through a confluence of social, cultural and economic capital, reinforcing this through an electoral process dressed up in the legitimacy of the universal franchise.

Seeing the approaching cataclysm of a partition in the early 1940s, Ambedkar may have adopted the prudent course of seeking political accommodation with the Hindu Communal Majority. But with his early efforts at forging a just order in independent India being thwarted, he felt compelled to deliver on a promise made in 1927, when his assertion of the right of equality in the Mahad Satyagraha had invited a violent backlash from caste Hindus. Though born a Hindu, he had declared then, he would not die one. In October 1956, he led his followers in a mass conversion to Buddhism, which he saw as the lone faith that enshrined equality as a core principle. He died within two months, unable to carry forward that final act of cultural rebellion.

Since the creation of the contemporary global mosaic of nation states, promises made to citizens have frayed. Civil society solidarities, a basic prop of the nation state system, have unravelled. And the nation has been rebuilding its crumbling foundations. The erosion of liberalism in politics and the menace of right-wing populism have since been much talked about. But is this integral to the politics of nationalism, requiring in some senses a transcendence of that narrow ideology? Or is nationalism an ideology that can be repaired and restored to the role it once played as a passage to well-being for large masses of people? That is a question to be examined in some depth.

Notes

1 Payne, Robert, *The Life and Death of Mahatma Gandhi*, Rupa Publications, New Delhi, 1969, pp. 205–6.
2 Ibid.
3 Pradip K. Datta, in his book *Heterogeneities, Identity Formations in Modern India* (Tulika, Delhi, 2010, pp. 120–35), provides a dissection of how Savarkar's construction of Indian nationalism, supposedly drawn from history, was a mix of myth and pretence at empirical evidence. It is a trait inherited by contemporary practitioners of the ideological doctrine of Hindutva that he spawned. He is described, in fact, as a 'nationalist' who spins a historical yarn to 'shock readers into action'. His early celebration of the 1857 Uprising against British colonialism as the 'first war of Indian independence' and the seeming recognition of the Muslim identity as integral to India, came with a premise: that the Muslims by then had accepted the supremacy of Hindu culture. Incarceration in the Andamans and the communal disputes that surged to the surface after the issue

of political representation became key in pushing him into the sectarianism that was his basic identity.

4 A.G. Noorani, in his book *Savarkar and Hindutva: The Godse Connection* (LeftWord Books, Delhi, 2002), provides a summary of all available information on this fateful final encounter between Savarkar and Gandhi.

5 Desai, Ashwin, and Ghulam Vahed, *The South African Gandhi, Stretcher-Bearer of Empire*, Navayana, Delhi, 2015.

6 *The Collected Works of Mahatma Gandhi*, Volume 19, Navajivan Publishers, Ahmedabad, pp. 277–78.

7 *The Collected Works of Mahatma Gandhi*, Volume 10, Navajivan Publishers, Ahmedabad, p. 13.

8 Eaton, Richard, *India in the Persianate Age, 1000-1765*, Allen Lane, 2019.

9 Datta, Pradip Kumar, 'Dying Hindus: Production of Hindu Communal Common Sense in Early 20th Century Bengal', *Economic & Political Weekly*, vol. 28, no. 25, 19 June 1993, https://bit.ly/3yM1lT5. Accessed on 17 May 2022; Bhagat, R.B., 'Census and the Construction of Communalism in India', *Economic & Political Weekly*, vol. 36, no. 46-47, 24 November 2001, https://bit.ly/3FUBV7p. Accessed on 17 May 2022.

10 Gould, Harold A., 'Local Government Roots of Contemporary Indian Politics', *Economic & Political Weekly*, vol. 6, no. 7, 13 February 1971, https://bit.ly/39ZAZTb. Accessed on 17 May 2022.

11 Ambedkar, B.R., 'Pakistan or the Partition of India', *Dr Babasaheb Ambedkar, Writings and Speeches,* Volume 8, Vasant Moon (ed.), Education Department, Government of Maharashtra, Mumbai, 1990, pp. 249–50.

12 Robinson, Francis, 'Municipal Government and Muslim Separatism in the United Provinces, 1883 to 1916', *Modern Asian Studies*, vol. VII, no. 3, 1973.

13 Sarkar, Sumit, *Modern India, 1885–1947*, Macmillan, New Delhi, 1990, p. 21.

14 Ibid. 79.
15 Robinson, Francis, 'Municipal Government and Muslim Separatism in the United Provinces, 1883 to 1916', *Modern Asian Studies*, vol. VII, no. 3, 1973, pp. 414–15.
16 Tilak, Bal Gangadhar, 'The Greatness of Hinduism', *Samagra Lokmanya Tilak*, Volume 7, Kesari Prakashan, Pune, 1975, p. 633.
17 Ibid. 634.
18 Tilak, Bal Gangadhar, 'A Standard Character for Indian Languages', *Samagra Lokmanya Tilak*, Volume 7, Kesari Prakashan, Pune, 1975, p. 641.
19 Ibid. 642.
20 Cashman, Richard, 'The Political Recruitment of God Ganapati', *Indian Economic and Social History Review*, vol. VII, no. 3, 1970, p. 353, p. 358.
21 Keer, Dhananjay, *Lokmanya Tilak: Father of the Indian Freedom Struggle*, Popular Prakashan, Bombay, 1959, pp. 92–100.
22 Ambedkar, B.R., *What Congress and Gandhi Have Done to the Untouchables*, Thacker, Bombay, 1946, pp. 13–14.
23 Rai, Lajpat, 'Reform or Revival', *Writings and Speeches*, Volume I, University Publishers, Delhi, 1966, p. 51.
24 Rai, Lajpat, 'The Religious Unity of Hinduism', *Writings and Speeches*, Volume I, University Publishers, Delhi, 1966, p. 37.
25 Ibid. 32.
26 Pal, Bipin Chandra, *Beginnings of the Freedom Movement in India*, Yugayatrik Proksshak Ltd, Calcutta, 1959, pp. 37–50.
27 Tilak, Bal Gangadhar, 'Orion, or Researches into the Antiquity of the Vedas', *Samagra Lokmanya Tilak*, Volume 2, Kesari Prakashan, Pune, 1975, p. 157.
28 Tilak, Bal Gangadhar, 'The Arctic Home in the Vedas', *Samagra Lokmanya Tilak*, Volume 2, Kesari Prakashan, Pune, 1975, p. 381.
29 Rai, Lajpat, 'A Study of Hindu Nationalism', *Writings and Speeches*, Volume I, University Publishers, Delhi, 1966, p. 40.
30 Gail Omvedt's book *Cultural Revolt in a Colonial Society: The Non-*

Brahman Movement in Western India (Manohar, Delhi, 1976) deals with this theme, as do several other authors.

31 Phule, Jyotirao, 'Ghulamgiri', *Selected Writings of Jyotirao Phule,* G.P. Deshpande (ed.), LeftWord Books, Delhi, 2002, p. 27.

32 Zaidi, A.M. (ed.), *Congress Presidential Addresses*, Indian Institute of Applied Political Research, Delhi, 1985, p. 89.

33 Ibid. 114–15.

34 Ibid. 214.

35 Nehru, Jawaharlal, *An Autobiography*, Oxford University Press, Delhi, 1989, p. 32.

36 Rai, Lajpat, 'The Hindu Muslim Problem' *Writings and Speeches,* Volume I, University Publishers, Delhi, 1966, p. 211.

37 Nehru, Jawaharlal, *The Discovery of India*, Oxford University Press, Delhi, 1989, p. 354.

38 *Census of India*, Volume 1, Part I, Government of India, 1911, p. 116.

39 Ibid. 117.

40 Ibid.

41 Rai, Lajpat, *The Arya Samaj: An Account of Its Origins, Doctrines and Activities,* Longmans, London, 1915, pp. 227–28.

42 See, for instance, Kaviraj, Sudipto, 'The Imaginary Institution of India', *Subaltern Studies VI: Writings on South Asian History and Society*, P. Chatterjee and G. Pandey (eds), Oxford University Press, Delhi, 1992, pp. 1–39.

43 Haan, Michael, 'Numbers in Nirvana: How the 1872-1921 Indian censuses helped operationalise "Hinduism"', *Religion*, no. 35, 2005, p. 18.

44 Ibid. 22.

45 Ibid. In some despair at arriving at a consistent set of standards, the British commissioner of Punjab in 1881 noted that 'the Hindus of the plains worshipped the saints of their Muslim neighbours; the Hindus of hill worshipped the devils and deities of the aborigines; and the godlings of the peasants were divided into classes of pure and impure'.

46 Datta, Pradip Kumar, 'Dying Hindus: Production of Hindu Communal Common Sense in Early 20th Century Bengal', *Economic & Political Weekly*, vol. 28, no. 25, 19 June 1993, p. 1305, https://bit.ly/3yM1lT5. Accessed on 17 May 2022.
47 Ibid. 1307.
48 Ibid. 1305.
49 Quoted in: Lee, Joel, *Deceptive Majority: Dalits, Hinduism and Underground Religion*, Cambridge University Press, Cambridge, 2021, p. 95.
50 Ibid. 125.
51 Ambedkar, B.R., *What Congress and Gandhi Have Done to the Untouchables*, Thacker, Bombay, 1946, p. 15.
52 Ibid.
53 Gandhi, M.K., *Hind Swaraj*, Prabhat Prakashan, New Delhi, 2009, p. 24.
54 This is as recorded in a 1920 letter from P.C. Mahalanobis, who was, aside from being a statistician, a scholar with 'unrivalled' knowledge of Tagore. It is quoted in E.P. Thompson's introduction to a 1991 edition of Rabindranath Tagore's *Nationalism* (Macmillan, London).
55 Both quotations are from the translation of *Ghare Baire* by Surendranath Tagore, which was later revised by Rabindranath. 'The Home and the World', *Rabindranath Tagore Omnibus III*, Rupa Publications, Delhi, 2005, p. 230.
56 Ibid. 312–22.
57 Ibid. 330.
58 Tagore, Rabindranath, *Nationalism*, Macmillan, London, 1991, p. 51, p. 53.
59 Ibid. 56–57.
60 *The Collected Works of Mahatma Gandhi*, Volume 10, Navajivan Publishers, Ahmedabad, p. 280.
61 Sarkar, Sumit, *The Swadeshi Movement in Bengal: 1903–08*, Macmillan, Delhi, 1973, p. 60.

62 *The Collected Works of Mahatma Gandhi*, Volume 10, Navajivan Publishers, Ahmedabad, p. 12.
63 Ibid. 29.
64 *The Collected Works of Mahatma Gandhi*, Volume 21, Navajivan Publishers, Ahmedabad, n.d., p. 48.
65 Tagore's reflections on non-cooperation, in the form of a series of letters to C.F. Andrews, were carried in the Calcutta journal *Modern Review* in May 1921. Quoted in: Bhattacharya, Sabyasachi, *The Mahatma and the Poet: Letters and Debates between Gandhi and Tagore, 1915–1941*, National Book Trust, Delhi, 1997, p. 55.
66 Ibid.
67 Ibid. 57.
68 Ibid. 62.
69 *The Collected Works of Mahatma Gandhi*, Volume 21, Navajivan Publishers, Ahmedabad, p. 47; *The Collected Works of Mahatma Gandhi*, Volume 23, p. 215, https://tinyurl.com/ycvjwd4j. Accessed on 23 June 2022.
70 Bhattacharya, Sabyasachi, *The Mahatma and the Poet: Letters and Debates between Gandhi and Tagore, 1915–1941*, National Book Trust, Delhi, 1997, p. 64, p. 66.
71 Thompson, E.P., Introduction, *Nationalism,* Rabindranath Tagore Macmillan, London, 1991.
72 *The Collected Works of Mahatma Gandhi*, Volume 27, Navajivan Publishers, Ahmedabad, p. 204.
73 *The Collected Works of Mahatma Gandhi*, Volume 21, Navajivan Publishers, Ahmedabad, p. 246.
74 Ibid.
75 *The Collected Works of Mahatma Gandhi*, Volume 24, Navajivan Publishers, Ahmedabad, p. 585.
76 *The Collected Works of Mahatma Gandhi*, Volume 37, Navajivan Publishers, Ahmedabad, p. 194.
77 Ibid. 181.
78 Ibid. 234.

79 In *An Autobiography* (Oxford University Press, Delhi, 1989, p. 194), Jawaharlal Nehru speaks of the drama that preceded his anointment as Congress president. Gandhi's refusal of the post seemed emphatic, but 'seemed to leave some room for argument'. There was some hope that he would change his mind, which remained alive 'almost to the last hour'. At the last moment, he 'pressed forward' Nehru's name, throwing the Congress into some confusion and irritation, though with no other person stepping up, they finally gave in. Though 'annoyed and humiliated' at how he had gained the honour, Nehru had no option but to accept it. Subhas Chandra Bose, who counted Nehru among his allies on the left wing of the Congress, observed in *The Indian Struggle, 1920–34* (Kindle edition, p. 57), that this may have been a canny strategy by Gandhi to divide the emerging radical line in the party.

80 In *An Autobiography* (Oxford University Press, Delhi, 1989, pp. 174–75), Nehru refers to the 'phenomenon of Bhagat Singh' and 'his sudden and amazing popularity in north India'. This surge in popular fascination did not stem from the supposed act of 'terror' that Bhagat Singh had carried out. Terrorism had existed in India for long years, and most people realized that it was 'an outworn and profitless method which comes in the way of real revolutionary action'. Bhagat Singh's popularity, Nehru concluded, was because he 'seemed to vindicate' the honour of Lajpat Rai, who had died in November 1928 after a brutal beating at a protest against the Simon Commission in Lahore. And through his act of honouring Lajpat Rai, Bhagat Singh had spoken for the nation. Bhagat Singh became a symbol: 'the act was forgotten, the symbol remained, and within a few months each town and village of the Punjab, and to a lesser extent in the rest of northern India, resounded with his name.'

81 *The Collected Works of Mahatma Gandhi*, Volume 45, Navajivan Publishers, Ahmedabad, p. 373.

82 *The Collected Works of Mahatma Gandhi*, Volume 21, Navajivan

Publishers, Ahmedabad, p. 552. Gandhi had fairly permissive views on social intermingling, but he drew the line on intermarriage. 'Many Hindus and Muslims eat together of their own free will and Hindu society tolerates this. But nowhere do we find marriages as between Hindus and Muslims; if such a thing were to be encouraged, the Hindu religion would die out. I think it is impossible for a Hindu and a Muslim to marry and yet follow his or her religion properly. Men devoid of the religious feeling live to no good purpose' (*The Collected Works of Mahatma Gandhi*, Volume 17, Navajivan Publishers, Ahmedabad, pp. 60–62).

83 This issue has been dealt with in the context of the disputes over the franchise reform, in particular, the proposal to have a separate electorate for the untouchables in an earlier article by this author, 'Patriotism Without People: Milestones in the Evolution of the Hindu Nationalist Ideology', *Social Scientist,* vol. 22, May–June 1994, pp. 5–6.

84 *The Collected Works of Mahatma Gandhi*, Volume 21, Navajivan Publishers, Ahmedabad, p. 554.

85 Ambedkar, B.R., *What Congress and Gandhi Have Done to the Untouchables*, Thacker, Bombay, 1946, pp. 134–35.

86 Ibid. 139.

87 Ibid. 131.

88 Quoted in: Lelyveld, Joseph, *Great Soul: Mahatma Gandhi and His Struggle with India*, Alfred A. Knopf, New York, 2011, p. 230.

89 Ibid. 233–34.

90 Lee, Joel, *Deceptive Majority: Dalits, Hinduism and Underground Religion*, Cambridge University Press, Cambridge, 2021, p. 141.

91 Ibid.

92 Ambedkar, B.R., *What Congress and Gandhi Have Done to the Untouchables*, Thacker, Bombay, 1946, p. 145.

93 Ambedkar, B.R., 'The Annihilation of Caste', *Dr Babasaheb Ambedkar, Writings and Speeches,* Volume I, Vasant Moon (ed.), Education Department, Government of Maharashtra, Bombay, 1979, pp. 47–49.

94 Ibid. 50–51.

95 Ibid. 75–77.

96 *The Collected Works of Mahatma Gandhi*, Volume 63, Navajivan Publishers, Ahmedabad, pp. 134–35; Ambedkar, B.R., 'The Annihilation of Caste', *Dr Babasaheb Ambedkar, Writings and Speeches*, Volume I, Vasant Moon (ed.), Education Department, Government of Maharashtra, Bombay, 1979, p. 83.

97 *The Collected Works of Mahatma Gandhi*, Volume 63, Navajivan Publishers, Ahmedabad, pp. 152–53.

98 Ambedkar, B.R., 'Federation versus Freedom', *Dr Babasaheb Ambedkar, Writings and Speeches*, Volume I, Vasant Moon (ed.), Education Department, Government of Maharashtra, Bombay, 1979, p. 352.

99 *The Collected Works of Mahatma Gandhi*, Volume 63, Navajivan Publishers, Ahmedabad, pp. 153–54; Ambedkar has a rejoinder to this Gandhian case in 'The Annihilation of Caste', *Dr Babasaheb Ambedkar, Writings and Speeches*, Volume I, Vasant Moon (ed.), Education Department, Government of Maharashtra, Bombay, 1979, p. 83.

100 Ambedkar, B.R., *What Congress and Gandhi Have Done to the Untouchables*, Thacker, Bombay, 1946, p. 184.

101 Ibid. 179.

102 Ambedkar, B.R., 'Pakistan or the Partition of India', *Dr Babasaheb Ambedkar, Writings and Speeches*, Volume 8, Vasant Moon (ed.), Education Department, Government of Maharashtra, Mumbai, 1990, p. 187.

103 Ibid. 184.

104 Ibid. 235. Ambedkar's work on Partition offers ample grist to the religious chauvinist today. He holds both communities responsible for the unending cycle of violence, but, on balance, seems to suggest that the Muslims have been the more aggressive. He condemns religion and tradition for holding both communities in thrall to the worst social practices but concludes that the Muslims have perhaps

the worse record. The supposition that Ambedkar harboured a deep-seated animosity towards the Muslim faith has also lately been greatly publicized. Ambedkar, though, framed his perceptions in as wide a context as possible and saw contemporary realities in terms of their historical and sociological determinants. He had little use for the argument that saw Islam in its basic characteristics as the antithesis of science and progress. If that were the case, he argued, it would be impossible to 'account for the stir and ferment that is going on in all Muslim countries outside India'. He then concludes that the reasons 'for the absence of the spirit of change' in the Indian Muslim was to be sought 'in the peculiar position he occupies in India': 'He is placed in a social environment which is predominantly Hindu. That Hindu environment is always silently but surely encroaching upon him.'

105 Ambedkar, B.R., 'Federation versus Freedom', *Dr Babasaheb Ambedkar, Writings and Speeches,* Volume I, Vasant Moon (ed.), Education Department, Government of Maharashtra, Bombay, 1979, p. 310.

106 Ambedkar, B.R., 'Ranade, Gandhi and Jinnah', *Dr Babasaheb Ambedkar, Writings and Speeches,* Volume I, Vasant Moon (ed.), Education Department, Government of Maharashtra, Bombay, 1979, pp. 218–25.

107 Ibid. 217.

108 Franco, Fernando, Jyotsna Macwan and Suguna Ramanathan, *Journeys to Freedom: Dalit Narratives,* Samya, Kolkata, 2004.

109 Hobbes, T.R., *Leviathan or the Matter, Forme, & Power of a Commonwealth Ecclesiasticall and Civill,* McMaster University Archive of the History of Economic Thought, Hamilton, 1998.

110 Ambedkar, B.R., *What Congress and Gandhi Have Done to the Untouchables,* Thacker, Bombay, 1946, p. 169.

5
NATION, STATE AND CIVIL SOCIETY

In his foreword to the second edition of a groundbreaking work on the nation as an 'imagined community', Benedict Anderson observes that the years since 1983, when his book first appeared, had witnessed an explosion of theoretical work on nationalism.[1] In insight and authenticity, all earlier scholarship on nationalism just did not match the post-1980s literature.

It is a compelling point, though perhaps in need of a caveat. Scholarship on nationalism, perhaps because the subject is so emotionally fraught, does allow for wide divergences in interpretation and seriously miscued forecasts. In 1990, the audience received the historian E.J. Hobsbawm's pronouncement that nationalism as a vector of historic change, for all its glorious pasts, has few presents and no futures, with a degree of respect. Within months of its publication, a new wave of ethnic and cultural assertion was thoroughly rearranging the mosaic of nation states created in the decades following the Second World War. Yet, his work on nationalism continues to be recognized, over three decades since publication, as authoritative, indeed invaluable.[2]

Nationalism, on the terrain of political ideology and practice, ran alongside industrialization, a process that in the late nineteenth century broke down barriers between traditional communities, creating economic aggregations of widening expanse. Nation formation was no tranquil path but often a violent and bloody suppression of ethnic and cultural diversity, which enabled one dominant culture to emerge through agreement amongst a national elite.

Suppressed cultures, to the extent they retained a distinct identity, emerged anew in the early twentieth century, being one of the forces—aside from the rampant envies between the imperial powers—propelling the world towards the catastrophe of the First World War. The unravelling of four large empires of mixed language and ethnicity in the First World War—the Ottoman, Austro-Hungarian, German and Russian—did not lead to a settled new order of nation states. That had to await the global cataclysm of the Second World War and the brief concord that followed.

Politics tends to treat identity as innate and argue that nationhood cannot be erased. The alternative view is simply that 'innatism' is a construct of modernity, and that identity, in fact, is an individual choice.[3] Innatism argues that the nation state is an immutable part of being, with an axiomatic claim to an individual's loyalty. The alternative view points out that the nation state has undoubtedly been the agency of an enormous transformation of the world map but cannot be regarded as eternal. As Karl Deutsch observes: 'The nation state offers most of its members a stronger sense of security, belonging, or affiliation, and even personal identity than does any alternative large group'.[4] But the many tensions that fester within the nation today also call out for attention, particularly in those that emerged out of colonialism.

Ethnicity as Indispensable Condition

Anthony D. Smith, a particularly consistent advocate of ethnic origins, believes that the nation state will remain indispensable because it reflects a prior form of solidarity. 'If nations are modern, at least as mass phenomena', he argues, 'they owe much of their present form and character to pre-existing ethnic ties which stemmed from earlier *ethnies* in the relevant area'. Smith concedes that 'many earlier *ethnies* disappeared, or were absorbed by others or dissolved into separate parts'. Yet, 'some ethnic ties have survived from pre-modern periods, among at least some segments of given populations, and these have often become the bases for the formation of latter-day nations and nationalist movements.'[5]

Nationalism, Smith says, has indeed generated 'widespread terror and destruction.' Yet, 'the nation and nationalism' enjoy a unique status as 'the only realistic socio-cultural framework for a modern world order'. There are no rivals today for nationalism as a doctrine that satisfies an individual's need for 'cultural fulfilment, rootedness, security and fraternity'. Nations are linked by the 'chains of memory, myth and symbol, to that widespread and enduring type of community, the ethnie, and this is what gives them their unique character and their profound hold over the feelings and imaginations of so many people'.[6]

It would be a 'folly', says Smith, to 'predict an early supersession of nationalism and an imminent transcendence of the nation'. A global cosmopolitanism would clearly be 'unable to offer the qualities of collective faith, dignity and hope that only a religious surrogate, with its promise of a territorial culture community across the generations, can provide'. Beyond the obvious economic and political benefits, 'ethnic nationalism' promises 'collective but terrestrial immortality', a unique and undeniable sense of anchorage that would sustain diversity and renew minorities otherwise 'doomed in an era of technological uniformity and corporate efficiency'.[7]

In Smith's description, the nation is the focus of collective loyalty because of its unique property of permitting finite human beings to reconcile their brief presence on the planet with the immortality of wider relationships. Nationalism as an ideology has this 'ability to satisfy a more general craving for immortality', which has enabled an alliance with religion, and in other contexts, 'to substitute itself for crumbling traditions'. Nationalism, in essence, becomes a surrogate for religion, and the nation, in turn, 'a continuation, but also a transformation, of pre-modern ethno-religious community'.[8]

Smith's hymns of praise for ethnicity fail to account for the impermanence of memory. Collective memories are transformed from one generation to another, and mythology is easily able to secure a place in the human understanding where directly lived experiences fail. To turn Smith's metaphor around: how durable, really, are the 'chains of memory, myth and symbol' in binding a nation together? How grounded are they in historical fact as opposed to nationalist mythology?

There was perhaps a time when smaller nationalities accepted imminent demise as their destiny, when they recognized the need for assimilation into larger units as a matter of pragmatic choice. There was no identity so deeply held and valuable that could not be submerged in a larger community of language and culture. The choice was to be determined by a simple calculation premised on the imperative needs of human progress, a reified notion in the late nineteenth century, which spoke of transcending the mortal existence of man and the temporary and contingent existence of his culture.

Hobsbawm describes how mainstream liberals like John Stuart Mill and left-wing radicals like Friedrich Engels looked with complete equanimity at the prospective demise of smaller cultures that had not attained the hallowed status of 'nations'. It was accepted, 'even by people far from hostile to national liberation in principle, or practice' that some 'small nationalities and languages had no independent future'.[9] Yet, no manner of consensus really could be forged to separate the cultures that have the claim to nationality and those that have to just accept extinction or assimilation. History often writes retrospective judgments repudiating decisions made in earlier junctures. Illustratively: when the Czech people obtained a state of their own that was relatively stable, even if it was a political space shared with the culturally distinct Slovaks, a retrospective judgment on history was exercised, rendering Franz Kafka a Czech writer. Yet, as the Czech-born novelist Milan Kundera points out, Kafka never was anything of that sort: 'all his work is in German and he was, by his own lights, a person of German culture.'[10]

The Euthanasia of Small Cultures

Looking back from the vantage point of the early twenty-first century, what is deemed an academic inquiry was, for those living through the turbulence of the times, a matter of political urgency, the difference, indeed, between existence and its opposite. The bitterness and rancour of thwarted cultural ambitions became especially acute in the years preceding the First World War and provided the context in which the revolutionary leader Vladimir Illyich Lenin intervened repeatedly and decisively. Tsarist Russia then oversaw the destinies of a mass of nationalities and—as Lenin pointed out—no more than 45 per cent of the empire was composed of the 'Russian nation'. It was a circumstance under which the preservation of the 'right to self-determination' of nations was an absolute necessity.[11]

Yet, while upholding the right of national self-determination, Lenin argued the case for understanding culture in its impermanent and continually evolving nature. There was nothing innate there: culture was, rather, in constant and continual definition through myriad individual actions. Capitalism had advanced the process of creating cultures that could claim the title of internationalism, but only socialism could complete the process. And this programme went beyond old nostrums of assimilation and the euthanasia of smaller cultures, since it began with the assurance that all cultures have a legitimate place in the sun, irrespective of numbers and volubility. It then proceeded to invite them all to contribute to the evolution of an international culture that was more than the arithmetic sum or an eclectic mix of national cultures.[12]

However, the questions that dominated international political theory and practice were narrower, hardly focused on the institutional forms that would unfetter popular creativity. What grouping has a legitimate right to call itself a nation? Is the nation a community of language, ethnicity or religion? Is shared history the criterion, with all the difficulties that could arise from rival perspectives in reading and reconstructing history? To choose a still more voluntary form of association, could a shared ideology be the basis of defining nationality? Beyond these, in a more mundane sense, the nation was identified with the economy and the aspiration towards industrial progress. This required certain conveniences, such as homogeneity in language, in weights and measures, in tariffs and taxes, to enable greater facility in commodity exchange.[13]

A manner of homogeneity is required in the practical realm for the success of the nation state. The deeper cultural markers of shared identity are often created post facto. Political convenience may have dictated, at various times, that one or the other criterion was accepted as decisive. Yet, the verdict from any objective reading of history has to be that all these have had a role, though none is sufficient in itself. To take the criterion most easily accepted today, Hobsbawm has shown that the claims of language as the basis of nationality are tenuous, since nation formation typically precedes the crafting of a national language.[14]

Modern France is a nation with a strong sense of linguistic identification. Yet, at the time that the French Revolution was bringing the nation into being, '50 per cent of Frenchmen did not speak French and only about 12-13 per cent spoke it "correctly"'. Likewise, Italy today is a nation with an entrenched sense of solidarity around a shared language. But at the time of

Italian unification, 'only 2-1/2 percent of the population used the language for everyday purposes'.[15]

The French Revolution birthed the political slogan of the nation as a form of organization that spoke for all against the monarchy. In seeking its destiny, the nation ended up in another form of absolutism. Between the two forms of absolutism, other elements within the power structure were squeezed out to allow the bourgeoisie or the Third Estate—townsmen, traders and incipient industrialists—room for their expanding horizons. Driven by different motivations, the monarchy and the Third Estate had a shared interest in the dilution of aristocratic power and privileges. For the monarchy, the aristocracy stood in the way of an assertion of absolute authority. And the Third Estate viewed the aristocracy as an obstacle to growth, its power to impose various duties, tithes and taxes being an impediment to the flow of commerce across French territory.[16]

The revolutionary upheaval of 1789 began very innocuously with a fiscal crisis. The royal court sought a way around the crisis that would not undermine aristocratic privileges, but the Third Estate would have none of it, since the tradesmen and industrialists who saw themselves as the productive elements in society had little inclination to bear the burdens imposed by a parasitic aristocracy. As the conflict sharpened, the Third Estate saw little amiss in declaring their representatives within the Estates General—a consultative body established by the monarchy to facilitate governance—as the National Assembly. The Third Estate was, in short, snatching a higher mantle of nationalist legitimacy from the feeble hands of the monarchy. But that presumed status could only be won by the recruitment of the large mass of people, the sans-culottes, into the revolutionary endeavour.

Sans-culottes literally means 'men without fancy breeches', which, in the first flush of the revolution, came rhetorically to represent an entire social and political movement through a minor sartorial attribute. These were the working classes, the small-holding peasant, the urban artisan and the wage worker, with few affectations, whose political philosophy remained largely unarticulated, except as an aspiration towards an egalitarian order. In his classic work on the French Revolution, French historian Georges Lefebvre identified the 'lesser bourgeoisie', made up of 'handicraft workers and shopkeepers', as the main source of strength of the insurrectionary movements. They were the permanent personnel around which insurrections formed, with their subordinates 'gathered behind them, not as a separate class, but as associates'.[17]

Recruiting Mass Loyalty: Values versus Identity

The recruitment of mass loyalty, essential to sustain the revolution against aristocratic reaction and foreign intervention, required the poor and the dispossessed being conferred a semblance of rights within the incipient nation. This imperative was reflected in the constitutional politics of the time. The 1789 revolutionary upsurge was first encoded in the 1791 Constitution, part of an effort to create a political order immune to three identified perils: royal 'despotism', aristocratic privilege and popular 'licentiousness'. This charter allowed for the survival of the monarchy, though strictly in a ceremonial role. Since it mirrored the fear of social disorder of the rising French bourgeoisie, it restricted popular participation in politics by instituting indirect elections and high property thresholds for the right to vote.[18]

With armed intervention from abroad a clear and present danger in 1792, a more radical charter of citizen rights was thought essential to rally the masses. The outcome, consummated after serious internal turmoil, insurrection and the beginnings of the Reign of Terror, was the June 1793 Constitution, a document described as:

[A] charter of the greatest historical significance in that, for the first time, a nation was provided with a system of government both republican and democratic, under which all male citizens had the vote and a considerable measure of control over their representatives and governors.[19]

Inclusive nationhood and equal citizenship were vital parts of the political programme that summoned the deprived and disenfranchised to the defence of the revolution. The army of the French Republic, as it mobilized to fight the forces of reaction—both domestic and foreign—waxed hugely in numbers with the enlistment of a new breed of 'citizen-soldiers'. By August 1793, it was vastly larger than the army bequeathed by the Ancien Régime and comfortably outnumbered its adversaries.[20] This was key in defending the revolution against the concerted efforts of neighbouring powers, including Britain, Austria and the Germanic states, to reinstate the Ancien Régime. With the gains of the revolution secured through 1793 and 1794, the upward spiral of political radicalism stalled and soon went rapidly into descent. The overthrow of the Jacobin dictatorship and Robespierre's execution in June 1794 were followed by the disenfranchisement of the sans-culottes and the forging of another identity for the French nation—as 'a republic of proprietors'.[21]

The Constitution introduced in 1795, sought to preserve and protect this character of the nation in an enduring charter of rights and responsibilities. Despite periodic outbursts and demands that the 1793 Constitution be retained, the 1795 charter significantly diluted the franchise. Property thresholds and tax eligibility levels specified in 1791 were reintroduced and indirect elections reinstated to insulate legislative bodies from intimate contact with the masses. The sans-culottes who had been in the forefront of the campaign for preserving the 1793 Constitution were, by now, rapidly fading as a political force on account of the dual deficits of leadership and organizational skills.

Beginning then, the wars of the French Republic began to alter in character. Soboul points out that the 'war of revolutionary defence' the Jacobins had waged, 'passed, by almost imperceptible stages, into one of annexation and conquest'.[22] During the long quest for stability, between unfettered mass aspirations and entrenched privilege, the constitutional position oscillated wildly. An assurance of equality was part of the republican compact that defined the nation, subject to the defence of property. But when threatened by external subversion, the French Revolution took a further and decidedly more radical step in the assurance of substantive equality by writing into its Constitution the right of insurrection. The final equilibrium that the revolutionary tide settled at was much closer to the defence of privilege than the ideal of equality.

Community implies a willing surrender of interests regarded, otherwise, as indispensable for an individual's self-fulfilment. And the main conflict that propagandists of the nation faced was of reconciling the ideology of the bourgeoisie—which conferred rights and privileges on a narrow stratum while excluding the majority—with the sense of community a nation implied.

Competition and Concord

A market society exalts an individual's private gain—if necessary, at the expense of society at large—as the decisive criterion of rational behaviour, though it ultimately falls back upon a quasi-religious belief of inherent harmony between individual self-interest and the social good. Working with this imperfect model, it is conceivable that in the real world of community identification, an individual could cede his own need for material fulfilment to a larger kinship network. On the broader canvas of liberal democracy, an individual could be won over by a vicarious sense of participation in the material advancement of his community.

Could this be the foundation of concord in a bourgeois society, which otherwise celebrates the competition of each to get ahead of the other and sees in the mutual antagonisms of individuals in society, the singular key to human progress? Could this be the basis of the mutual bonding between individuals who, in various other ways, are divided by class, rank and status? Is this the ticket that those excluded from the nation are given as a serviceable substitute for a true sense of belonging?

These matters have never been thought through with any rigour or clarity. Consider Adam Smith, who wrote a treatise on the wealth of the nation while disregarding the question of what made the nation. For Smith, the nation is a territorial entity that happens, by historical accident, to be under a unified system of government. The fuzziness is evident: government is peripheral, and territoriality, inconsequential. Indeed, Smith's system is strongly imbued with a suggestion of extraterritoriality—or a political jurisdiction beyond the nation—in the sense that the wealth of the nation is determined by the extent of the market, which, in turn, is a function of the ease with which goods transit over geographical space. National frontiers are no obstacle, or rather should not be, in augmenting the wealth of nations.

The division of labour, an archaic reference to technological change, could cut through space, uniting nations—however they are defined—in a shared cycle of economic activity. The nation is the territorial and administrative unit that promotes the accumulation of capital. It is potentially unlimited in a spatial sense, though certain bounds are accepted for contingent and mostly unexplained reasons. Smith's understanding evidently is that the competitive rules of engagement within the nation state are operative also in its external relations, contributing to equilibrium at the international level too.

Competition between equals, though, is not the operative principle in matters involving the colonies. And this is because the colonies have certain advantages in being 'so thinly inhabited that the natives easily give place to the new settlers', allowing them to advance 'more rapidly to wealth and greatness than any other human society'. Colonists take with them the 'knowledge of agriculture and other useful arts, superior to what [exists] among savage and barbarous nations'. Moreover, with land being plentiful—unlike in their home countries—the colonists would be spared the burden of yielding large shares of their produce as rent.[23]

Smith provides an early flavour here of a tendency that was to become, roughly a century later, a powerful strain within the human sciences (as they were then called). And there has been no better commentator on this proclivity in modern times than Edward Said. Nationalist consolidation in much of Europe through the latter half of the nineteenth century, Said observes, led to the commonly held view of the Orient as a 'geographical space to be cultivated, harvested and guarded'. A French ideologue of the imperial mission put it with a considerable flourish: 'A society colonises, when itself having reached a high degree of maturity and of strength, it procreates, it protects, it places in good conditions of development, and it brings to virility a new society to which it has given birth.' The societies at the outer peripheries of the West, in other words, had no prior existence.[24] For European ideologues gazing at the world map, there seemed vast blank spaces that needed to be filled in with the cultural energy of the West.

As capital expanded beyond countries of origin, bringing larger territories under its sway, subjugating ever more communities to the relentless dynamic of its expansion, it fostered the values supposedly fundamental to its growth: individual liberty, civic solidarity and the private appropriation of the social product. Communities pulled into the orbit of capital responded in their own ways: resistance being the first option, followed by an effort at reconciliation. Civic equality was often the first principle on which people in the colonies sought an engagement with capital. When that proved impossible, there was an effort to forge new collective identities from a reconstructed past, from an ostensible golden age when the country was free of the baneful grip of capital. These refurbished and recovered identities were, in turn, rendered into the organizing principles of proto-nationalist movements that sought to mobilize a colonized people around the demand for political autonomy.

Capital in Its Spatial Dimension

Capital accumulation or the division of labour has its spatial dimension. Though opinions on modern economic theory vary, there is general agreement that its approach to questions of growth and development lacks a spatial perspective. David Harvey puts it well: economics as a discipline tends to view all processes of growth and accumulation as taking place 'on the head of a pin', instantaneous in time and confined to a singular point in space.[25] Clearly, this approach will have little ability to account for the actual growth of capitalism, which is all about the conquest of space and the dynamics of the circuit of investment, production and consumption, squarely enfolded within the passage of time. The growth of capitalism as the division of labour is about money power flowing 'through space and over borders in the search for endless accumulation'.[26]

Borders were entirely fluid in the early years of nation formation: they were, in fact, defined by the rate and spread of capital accumulation. As capital washed over the vast spaces inhabited by 'lesser people' awaiting the western civilizational mission, it created an economic identity of interests with clients within the colonies. It also engendered hierarchies of value addition, creating distinct patterns of capitalist relations between metropolitan centres and colonies, and within the colonized territories. Political boundaries were established where remembered history and modern constructs of identity intersected with the compelling influence of capital. Military might was often the arbiter, as during the prolonged conflict between British and French commercial firms for a trading monopoly in India, a tussle that both sides engaged in with armies quickly mobilized from among the native peoples.[27]

Nation then is the spatial dimension of the capitalist order. Economic theory in the classical phase sought an understanding of capitalist accumulation in both its spatial and temporal dimensions. Adam Smith's expansive view of development and the progress in the division of labour was, within one generation, transformed in the perception of David Ricardo into a gloomier picture of a capitalist order headed towards 'stationary state'. Even with wages restricted to bare subsistence, the growth of population would cause greater shares of the national product to go towards immediate consumption. And spatial expansion towards newer territories would inevitably reach a limit of added productivity. When the territorial frontier of capital accumulation is reached, the rent paid for the mere use of land would absorb the entire product. With nothing available to reinvest in intensifying resource utilization through innovation, the economy would effectively be in stagnation, or as Ricardo put it, the 'stationary state'. In the years that followed, the British capacity to open up new frontiers through hard-nosed business relationships coupled with the revolution in shipping, railways and the telegraph, made the stationary state a remote prospect. Internally, by abolishing the Corn Laws, which protected the older landed aristocracy from the competition of external producers of food grain, Britain achieved a state of political accord.[28] The wide-open frontiers of India, China and the Americas could be conquered through force or trade, both of which enjoyed their legitimacy within the bourgeois enlightenment. Force, after all, was merely trade by other means. The lesser people in these territories could legitimately be coerced into subjection or even eliminated in large numbers. Within the nation, though, coercion had to give way to consent, to a social contract that bound together all classes.

For all the complex explorations that his questions prompted, Adam Smith's main focus was not so much on the spatial dimension of how a nation is organized but on determining how the 'wealth' of the nation is distributed within the political and social order. The bourgeoisie, landholders and workers, receive their shares in the national wealth in proportion to three component parts of price: profit, rent and wages. Between the production of the 'wealth of the nation' today and its reproduction tomorrow, lay the intervening stage of circulation and distribution. Every element in the nation—whether an individual or class—had to be assured of a fair share within the wealth produced today to partake of the productive process the following day. And the distribution of the national product followed certain norms and conventions, determined by a contract between the three main classes comprising the social order.[29]

Smith's main endeavour, since he was also a moral theorist deeply concerned with justice, was to find a fair basis for distribution between the three classes, consistent with an objective theory of 'value'. He had no doubt at all that the terms of the contract would be far more to the advantage of the profit component of price, to the exclusion of the wage component.[30] He conceded that this morally dubious arrangement had a strong force of ideology and legality propping it up. From within his chosen discipline of economic theory, Smith was in a way reflecting an identical sensibility, though with a greater sense of moral turmoil, as Voltaire some decades back. Voltaire found in the country he inhabited several who simply did not belong. The French revolutionary Abbe Sieyes had little hesitation about appropriating for the Third Estate the mantle of the nation. Smith established, though with greater self-doubt, that working-class disentitlement is encoded in the meagre share that it secures, even in the best of circumstances, in the 'wealth of the nation'.[31]

In relation to prior theorists of the bourgeois-liberal tradition, Smith makes a conceptual breakthrough in positing a model of man as inseparable from society. Though he is not yet completely rid of the tendency, so evident in his predecessors, to posit 'human nature' as inherent and distinct of the social existence, Smith comes to the verge of recognizing that human nature is itself determined by the socialization process. Far from being naturally hostile to society or destined by divine will to inhabit a station ordained by prior conduct, good or bad, man was impelled by the balance of his own calculations of utility and otherwise to respect the norms of his social existence. 'Man, it has been said, has a natural love for society, and desires that the union of mankind should be preserved for its own sake', he writes, 'though he himself was to derive no benefit from it.' For obvious reasons, any person would consider the 'orderly and flourishing state of society' more 'agreeable' than one that is 'disorderly and confusing'. This is because any person would be 'sensible' that 'his own interest is connected with the prosperity of society, and that the happiness, perhaps the preservation of his existence, depends upon ...(society's) preservation.'[32]

The nation, in other words, was cemented by the mutual compact of its citizens to maximize its wealth. Adam Smith recognized every manner of exception to this optimistic construction, candidly conceding that in most instances he could observe the rules of association of the nation worked to the disadvantage of those without means. Smith was not quite equal to resolving this dilemma, except by positing a sense of human empathy that neutralizes the worst effects of naked self-interest. Civil society emerged as a possibility from this impulse towards sobriety in judgment and action. Adam Smith spoke often of the human sense of 'approbation and disapprobation' on which society is sustained, but was unable to decide if it came from rational calculation or from an innate sense of empathy that every human bears towards others.[33]

Smith's Germanic contemporary, the philosopher Immanuel Kant saw things differently, believing the 'antagonism of men in society' as nothing less than the means nature had decreed 'to accomplish the development of all (human) faculties'. Ends that individual human beings would 'care little for' are promoted by 'each pursuing his own ends according to his inclination and often one against another (and even one entire people against another)'.[34]

There are similarities with how Smith sees things but also clear divergences. In Kant's judgment, it was simply futile to seek the faculties of perfect rationality and logic in the individual. As the only rational creature on earth, it was only 'in man... [that] those natural predispositions which aim at the use of reason shall be fully developed in the species, not in the individual'. Man is not a free agent. Rather he is, even if free, subject to the irresistible laws of nature, applied through social norms. Kant clearly is setting course here, towards an understanding of the nation as the collective entity in which values inherent in the human species would be realized. He posits a superior, hidden purpose that guides man's actions, an intent which is not part of individual human nature but drawn from the species characteristics of humanity. He sees the antagonism of men in society becoming, 'in the end, the cause of a lawful order of this society'.[35] With all their mutual hostility, every individual, 'each pursuing his own ends according to his inclination and often one against another (and even one entire people against another)', manages to 'unintentionally promote... an end of nature which is unknown to them'. In this manner do they work, impelled by species properties, to 'promote that which they would care little for if they knew about it.'³⁶

In other words, the individual could only fulfil his potential in a larger human collective. Nature, Kant said, had set the 'supreme test' for mankind in the evolution of a 'perfectly just civil constitution'. Only that regime of law could ensure the 'development of all faculties of man by his own effort'. The greatest degree of freedom should be assured under the law so that there is a 'very general antagonism' among the members of a society. Alongside, there should also be a 'precise determination and enforcement of the limit of this freedom', which alone would make the sustenance of society and the coexistence between societies possible. Species characteristics of humanity, Kant proposed, would be realized in the collective will and embodied in a civil constitution, represented by the institutions of the State. Despite shared allegiance to the values of a civil constitution, the freedom enjoyed by individuals within society was represented in its magnitude by the prevalence of conflict. Restraints were needed, but these could not be applied externally, but would rather emerge internally, from the human faculty of reason. Order and harmony within the nation, in turn, would only be attained within a context of stable international relations. The 'same unsociability' that impelled man into continuous conflict within his own milieu would create conditions of 'unrestricted freedom' and consequent disharmony in relations between nations. 'Wars (and) the excessive preparation for wars' and the sense of deprivation that people in all societies must feel in a state of war are the means through which 'nature instigates attempts' to accomplish that which 'reason could have suggested': that it would be in everybody's interests to leave the 'lawless state' and to 'enter into a union of nations wherein each, even the smallest state, could expect to derive its security and rights'. Reason, though, does not dawn without prolonged conflict and arduous suffering. Wars between societies are part of the design of 'nature' to 'bring about new relations among the states'. This dynamic of internal necessity and external compulsion through war would have to work itself out. The ultimate objective would be 'a state which, like a civil commonwealth, can maintain itself *automatically* [emphasis added]'. In this sense, war may be an essential part of the civilizing mission, since it compels the formation of 'new bodies by the breakup of the old states'. And these wars would continue till old states reconcile themselves to the reality that they cannot be maintained except by 'suffering revolutions'. These convulsions would continue until peace between the nations is established, 'partly through the best possible arrangement of the civil constitution internally, and partly through the common agreement and legislation externally'.[37]

How does harmony emerge, by some miracle, from the collisions of infinitesimal individuals who share nothing except the instinct for acquisition and a tendency to allow their egos to take over their existence?

In his *Critique of Practical Reason*, Kant proposed that the human will should 'freely' submit itself to the law. In this sense of 'free' submission lay the preservation of individual liberty. Every individual, under the reign of reason, would be enjoined to act as though the exercise of his will could 'always at the same time hold good as a principle of universal legislation'.[38] A state of enlightenment, for Kant, involved mankind escaping the tutelage of older authorities—typically of the ecclesiastical sort—and each individual acting with a sound and well-formed judgment of the principles of 'universal legislation'. Kant was not a theorist of civil society in the manner Hegel was. But his notion of a settled and agreed pattern of social practice that would be in conformity with civilized reason, independent of the State and the coercive power it holds in reserve, is as clear a construct of 'civil society', as can be found in the thicket of conceptual confusion that has sprouted around the term over the years.

In a later work, titled *To Eternal Peace*, Kant sought to work out a definitive list of the conditions that would preserve harmony within the nation and ensure its untroubled coexistence with others. Conditions for peace external to the nation, he pointed out, are the same and logically contiguous with those required internally. As with individuals in society, the 'state of peace' must be founded among nations too, 'for the mere omission of the threat of war is no security of peace'. Foremost among the conditions for 'eternal peace' would be the adoption by every state of a 'republican constitution'.[39]

In later years, Kant's system was prised open at that singular point of vulnerability—the transformation of infinite human actions by finite individuals, each with deeply disruptive effects, into an outcome that is equitable for society. Hegel recast the function of laws: no longer were these seen as arising from the need to create a climate of coexistence nor as the expression of a natural state of harmony but as the expression of a supernatural 'Idea' in the finite world. The most striking feature of Hegel's philosophical thought, including his political theorizing, is his perception that human activity is the mere manifestation of the many processes by which the grand supernatural entity called the 'Idea' makes its will known. The point is made with absolute clarity in *The Philosophy of Right*: 'Against the doctrine that the idea is a mere idea, figment or opinion, philosophy preserves the more profound idea that nothing is real except the idea'.[40]

What Kant identified as the freedom of the individual to act within society in a manner of his choosing, in pursuit of his self-interest, was for Hegel, mere 'caprice'. To 'take caprice as freedom may fairly be named a delusion', he says, as he takes direct aim at the Kantian doctrine. Hegel poured subtle scorn on the tendency to identify 'freedom' with 'this formal self-activity': 'Since I have the possibility of determining myself in this or that way, since I have the power of choice, I possess caprice, or what is commonly called freedom. This choice is due to the universality of the will, enabling me to make my own this thing or another.'[41]

These locutions represent the merger of several motifs: the supposed collisions between various social actors over resources and the reproduction of society within the sphere of 'nature' are all illusory. Hegel says that, in fact, there is no such collision. The 'shallow-minded' believe that when a 'nation' is 'ruled by a common spirit, then from below, out of the people, will come life sufficient for the discharge of all public business'. In Hegel's rather contemptuous description, the shallow empiricists who believed that they had ascended to philosophical virtue were guilty of the greatest impudence.[42]

In effect, Hegel is making a case against the notion that 'empathy', as Adam Smith may have put it, could be a solvent for the antagonisms between individuals locked in a bourgeois order. Neither, it appears, does he have any sympathy with Kant's formulation that individuals would in their own enlightenment submit willingly to a social compact they could design in perfect consonance with personal longings and desires. Hegel was convinced that this was a 'kind of evil consciousness' cloaked in 'wishywashy eloquence'.[43] Just when it exhibits the 'greatest self-seeking and vanity', it invokes with great fervour and conviction the cause of the people and the nation. But it is not quite able to conceal the malignant sources of its origin, since its 'peculiar mark, found on its very forehead, is its hatred of law'. It was the greatest conceit, or more charitably put, self-delusion, that a rightful system of organizing a nation state could be found in the struggles of ordinary human beings.

Hegel evidently found the turbulent political environment of his time deeply disturbing. And he was repelled by the philosophical thinking that ascribed a higher purpose to the seemingly endless social contention. The notion that social harmony could be achieved with an agreed underpinning of law, that this state would evolve out of the competition between individual egotisms, was the 'last degree of shallowness'. The fundamental mistake of this brand of thinking was that it looked upon science as developing 'not out of thought or conception, but out of direct perception and random fancy'. It was simply illusory to believe that a viable political compact could emerge out of the process of negotiation, with individuals and social classes accepting limitations on their 'freedom or caprice', so that, in a social framework, these would be able to 'subsist alongside of every other individual's caprice in accordance with a universal law'.[44]

Law and State as Expressions of a Superior Will

The nation was not Hegel's focus so much as the State, the political embodiment of the collective will. And he was deeply unsettled by what he perceived to be the 'purest charlatanism' winning the name of philosophy and making it 'almost a disgrace to speak in a philosophic way about the state'. Unlike in ancient Greece, a constant referent for the European enlightenment, Hegel saw philosophy in his time not as a 'private art' but as an activity with a 'public place', which should always be 'employed only in the service of the State'.[45]

Recent years have seen a resurrection of the debate over Hegel's place in the history of ideas, particularly over the uneasy suspicion that his dense and mystifying idiom of expression may have been a cloak for lame political conformism. Irrespective of the academic value of this discussion, it clearly seems the case that locutions such as this from the *Philosophy of Right* create a solid case for inquiry:

> The state is the march of God in the world; its ground or cause is the power of reason realising itself as will. When thinking of the idea of the state, we must not have in our mind any particular state, or particular institution, but must rather contemplate the idea, this actual God, by itself.[46]

Mystically endowed as it is, the State cannot exist without an antecedent condition of civil society. The latter, in turn, is premised upon the existence of the State. This is a seeming tautology, but in reality, an illustration of the Hegelian dialectic playing out in the material world, with various aspects of reality always being in a process of emerging in their mutual interrelations. Here is how Hegel expresses himself:

> The concrete person is a totality of wants and a mixture of necessity and caprice. As such he is one of the principles of the civic community. But the person is essentially connected with others, and so must call in the assistance of the form of universality. This universality is the other principle of the civic community.[47]

Separate, individual existences were united in civil society, which represented the fusion of 'particular subjectivities'. And above all this, the State represented the universal objectivity. In achieving this higher synthesis, Hegel transits through several intervening moments. At the foundation are the family and 'the corporation', the latter referring not to commercial enterprise as currently understood but to voluntary groupings such as guilds and associations of workmen. For advocates of a liberal economy then, these were remnants of an older time that needed to be replaced or superseded by institutions more in tune with the times. Hegel viewed this with some alarm: the dismantling of the 'corporation', he warned, was a prescription for destroying civil society and opening the doorway to chaos.[48]

Nation formation is incomplete without civil society being in place. The individual citizen goes through levels of mediation in his engagement with the State. These serve to harmonize diverse interests and convert potential sources of conflict into a superior harmony. Hegel gets his perceptions upside down, banishing the real world to the ethereal space and investing a transcendent being, which has no existence outside his imagination, with ultimate and decisive powers over matters great and small. This inversion infects his entire system and colours his construction of civil society. Hegel proved thoroughly indifferent to stratification by class as he brought all the diversities of the social milieu into a mystical union that served the higher purposes of the State. Where civil society did not have the means to bring all individuals within the compact that would preserve unity and solidarity, Hegel invested the State with that coercive power— as in overriding parental authority when necessary, to provide all children with inoculations against disease or ensuring that they be sent to school for gaining at least the primary stage of education.

Endowed with a transcendental purpose, the State enjoyed a presumptive claim to the loyalty of its citizens. Inequalities of class and status, which Kant and others from the Enlightenment tradition recognized but chose to ignore, were swept aside as completely inconsequential, since the higher calling of every individual was that of serving the State.

Years later, as waves of political transformation swept across Europe, Karl Marx tried reckoning with this mystifying philosophical legacy. He noted that man had a dual existence in Hegel's doctrine: he lived in the political community as a 'communal being' and in 'civil society', 'as a private individual'. In the latter incarnation, 'man regards other men as means, debases himself to a means and becomes a plaything of alien powers'. 'The relationship of the political state to civil society', Marx concluded with some irony, was 'just as spiritual as the relationship of heaven to earth'.[49]

In his *Critique of Hegel's Doctrine of the State*, Marx had, without quite calling the authority of the sage into question, wondered at the contrary propositions inherent in his philosophy. 'He may not measure the idea by what exists, he must rather measure what exists in accordance with the Idea'. The material world, its institutions, its political structures were all various stages in the development of the Idea, its grand coming-into-being. And in dealing with legislative institutions and their power to determine the constitutional order for functioning societies, Hegel ties himself in knots of amazing complexity. At the root of the muddle is his aversion towards recognizing material reality and human agency as anything other than manifestations of an unseen divinity.[50]

Civil society as a theoretical construct, in Hegel's doctrine, was about submerging antagonisms into a higher, divinely ordained sense of concord. To the extent that the Hegelian perception has a bearing on contemporary understanding, civil society—as a process of transforming minute particularities in a complex society into a unified perception which feeds into state policy—is an infirm concept. Since being dismissed as a vacuous theoretical construct by Marx, civil society receded into the background of active theoretical engagement. But the maturing of bourgeois society meant that it acquired a practical relevance that could not be ignored. For a later generation of Marxist thinkers, civil society was a fact of life, associated with part of the hegemonic apparatus of bourgeois society.

Bourgeois society deemed those without means as less than sovereign individuals and, by that token, incapable of exercising the rights and liberties of citizenship. This doctrine, though, conflicted with the practical compulsions of bourgeois society. Working-class people had to volunteer to serve in the armies that fought national wars and make their labour power available for wages to perpetuate capitalist accumulation. This identity of interests between the bourgeoisie and the working class was contingent and tenuous, prone to violent disruption at regular intervals.

Equality in Civil Society: Illusion and Reality

Years after Hegel, the Marxist philosopher Jürgen Habermas rendered much-needed clarity, both in terms of concept and historical fact, with his construct of the 'public sphere'. The public sphere, he said, takes on political functions specific to that period of 'the developmental history of civil society as a whole in which commodity exchange and social labour became largely emancipated from government directives.'[51]

Coercion yields to consent in perpetuating the commodity exchange on which the bourgeois order rests: the recruitment of social labour in the reproduction of capitalist relations. It is a consensus arrived at in complex fashion, never conforming to any predetermined template, determined by the manner that social forces are represented in political institutions and the bargains struck over social welfare and economic policy. Civil society, here, departs from its Hegelian roots, where it is the embodiment of a divine will acting through family and corporation to achieve a fusion with the State. It becomes a public sphere where social groups contend and engage through organized apparatuses of information exchange and bargaining. The outcome of this engagement is, in the happiest instances, the stable liberal order seen in many variations on the European continent in the twentieth century, where a gradual widening of the franchise fostered the illusion of an inclusive polity. The transition to the welfare state, beginning with the Great Depression of the 1930s, opened a phase of active consensus-building between capital and labour, with the elected authorities being compelled to act the honest broker. When ordained as official policy following the Second World War, the welfare state was responsible for the subtle but significant transformation of the public sphere.

Habermas was convinced that the public sphere 'stood or fell with the principle of universal access', since a space that excluded specific groups on account of identity or economic status was indeed 'not a public sphere at all'. As a construct, the 'public sphere' needed the necessary safeguard that nobody would be denied admission by 'economic and social conditions', that all who desired could 'earn the qualifications for private autonomy that made for the educated and property-owning person'.[52]

Liberalism proclaimed its moment of triumph in Europe in the mid-nineteenth century. The 1848 revolutions that ran like a 'brushfire across frontiers, countries and even oceans'[53] represent the point of transition, 'potentially the first global revolution', which, within a matter of weeks, had overturned governments 'in an area of Europe which is today occupied by all or part of ten states'. And yet, within six months, its 'universal defeat was safely predictable'.[54]

The 'age of empire' began as the revolutionary tide ebbed and Europe fell back into the comfort of a settled bourgeois–liberal order. Consolidation of domestic political harmony was the other side of imperial expansion. France had ventured into a system of universal suffrage during the fervour of its revolution but soon found the practice ill-suited to the sustenance of privilege and wealth. Over the decades that followed, as its far-flung empire began absorbing its industrial products and bringing in assured supplies of vital raw material, the sharp edges came off the confrontation between the bourgeoisie and the working class. Democratization of politics at home became a much more realistic prospect, one that would create social harmony while not undermining an order based on privilege.

Settled times allow greater latitude for political reform. From the second half of the nineteenth century, the franchise gradually began to be expanded in most west European countries, principally Germany and France, till, by the later decades, both could claim that they had instituted systems of universal suffrage. 'Universalism' as a term did not, of course, include women then, since it was considered far beyond the realm of imagination that women should be participants in the public sphere. In the 1870s, Hobsbawm estimates from the example of Germany, France and the US, which had instituted the unrestricted franchise for the adult male population, that a European country with roughly similar demographics should have between 20 and 25 per cent of its population as enfranchised voters. Yet, for Britain, the percentage of the population that had the right to vote remained at an abysmal 8 per cent and in the Kingdom of Italy, which had just been consolidated into a nation from a host of petty principalities, it was a purely token 1 per cent.[55]

Projects of overseas conquest gained a fresh impetus in the years that followed. With the entities now known as Germany, Italy and Spain having, in varying degrees, completed by then the process of 'national unification', there was intensifying competition for markets that could provide room for the burgeoning ambitions of national bourgeoisies. Particularly significant in their participation in the programme of aggrandisement of the nation were the middle strata, hitherto rather unsure of the loyalty they owed the nation and their place within its social and political hierarchy. Those who responded most ardently to the 'nationalist bugles', says Hobsbawm, 'were to be found somewhere between the established upper classes of society and the peasants and proletarians at the bottom'. Service in expanding the reach of the empire, often in military uniform, gave them the status, in the ironic term used by the British upper class, of 'temporary gentlemen'.[56]

The mutual accommodation between Europe's imperialist powers, as worked out at the Congress of Berlin in 1878, had established a tenuous peace within the continent. Britain, France, Russia and Germany—and the lesser players who participated eagerly in the chorus of consent—then forced the debilitated Ottoman Empire to retract its territorial claims and the smaller nationalities to yield to their voracious expansionism. Yet, imperialist ambitions and rivalries remained uncontained. In November 1884, Germany, under Otto von Bismarck's stewardship, hosted another Congress of Berlin to discuss burgeoning disputes over Africa.

Through prolonged deliberations that stretched from November 1884 into the early months of the next year, the Berlin congress evolved an agreed blueprint for the division of Africa. The latter half of the nineteenth century was a period of gigantic global movements of people and capital. It was, in this sense, the first wave of globalization, and with the imperial nations being in absolute control both in the physical realm as well as the ideological, there was no challenge to the pretence of a benefit for all, since 'lesser nations' were not regarded to have a part in the bargain. Between 1820 and 1920, it is estimated that the territory today constituting the United States of America drew a total of 33.6 million immigrants from various parts of Europe. The largest number, over half of the total, came from the British Isles. Earlier immigrants had suffered some moral qualms about their relationship with the native inhabitants of the American continent. These ambiguities were banished by the second half of the nineteenth century, as the immigrant wave swelled and settlements spread rapidly towards the Great Plains of the American continent.[57] Darwin's evolutionary theory was, by now, established in the realm of science, and it was not an impossible feat to leap from the competitive struggle for survival that was understood to be the fundamental impetus of species evolution to a 'devil take the hindmost' theory of social development.

Capital Hits Its Limits

By the early years of the twentieth century, Africa had been devoured and the American frontier had been reached. With this, the putative 'neutral ground' on which the imperialist powers could sate their appetites for conquest had effectively run out. The urge for acquisition and territorial aggrandisement, incubated and bred in Europe, began rapidly turning in upon the continent. The Boer War, fought with ferocious determination by rival sides among white settlers in southern Africa, offered an early foretaste of what was to come. In 1914, as Germany and Britain formally declared war, and he watched the gaslights being turned off in the streets of London, a British Cabinet Minister observed rather gloomily, that 'the lamps were going out all over Europe'. There was little likelihood, he said, that they would be lit again during his lifetime.[58]

Variously called the Great War or the first inter-imperialist conflagration, the conflict in Europe between 1914 and 1918 is now referred to almost universally as the First World War. For this name to stick, it is, of course, necessary that there should have been a second visitation on the same scale. And this knowledge does not occur prospectively. Between 1918—when an armistice was concluded between the belligerent powers of Europe—and 1939, when conflict once again broke out, it could be argued that the world never really ceased fighting. First there was the Russian Revolution and the civil war that followed, with all the European powers seeking to turn back the tide of socialist revolution. All through this period, there were unending battles waged in the Balkans. Italy brought Libya under its iron heel through a series of campaigns that went on till the late 1920s and then invaded Ethiopia in a reckless military adventure that created a brief moment of concerted outrage among otherwise scattered anti-colonial movements. Meanwhile, the British mandate in Palestine and Mesopotamia (as it was then called), not to mention the authority that the French had garnered from the pompously named League of Nations to administer the Syrian Arab territories, were precipitating a series of armed skirmishes and full-scale insurrections. To add to this chronicle of incessant strife, there was the Japanese invasion of China beginning in 1931 and the Spanish Civil War breaking out in 1936.

Relations between the industrial world and the lesser people, enshrined in the charter of the League of Nations, meanwhile, imposed a philosophy of tutelage.[59] Because the lesser people had not yet awoken to a state of enlightenment when they would be able to take charge of their own affairs, their custody was an onerous burden that the industrialized West had to accept. As Article 22 of the Covenant of the League of Nations put it:

> To those colonies and territories which as a consequence of the late war have ceased to be under the sovereignty of the States which formerly governed them and which are inhabited by peoples not yet able to stand by themselves under the strenuous conditions of the modern world, there should be applied the principle that the well-being and development of such peoples form a sacred trust of civilisation and that securities for the performance of this trust should be embodied in the Covenant.[60]

War resumed between the European powers in 1939, when the scars were yet to heal from the earlier conflagration. The guns finally fell silent in 1945, ending a traumatic period that has, with some justice, been characterized as the 'thirty-one years' world war'.[61] The lights that had gone out all over Europe had been lit once again, though not with the old luminescence. Europe was now very much an understudy in the imperial pecking order, having yielded pre-eminence to its creation on the other bank of the Atlantic Ocean.

British, French and Dutch colonies that had fallen to hostile powers during the Second World War were soon reoccupied. Colonies in Africa that had not been direct theatres of war began to feel the bite of colonial exploitation more sharply than before, as imperial powers sought to embellish rapidly fading glories. The days of European colonialism were irretrievably past, though the powers that had determined the destinies of millions of subjects were yet to realize it. The Dutch made an effort to bring Indonesia back under their sway, as did the French in Vietnam and the British in the Malayan Peninsula.

Africa rose up in a mass upsurge against Europe in the years after the Second World War, but the colonial masters were again not inclined to let go. In Kenya, the British fought the uprising of the Kenya African Union—the rather derogatorily named Mau Mau rebellion—through an overt policy of pacification and racial re-engineering. The demand that the colonial expropriation of land—which reserved the most fertile tracts for the white settler community—be overturned and appropriate restitution be made to the African population was met with a strategy of destroying existing patterns of habitation and clustering all the troublesome natives into designated sites that could be garrisoned by occupation forces. In Algeria, the French began a systematic process of targeted killing against recalcitrant natives, justifying the harshness of their measures by merely invoking the complete ignorance, if not disdain, that the rebels displayed towards civilized rules of engagement in warfare. In every such confrontation between the fading powers of colonialism and organized nationalist resistance, the job of managing the integration of the newly liberated territories into the global system of power was left to Europe's lineal descendant across the Atlantic.

Nationalism was the mode of political organization forged by the European enlightenment, and its obverse side was imperialism. Within the colonies of Europe, popular resistance crafted a new idiom of nationalism. Ethnic homogeneity was consciously downplayed as a necessary aspect of the newly independent nations. More central to the sustenance of the new nationalism and its growing legitimacy was the popular determination to be free and the shared experiences of struggling for liberation from colonial oppression. There were several respects in which the new wave of nationalism was distinct from the old. To name just two: it was inclusive on grounds of language or ethnicity and focused on the State as an embodiment of the collective will of the national community. Not surprisingly, the nations that came into being after the terminal crisis of European colonialism invested great legitimacy and power in the State.

The New Global Order: Pax Soviet-Americana

However, these nations also inherited a status in the global division of labour that was deeply embedded in colonialism, serviced by a financial system whose levers were entirely in the hands of imperial powers, old and new.[62] Certain among the post-colonial States began their own nation-building efforts with the promise of lifting vast populations out of poverty by the bootstraps. These efforts, though, were severely impaired by resource scarcities, technological lacunae and infrastructural gaps that led to very poor returns on initial investment for capital-scarce countries.

In the western industrialized states, the years after the Second World War were also a time for rethinking the role of the State in public affairs. The impetus here came from the mass enlistment of the working classes in the armed forces during the war and the promise held out that victory would bring immense rewards for those at the bottom of the social hierarchy. As Hobsbawm puts it, the Second World War was 'for those on the winning side, not merely a struggle for military victory, but—even in Britain and the USA—for a better society.'[63] Simply for this reason, the British wartime government under the arch social conservative and political reactionary Winston Churchill had to perforce commit itself 'to a comprehensive welfare state and full employment'. It was no coincidence, indeed, that the Beveridge Report (named after a minister in the Churchill Cabinet), which laid out the contours and parameters of a welfare state, was published in 1942, 'as black a year as any in Britain's desperate war'.[64]

Welfare State

The welfare state has been variously conceived and constructed. The legal status welfare claimants enjoy may differ widely, as too would the level and coverage of benefits. But there are certain similarities and convergences in the manner in which the welfare principle has been operationalized in different countries.[65] One of its key features is redistribution through progressive taxation; another is a compulsory and collective arrangement whereby today's economically active population pays for the welfare of senior citizens, and, in turn, sets apart sufficient savings to provide for themselves and their peers in years of retirement. A reaction against this system of welfarism began in the 1970s, principally in the US and the UK. Full employment, it was found, was a good advertisement for the capitalist system—then under challenge from the ostensibly socialist endeavour of the Soviet Union—but it also added to the strength of trade union movements, enabling them to drive hard wage bargains. In a situation where employers sought to protect their profits despite high wage bills, this led to what is called the wage-price spiral and rampant inflation through the 1970s, a problem considerably aggravated by the surge in international commodity prices, led by the oil producers' initiative through the Organization of the Petroleum Exporting Countries (OPEC).

An attack on the welfare system began in the 1980s, often called the Reagan–Thatcher Revolution. Counter-revolution, though, would be the more appropriate description, for it successfully accomplished a regression in human thought by a century (if not more), to the ill-remembered days of Social Darwinism. The central components of this counter-revolution were a sharp cut in taxes for those at the upper end of the scale of income and wealth, a hike in the compulsory payments required from the working class for the sustenance of the social welfare system and a cutback in public expenditure in areas deemed better served by private enterprise.

Between them, these policy changes induced a crunching recession in the industrialized world in the early 1980s, which soon spread to the global economy. The concurrent massive build-up in military expenditure in the US led to a bloating of the budget deficit, which sucked in a large part of global savings and hardened interest rates. Developing countries, which had borrowed to support ambitious development schemes in the 1970s, were suddenly obliged to deal with a huge increase in interest payments and, quite possibly, a default on debt servicing. At the same time, because of the recession in the industrialized countries, demand for primary commodities fell precipitously and, with it, the prices that developing country exporters could command.[66]

Over the next decade, one developing country after another was sucked into the international debt crisis and forced to adopt 'structural adjustment programs' dictated by the International Monetary Fund (IMF) and the World Bank. The crisis began in Latin America and soon spread to Africa. Both these continents suffered significant drains of capital through the decade of the 1980s. Asia continued to have positive flows, with China and India, particularly, entering the international finance market as big borrowers in the 1980s. But for India, at least, the good fortune ran out by 1990, with the explosion of international petroleum prices following Iraq's aggression against Kuwait. Having tentatively stepped into the tutelary orbit of the IMF in 1982, India chose, in 1991, to accept the firm embrace of its structural adjustment policies.

By the 1980s, promises made by the developmental state were hollowed out. Ethnic strife engulfed many of the newly liberated nations, and a financial crisis, which discredited—if it did not directly indict—the ruling elites, had begun to devastate all their pretences of policy autonomy. By the late-1980s, the nation state, as constituted in the struggle against colonialism, was facing seemingly lethal challenges both from above and below. The demands of international finance were beginning to drain it of precious capital. And from below, the burgeoning strife between communities—ethnic, linguistic and religious—accentuated by the famine of resources, had begun to seriously erode the democratic commitments these States were founded on.

Where did these tendencies lead? What directions did they take? And what do these foretell for the future?

Notes

1 Anderson, Benedict, *Imagined Communities: Reflections on the Origin and Spread of Nationalism*, Verso, London, 1983, p. xii.
2 Hobsbawm, E.J., 'Chapter 6: Nationalism in the late twentieth century', *Nations and Nationalism since 1780: Programme, Myth, Reality*, Cambridge University Press, 1992.
3 Amartya Sen, in his book *Identity and Violence: The Illusion of Destiny* (Penguin, Delhi, 2006), has drawn attention to the multiple identities that any one individual could lay claim to and the contextual nature of the assertion of any one of these.
4 Quoted in: Horsman, Matthew, and Andrew Marshall, *After the Nation-State: Citizens, Tribalism and the New World Order*, HarperCollins, London, 1995, p. ix. That assessment obviously needs to be qualified by the insecurities that members of nation states suffer today because of extreme expressions of nationalism.
5 The term 'ethnies' here is used in the sense of ethnic groups. Smith, Anthony D., *Nations and Nationalism in a Global Era*, Oxford University Press, 1995, p. 57.
6 Ibid.
7 Ibid. 159–60.
8 Ibid.

9   Hobsbawm, E.J. *Nations and Nationalism since 1780: Programme, Myth, Reality*, Cambridge University Press, 1992, pp. 35–37.
10 Kundera, Milan, *The Curtain: An Essay in Seven Parts*, Faber & Faber, London, 2007, p. 38.
11 All quotes are from Lenin, V.I., 'Theses on the National Question', *Collected Works*, Volume XIX, Progress Publishers, Moscow, pp. 243–51; and Lenin, V.I., 'Cultural-National Autonomy', *Collected Works*, Volume XIX, Progress Publishers, Moscow, pp. 503–7.
12 Ibid.
13 Ernest Gellner in his book *Nations and Nationalism* (Cornell University Press, 1983) identifies industrialism as the context for the emergence of the nation. This is a condition of generalized movement and disorder, or as he puts it with a term borrowed from thermodynamics, 'entropy'. Older certainties of status and position under the unchanging norms of agrarian life vanish in the new industrial order. There is, rather, a generalized sense of entropy, of citizens of the nation drifting from one location or occupation to another in response to the compelling pulls of industrialism. Certain enclaves, though, would emerge in this process that resist that generalized sense of entropy, that insist on retaining their anchorage in older forms of life. These 'anti-entropic' islands, Gellner says, could, in time, emerge as autonomous nationalities on their own.
14 Hobsbawm, E.J. *Nations and Nationalism since 1780: Programme, Myth, Reality*, Cambridge University Press, 1992, p. 10.
15 Ibid. 60.
16 Soboul, Albert, *Understanding the French Revolution*, Peoples' Publishing House, New Delhi, 1989, pp. 197–98.
17 Lefebvre, Georges, *The Coming of the French Revolution*, Princeton University Press, Princeton, 1947, p. 98.
18 Rudé, George, *Fontana History of Europe: Revolutionary Europe: 1783–1825*, Fontana Press, London, 1985, pp. 108–14.
19 Ibid. 139.

20   Ibid. 207.
21   Ibid. 160.
22   Soboul, Albert, *Understanding the French Revolution*, Peoples' Publishing House, New Delhi, 1989, p. 168.
23   Smith, Adam, *An Enquiry into the Nature and the Causes of the Wealth of Nations*, Edwin Cannan (ed.), Random House, New York, 1965, pp. 531–32.
24   Said, Edward, *Orientalism: Western Conceptions of the Orient*, Penguin, London, 1995, p. 219.
25   Harvey, David, *The Enigma of Capital and the Crises of Capitalism*, Profile Books, London, 2011, p. 154.
26   Ibid.
27   Edward Said in *Orientalism: Western Conceptions of the Orient* (Penguin, London, 1995), for instance, puts this phase of conflict down to national competition, which would be accurate, since the vectors of the nationalist idea then were commercial enterprises seeking overseas monopolies. It bears recall here that the colonial state originated as a trading company.
28   Maurice Dobb, in his book *Theories of Value and Distribution since Adam Smith* (Cambridge University Press, 1973), provides an account of Ricardo's pessimism about the prospects of capitalist accumulation.
29   Book I of Smith's classic *The Wealth of Nations* begins with a close examination of what promotes the division of labour. Following this, Smith shifts his attention to the distribution question, seeking to find a fair and objective quantitative basis for the profits of stock, the wages of labour and the rent from land.
30   The point is made with little ambiguity by the man who is, in the vulgar understanding, portrayed as the father of laissez-faire economics. 'What the common wages of labour are', he argues, 'depends ever where upon the contract usually made between these two parties, whose interests are by no means the same...It is not, however, difficult to foresee which of the two parties must, upon all ordinary occasions, have the advantage in the dispute, and force

the other into compliance with their terms. The masters, being fewer in number, can combine much more easily, and the laws, besides, authorises, or at least does not prohibit their combinations, while it prohibits those of the workmen...' (Smith, Adam, *The Wealth of Nations,* Edwin Cannan (ed.), Penguin Random House, 2000, pp. 66–67).

31 Ibid. 48.
32 Ibid. 127.
33 Smith deals with the sense of 'approbation and disapprobation' at length in Part VII, Section 3, *The Theory of Moral Sentiments* (Penguin Classics, 2010). He examines three possible sources for mankind's sense of what is right and wrong: self-love, reason and sentiment. None of these, he finds, stands up to a rigorous examination. Finally, then, it is a characteristic of man as a social species, who only finds his individuality within a community.
34 Kant, Immanuel, 'Idea for a Universal History with Cosmopolitan Intent', *Basic Writings of Kant*, Allen W. Wood (ed.), Random House, New York, 2001, p. 119.
35 Ibid. 122.
36 Ibid. 119.
37 Ibid. 126–27.
38 Kant, Immanuel, 'Critique of Practical Reason' *Basic Writings of Kant,* Allen W. Wood (ed.), Random House, New York, 2001, p. 238.
39 Kant, Immanuel, 'To Eternal Peace', *Basic Writings of Kant*, Allen W. Wood (ed.), Random House, New York, 2001, p. 440.
40 Hegel, G.W.F., *The Philosophy of Right*, Batoche Books, Ontario, 2000, p. 18.
41 Ibid. 39.
42 Ibid. 14.
43 Ibid. 15.
44 Ibid. 46.
45 Ibid. 15.

46 Ibid. 136.
47 Ibid. 96.
48 Jones, Gareth Stedman, 'Hegel and the economics of civil society', *Civil Society: History and Possibilities*, Sudipta Kaviraj and Sunil Khilnani (eds), Cambridge University Press, 2001.
49 Marx, Karl, 'On the Jewish Question', *Karl Marx: Early Writings*, L. Colletti (ed.), Penguin, London, 1977, p. 220.
50 Marx, Karl, 'Critique of Hegel's Doctrine of the State', *Karl Marx: Early Writings*, L. Colletti (ed.), Penguin, London, 1977.
51 Habermas, Juergen, *The Structural Transformation of the Public Sphere*, Frederick Lawrence and Thomas Burger (trans.), MIT Press, Cambridge, 1989, p. 304.
52 Ibid. 85–86.
53 Ibid. 22.
54 Hobsbawm, E.J., *The Age of Empire: 1875–1914*, Vintage, London, 1987, pp. 160–61.
55 Hobsbawm, E.J., *The Age of Capital: 1948–1875*, Abacus, London, 1988, p. 127.
56 Hobsbawm, E. J., *The Age of Empire: 1875–1914*, Vintage, London, 1987, pp. 160–61.
57 John Keegan, in his book *The Book of War* (Viking, London, 1999, p. xvi), seeks to rationalize the genocide of the Native Americans as a necessity forced upon the humane and altruistic legions of the European colonization project. It was on account of the Native American dedication to the 'warrior ideal', which went beyond rationality, that 'Europeans found only one recourse to assert their dominance, which was oppression to the point of extermination'. The newer vogue among imperial apologists, though, is to report the events without serious moral qualm or comment, as with Niall Ferguson (*Empire, How Britain Made the Modern World*, Penguin, London, 2003, p. 66).
58 Quoted in: Hobsbawm, E.J., *The Age of Empire: 1875–1914*, Vintage, London, 1987, p. 327.

59 Ibid. 265.
60 'Covenant of the League of Nations', The Avalon Project, Yale Law School, https://tinyurl.com/2p82s5yx. Accessed on 23 June 2022.
61 Hobsbawm, E.J., *The Age of Extremes: 1914–1991*, Abacus, London, 1995, p. 22.
62 These are themes very acutely dealt with in Thomas Piketty's book *A Brief History of Equality* (Harvard University Press, 2022).
63 Hobsbawm, E.J., *The Age of Extremes: 1914–1991*, Abacus, London, 1995, p. 161.
64 Ibid. 162.
65 See the entry under 'Welfare State' in Krieger, John, (ed.), *Oxford Companion to the Politics of the World*, Oxford University Press, New York, 1993.
66 Much of this sequence of events is sketched out in the report of the South Commission, set up under the initiative of the former president of Tanzania, Julius Nyerere. See: South Commission, *The Challenge to the South: The Report of the South Commission*, Oxford University Press, Oxford, 1990.

6
NETWORKS OF POPULISM AND THE UNEQUAL NATION

The nation is a community of anonymity. No single person in the nation knows all his or her associations. Traditional polities were bound by a stated or unstated oath of allegiance, of loyalty to the sovereign. But the nation is different, in that it is a polity in which all citizens are sovereign. Where it is defined by an identity criterion such as religion, there is usually—as with minority rights acknowledged under various systems of law—a way of bringing all who do not conform into a status of equality.

The nation is bound by ties of mutual dependence, a division of labour that embraces material spheres of production and intangible spheres of administration. Every identity is defined by an assigned role within the division of labour, and likewise, there is an entitlement prescribed for every citizen in accordance with the role he or she fulfils. Money is the easiest unit, the only medium in which a complex set of relationships could be expressed. Every person who earns a dollar or a rupee while performing his day's work earns an entitlement guaranteed by the sovereign national power, to a certain quantum of the necessities, conveniences and luxuries of life.

The reproduction of everyday life in the nation requires a contract between citizens, one that is sustained through recurrent cycles of time. Any individual's position in the distribution of tasks that makes up the nation is his or her identity. The task itself could be essential, life-sustaining, recreational or cultural, but that elusive attribute, 'identity', is often defined in terms of what a person does and what she has a reason to do. These are matters both thought through consciously but also, in most cases, an unreflective instinct.

The sociologist Pierre Bourdieu has made the concept of the 'habitus' a powerful explanatory element of his repertoire, and philosopher Anthony Appiah, in turn, has taken it over in his explorations of identity. As Appiah interprets the term, habitus refers to 'a set of dispositions to respond more or less spontaneously to the world in particular ways, without much thought'. It is something trained into a person, 'starting from childhood'.[1]

That predisposition could vanish when the citizen of the nation finds the contract unfulfilled, when he or she finds that the entitlements and rewards promised are not materializing. That is when the compact that keeps the individual functioning as a spontaneous participant in the cycle of social reproduction begins to strain. The nation then requires to renegotiate its internal compact, in ways that have a bearing on political representation, the organization of the economy and the distribution of the social product.

Today's global mosaic of nation states emerged out of the Second World War. The bipolar competition that began after the war and growing nationalist consciousness in erstwhile colonies were part of the dynamic driving change. For a while, integration in larger supranational bodies also seemed a possibility. From the 1980s, it seemed that globalization would be the destiny of all the world. And this was emphatically underlined when the alternative socialist system imploded in the early 1990s. Yet, by the second decade of the following century, that promise also seemed to be wearing thin. The miracles of globalization had begun to sour and, increasingly, people were agitating for a retreat into narrower identities, some congruent with national frontiers, some threatening to disrupt older nationalist solidarities.

The decades of globalization were a second wind for the political and economic order that emerged after the Second World War. It was the resolution devised by global capitalist powers for the crisis of the post-war 'miracle economy'. The moment when the miracle economy began to crumble could be variously identified, but the mid-1960s may have been a time when a wave of political disillusionment began to spread over much of the globe. In March 1968, US President Lyndon Johnson, after recklessly escalating the war against Vietnam during his term in office, appeared before his people in deep penitence to renounce a bid for re-election. The remaining months of his term in office, he announced, would be devoted to the moral imperative of bringing an 'ugly war' to an end. Unending war was exacting an economic price, since the very foundation of US prosperity since the Second World War was in peril. There was no way the US could meet its war expenditures without significant action to cut certain lines of domestic expenditure. When action was required, the US Congress dithered and the nation faced its 'sharpest financial threat in the post-war era—a threat to the dollar's role as the keystone of international trade and finance'.[2]

First Signs of Economic Turbulence

Years of turbulence followed since the miracle economy first signalled that its days were numbered. Politically, there was the Watergate scandal and a presidential resignation in the US, and deepening political turmoil in the UK, as organized worker unions clashed with a regime that seemed indifferent to the decline in living standards. In India, a government of seemingly unassailable parliamentary strength was reduced by civil unrest to paralysis. The US, UK and, in fact, most of the advanced capitalist nations weathered the storm without overt disruption to the political system. In India, the crisis occasioned a suspension of the Constitution and a period of authoritarian rule, the so-called Emergency, when civil liberties were severely abridged.

Key ingredients of the miracle economy, as Nobel laureate Paul Krugman identifies them, were the 'active management of the economy to achieve high employment, and a welfare state based on progressive taxation'.[3] Once the miracle wore out, the terms of engagement had to be renegotiated and the common sense of the post-war years, attributed in most part to the economist John Maynard Keynes, discarded in favour of a new orthodoxy. Governmental regulation—once the essential guarantor of equity within the nation—was now identified as the problem.

Despite having the proven remedies in the real world, Keynes never held the field unchallenged in the scholarly realm. Joseph Schumpeter, who celebrated the innovative entrepreneur as the mainspring of economic progress, dissented even from the time Keynesian remedies had their widest practical acceptance. Capitalism, for Schumpeter, grew through cycles of innovation followed by waves of 'creative destruction.' Keynesian remedies were little else than an artificial prop built for enterprises to eke out a precarious existence far beyond the time they serve a useful purpose. The better option would be to let them perish so that others could sprout in their place. Getting in the way of the inevitable demise of older enterprises and the slump that must accompany this collective extinction would only 'end up making it worse'.[4]

What Schumpeter failed to appreciate from his lofty perch as a political conservative was that waves of creative destruction washing over a country could trigger massive social upheavals. The franchise had expanded to include the vast working-class majority, and democracy was more than the shallow pretence it had been in the golden age of the capitalist entrepreneur. Creative destruction, unless managed through strategic State intervention, was little else than a formula for ripping up the consensus that held the nation together. And the international repercussions were another matter, since divergent growth rates across nations invariably had a bearing on the competitive dynamic between them, creating the potential for war and peace.

Schumpeter's Austrian phlegmatism was closely connected with another uniquely American strain in economic thinking that laid stress on sound monetary policies as the sole requirement to keep the national economy in robust health. The government's only role here was to provide the legal scaffolding and the medium through which contracts between capitalist entrepreneurs and all other economic agents could be negotiated and fulfilled. Balancing the budget was crucial, since a government that spent beyond its means and borrowed from the pool of money it was entrusted with safeguarding would only debase the currency and destroy all creative possibilities of sustaining the social contract.[5]

Monetarism as economic doctrine, translated into policy in 1931, caused the deepest depression in US history. Though the US was by no means alone, it was different in having the kind of exuberance on the stock market that concealed the reality for long. The European continent was already in the coils of a wrenching economic meltdown from the mid-1920s, impelling Britain and France towards unavailing experiments with austerity, and Germany towards a harsh authoritarianism that the business world fully supported and endorsed.

As the economist Joan Robinson remarked, 'Hitler had already found how to cure unemployment before Keynes had finished explaining why it occurred'.[6] In other capitalist economies, it was a hard-fought battle between conservatism and the new pragmatism that Keynes and his allies advocated. Finally, as Krugman puts it, the depression was 'ended by the one kind of public works program that even conservatives [were] willing to support: a war'.[7]

Older worries and conservative scruples over deficit financing and taxes on the rich were briefly buried as the world mobilized for war. And once the global carnage had abated, reconstruction afforded another cause in which the nation could be collectively mobilized. That momentum carried most of the early industrializing countries through the first two post-war decades, while freedom struggles, several of them successfully consummated, and the effort at creating new national development plans served a similar purpose for poorer, post-colonial parts of the world.

Years of high growth and employment created new parities in bargaining power between capital and labour, allowing workers' unions to seek a share in the national product that reflected their newly won importance in the nationalist compact. Conceding these demands was relatively easy through the early years when competition between the major economies was yet to sharpen. That reality altered as productivity gains started tapering off, notably in the US, and as years spent in the comfort zone of colonialism began to catch up with the UK.

Economic theory has no clue to understanding why growth takes place at 'different rates over time and across countries'. As Krugman puts it: 'Nobody really knows why the U.S. economy could generate 3 percent annual productivity growth before 1973 but only 1 percent afterward; nobody really knows why Japan surged from defeat to global economic power after World War II, while Britain slid slowly into third-rate status'.[8] How, indeed, did these divergences occur? There will be much effort spent in crunching the numbers to establish some posture of the professional and supposedly value-free economist, but little recognition that economics is not a pristine discipline amenable to numerical precision but a domain where politics and the nationalistic impulse are big players.

By the 1970s, economic reconstruction in Japan and West Germany (as it was then) had brought two new manufacturing powerhouses into the global arena. As the miracle economy began to wear thin, US President Richard Nixon, Johnson's successor, swore his eternal allegiance to Keynesian economics. It was, for a politician always identified as a conservative, an astonishing switch of loyalty. But as he tried dealing with eruptions of conflict between capital and labour, aggravated by the major spike in global energy prices, Nixon realized he was up against forces beyond his comprehension. Stagflation was the reality of the 1970s, one that defied Keynesian solutions because of the resistance on both sides—capital and labour—to a shrinkage in share of national output. Years of explicit commitment to the welfare state ideology had created uncomfortable parities in bargaining power, which had to be reversed for the reign of capital to be restored.

Every Man for Himself

Finally, the remedy for stagflation came from the US monetary authority—the Federal Reserve or Fed—after Paul Volcker was appointed chairman with a mandate endorsed by both Republican and Democrat parties to use all available means in the fight against inflation. Volcker responded with sharp increases in the interest rate between 1979 and 1981, sending the economy into a tailspin. The 1980s began under the shadow of the Volcker Shock, an overnight increase in interest rates that pushed the US into recession, playing no small part in propelling Ronald Reagan to a decisive win in the presidential election. And Reagan brought his unique brand of 'voodoo economics' to the mix, slashing taxes in the expectation of an increase in revenue and sharply raising defence expenditure to send the deficit soaring, interest rates went above a critical threshold, pushing nations around the globe, most so in South America and Africa, into debt-induced meltdown.

In the US, the interest rate shock also had the effect of transforming incentives: investment now flowed into financial assets, while fixed capital was taken out of commission as the US lost global manufacturing competitiveness. High interest rates attracted large inflows of foreign capital, sustaining the enormous US external deficit and also causing it. If the fabled laws of the market had actually been operative, the US Dollar should have been pummelled into a lower rate of exchange by the growing deficit. Yet, because the US still exercised powers of seignorage over the global currency, a privilege that rightly belonged to the feudal age, this cumulative causation, quite unlike anything foreseen by equilibrium theory, continued with no seeming limit.

Inflation was squeezed out of the system, but as Volcker let slip in an unguarded moment, this was an achievement that could almost entirely be put down to the crunching recession that the Fed managed to engineer, alongside the high levels of unemployment that effectively destroyed organized working-class power. It was not the impersonal hand of economic policy but the direct coercive power of politics that was key in the fight against inflation. 'The most important single action of the administration in helping the anti-inflation fight', he said later, 'was in defeating the air traffic controllers' strike'.[9]

In August 1981, just a few months into Reagan's term as president, 13,000 members of the largest air traffic controllers' union struck work. Reagan did not pause to bargain or negotiate, as had become the convention through the years when capital and labour played out their game of countervailing power. He simply fired the striking workers, replacing them with military personnel. Corporate resistance to union demands was strengthened with that signal from political leadership.[10] And as job losses accelerated over the months that followed, corporate managers were permitted almost a clear field for restructuring capital.[11]

Events on the stock markets foreshadowed much that was to come, with the excesses of junk bonds causing a buoyancy beyond anything warranted by the real economy. It was obvious from the very early days of the reign of right-wing economics that the growth achievements it registered were inevitably going to be accompanied by a perverse redistribution of income towards the upper strata. As Krugman observed in 1994:

> Once you correct for the ups and downs of the business cycle, the growth path of the economy was virtually the same before and after Ronald Reagan took office. But the conservative era was marked by a huge fanning out of the spread of incomes, with the rich becoming far richer, the poor a lot poorer, and the middle class going nowhere in particular.[12]

Inequality assumed an impersonal shape in the 1980s. As part of a determined assault on welfare, right-wing politics promoted a discourse of *merit* as the key to opening the infinite opportunities of the market economy. It was an argument that was a virtual truism: those who did well had merit, and those who did not lacked that vital attribute for success. In later variants, especially in the hands of those who were keen to take a hatchet to the foundations of the welfare state, the doctrine of merit came to be tied very closely to that of personal responsibility.[13] In 1996, a right-wing US Congress, elected in a massive backlash against Democratic incumbency in the White House, literally forced a bill titled 'Personal Responsibility and Work Opportunities Reconciliation' on to the table of the US president. Rather than confront the obvious bad intent, which included a lifetime ceiling on the welfare benefits any citizen could draw and the fanciful assumption that employment opportunities would expand infinitely irrespective of underlying economic conditions, President Clinton signed the bill in the belief that it represented the core demands of middle-America.[14]

Clinton sought a conventional remedy to the burgeoning deficit: he hiked the tax rate modestly but proved his fealty to the new ethos with a thorough deregulation of financial services. He had the good fortune of coming into office at just the time that the successor states to the Soviet Union were literally prostrate, in dire need of western patronage to get over the 1991 disintegration. The greater stroke of luck he had was in the arrival of the internet as a transformative technology, sparking innovation and a frenzy of speculation that propelled US markets into a giddy spiral. Minor fiscal tampering at the margins had created greater comfort for the US government budget, but just as borrowing from the rest of the world on the official account was beginning to fall, the corporate sector, with the promise of a glittering future of 'dot com' riches, eagerly began picking up enormous liabilities on their balance sheets.

As both parties tacked to the right in economics, culture became a terrain of battle. That afforded the leverage for George W. Bush, despite losing the national vote in 2000, to win back the presidency for the Republicans by a majority of one in an infamously partisan decision by the US Supreme Court. He inherited a budget in near balance, which he regarded as a luxury to be shared with his constituency of 'haves and have-mores.'[15] It mattered little that Bush was then taking the US into a war of indefinite duration and global expanse.

On 11 September 2001, the US mainland was attacked in a manner it had not been in close to two centuries. And even as Bush dealt with the imperatives of mobilizing to counter the threat, he pushed through a massive cut in taxes for the wealthy, predicted even then to be catastrophic for traditional notions of fiscal rectitude.

The dot-com boom turned bust just as the Bush tax cuts and reckless overseas military adventurism began to show up in a burgeoning deficit and growing working-class anxieties. But with the US engaged in a war on many fronts against an ill-defined adversary known only by the generic term 'terrorism', the nationalist sentiment proved Bush's ally through two terms in office. The economic foundations, already shaky and threatening to give way under the weight of hubris, had to be buttressed, for which a new bubble of asset prices was conjured up. The existing stock of real estate and the dream of home ownership for those at the bottom of the income scale afforded that opportunity. As Krugman observed in the early days of the boom that came apart with traumatic effect in 2008, Americans in the Bush presidency had begun making 'a living by selling each other houses, paid with money borrowed from China.'[16]

Clawing Back from Calamitous Times

In elections held within two months of the 2008 bubble-burst, the US elected, for the first time, an African-American as president. Barack Obama brought conventional Keynesian remedies back but with a difference: the massive rescue package he shepherded through Congress was financed almost entirely by the Fed buying up treasury bonds or by injecting new money into the system.[17] Inflationary worries were contained. Changes in economic structure over the preceding decades had ensured that fresh liquidity would find its way into speculative assets purchase rather than demand for basic commodities. Stock markets were soon booming again, emboldening the financial managers who had brought on the 2008 meltdown to hand themselves record bonuses. Obama issued a moral reprimand but admitted helplessness. He did institute a marginally more equitable taxation regime, but his legacy finally was a more rapid growth of inequality, measured by the Gini coefficient, than during prior Republican tenures.[18]

By now, the growing disparities were recognized as a matter of urgent concern even in mainstream economics. Nobel laureate economist Joseph Stiglitz spoke of urgent correction as a necessity, lest inequality cause a 'disorderly unwinding' and an unravelling of the global system of exchanges. What was most worrying about emerging global patterns was the chronic US deficit—an unrestrained binge of borrowing from the rest of the world—when the country needed to save to ensure the security in retirement years of the generation born immediately after the Second World War.[19]

The corrective remained elusive. In a 2019 work, economist Heather Boushey spoke of how economic inequality over the decades had hindered 'productivity and growth by blocking the flows of people, ideas and new capital.' Those at the top of the pyramid had succeeded in 'hoarding the best economic opportunities, [and] ensuring that their good look solidifies into ongoing privilege by putting up barriers to upward mobility for others'.[20] A weakening sense of community was the consequence—the elevation of rampant individualism to a hallowed status among the principles society should commit itself to.

Rubbishing distributive justice and welfare as basic principles of the nation state had always been a vigorous pursuit. It went mainstream with Reagan's campaign demagoguery about the 'welfare queen' driving a luxury car to collect her monthly benefits cheque and then squandering it all on intoxicants. The imagery was vivid even if devoid of any connection to reality, and it provided just the right infusion of racist grievance into the market-oriented paradigm of governance.

The continuing contest between white privilege and social justice saw periodic eruptions of civil unrest, mostly put down by an increasingly militarized police force. The arsenals of major police forces in the US and the UK became, through the neoliberal era, 'so well-stocked…that some critics complained the police were being transformed into a paramilitary service'.[21] With insecurities lurking just beneath the surface, even in years when prosperity seemed an unending prospect, the rhetoric of looming anarchy won a receptive audience in the US mainstream. That drift away from the fundamentals was destined to end in the surpassing crudities of Donald Trump's politics.[22]

Even before Trump was elected US president, Francis Fukuyama, famous for his prediction of the 'end of history' in the heady aftermath of the Soviet collapse, saw some reasons for concern in a growing 'democratic recession'. The capacity of the various nation states that embraced the democratic ethos, he worried, had failed to keep pace with 'popular demands for democratic accountability'. The State is the agency with a monopoly over legitimate coercion but necessarily constrained by rule of law, since violence unfettered would be a recipe for dictatorship. Building democracy was seen conventionally to involve the sustenance of civil society, to promote pressure groups that could check a drift towards State authoritarianism. Fukuyama saw this as essential but not sufficient for safeguarding democracy. The task indeed would only be complete if popular pressure and mobilization were to be 'institutionalized and converted into durable practices.'[23] This required 'the organization of social movements into political parties that can contest elections', and beyond that, the building of 'state capacity'. Democratic government would only survive if it were to really govern, i.e. 'exercise legitimate authority and provide basic services to the population'.[24]

Democratic values, for Fukuyama, are assessed in terms of their conformity with US strategic objectives. From that perspective, he loses sight of how deeply troubled democracy is in the country that purports to export it to the rest of the world. The problem is perhaps not one of a failure to institutionalize but of the erosion of all institutions in the cult of the market. The dissolution of older forms of collective organization, such as unions, was a singular objective of neoliberalism, the specific form taken by bourgeois democracy to surmount the crises of the 1970s. Civil society collectives were then reassembled in a manner that promised a restoration of the older forms of privilege embodied in capital.

Inequalities Fuel Discord

For all the power it projected on the world stage, the US was a superpower bitterly torn by discord within. The legacy of the 1980s was an economy out of joint: a growing fiscal gap and current account deficit. In the 1990s, with the internet and its associated forms of communication gaining global traction, this was not a major worry. Salvation, at least for the US, was promised in a structural change in the economy, a shift to the new generation of high technology that would pick up the slack left by the decline of older industries. That ambition seemed realistic through the boom of the 1990s in technology stocks, when inflation and unemployment remained in check and the buoyancy of the economy, despite low tax rates on the rich, filled government coffers.

The sense of community—of local bonds that serve as the foundation on which the larger solidarity of the nation is constructed—was already fraying through these years, in part because collective forms of association, such as the factory union and the local congregation, were losing membership. Neoliberalism invited all the nations of the world to partake of its promise.[25] And in the early 1980s, with the hardening of interest rates pushing several of the poorer countries into debt-induced distress, they were compelled to adopt policies dictated by the custodians of global finance. This included import liberalization and the dismantling of all domestic controls on investment. Unconstrained by national frontiers, capital could now seek the best sites for manufacturing, and China and other vast territories of low-cost labour offered great incentives for industrial relocation.

President George W. Bush seemed to have created a new sense of national cohesion with his calls, following the 9/11 terrorist attacks, to endless war against faceless enemies. But that fervour died a quick death, serving just long enough to ensure his re-election in 2004. The restoration of adult responsibility to the White House under Barack Obama was altogether too brief, before the politics of rage and resentment found their perfect expression in Donald Trump.

From then on, the hidden pathologies and fissures within the US were out in the open, fully mirrored in bitter political partisanship. Efforts by the co-equal elected branch of the government, the US Congress, to hold Trump to account for a term in office strewn with bigoted public statements, highly questionable policy decisions and outright corruption were throttled by a Republican Party that saw little amiss in standing rock solid behind their man.[26] When it came to nominating its standard bearer for the 2020 election, the Republicans deferred to the dubious authority of the incumbent. With little by way of policy ideas over four years than a record tax giveaway to the rich, the economy was poised precariously on a knife-edge. And on top of that, Trump bungled the official response to the Covid-19 pandemic, resulting in the US having the world's worst outbreak, till India gained that dubious honour in the spring of 2021. With seemingly little chance of winning a fair election, Trump had been preparing a case that a rightful victory would be stolen from him.[27]

Once the last ballot had been counted, confirming his defeat by a margin of over seven million, Trump mobilized legal teams to argue a case that the election had been severely corrupted by changes in the rules and procedures of voting. His main target was the early voting rules created to enable ballots to be cast without the infection hazards of people clustering at polling centres. At least one court observed on seeing the substance of Trump's plea that it smacked of racism, in that it sought to discard votes cast by blacks and other minorities.[28]

Soon afterwards, the electoral college, which under the US constitution is the body that formalizes the election of the president, voted to confirm that Joe Biden would be the next president. On 6 January 2021, the day the US Congress, in a largely ceremonial event, was scheduled to certify the election result, a violent mob instigated by Trump forced its way into the hallways of the legislative complex. As the assembled elected representatives fled in terror, a hasty summons to the armed National Guard succeeded in restoring order for the completion of the agenda for the day.

The day's events were conveyed to viewers across the nation in sharply variant hues. Research by a group that tracks the kind of messages shared on social media found that when the riotous mob invaded the Capitol, users of the social networking site Facebook 'saw the riot through very different lenses'. An analysis of 'Facebook feed data from hundreds of the panellists' who had volunteered for the study, found that those 'who voted for Joe Biden in the 2020 election were more frequently exposed to news stories from nonpartisan outlets directly covering the riot at the Capitol and the certification of Biden's win', while panellists 'who identified themselves as Trump voters in the 2020 election were more likely to be exposed to conservative news coverage'.[29]

This was, of course, only one in a sequence of events in recent years when technologies that made their debut promising a miraculous degree of connectivity proved, in practice, to promote a toxic polarization. The *network* permitting universal access was supposed to represent the acme of the participative public, the ultimate flowering of that guardian of freedom—and foundation of the nation—called civil society. How, then, did the network society take a turn towards promoting internal discord?

In his widely cited 2009 book, *Communication Power*, Manuel Castells speaks of the network society as a process of action through communication that creates 'meaning'. Communities bond on the basis of shared meanings and create the social sanctions for, and against, the political establishment. Castells sees the creation of networked meanings as defining 'the conditions for the legitimate exercise of power'. The basis of legitimacy is not fixed or absolute. In the manner it is exercised, power would necessarily have to represent 'the values and interests of citizens expressed by means of their debate in the public sphere.'[30]

Denying the Objectivity of Reality

In a 2018 work appropriately titled *Antisocial Media*, media scholar Siva Vaidhyanathan diagnosed the problem with social media platforms, such as Facebook, as their tendency to override truth and authenticity and 'solidify' a sense of 'tribe'. 'Because we yearn for those small bolts of affirmation—the comment, the like, the share—we habitually post items that have generated the most response', says Vaidhyanathan. 'Facebook also rewards us... and pushes that rewarding content out farther, faster, and more frequently'. When the network becomes a venue for asserting a sense of identity, 'disputable, divisive, or disreputable content [could] become even more valuable' than the relatively bland information that has gone through a rigorous fact-check.[31]

The US election of 2016 was a wake-up call, when the possibilities of a new century of American dominance were turned around and the architects of that promised techno-utopia found themselves under scrutiny. An early message that the whole cycle of events conveyed is that globalization and the network state could be heading towards a harsh new dystopia, far removed from early rosy forecasts.

India's great democratic experiment has also run a rocky course, all its own. The early years were flush with optimism about the Congress system succeeding in managing the diversities and conflicts inherent in the adoption of the universal franchise in India. The pioneering Indian political scientist Rajni Kothari has written the locus classicus on how the Congress has been a unique institution in combining the roles of ruling party and opposition within itself.

The success of the Congress as a 'system' hinged around its ability to draw in and involve 'traditional institutions of kin and caste' and evolve a viable 'structure of pressures and compromises'. Vigorous competition within the party, manifest at the local level and aggregated at the level of the respective states, imparted legitimacy. At the level of the states, 'individuals who had risen to power in the Congress organisation sometimes constituted the chief opposition to the government [and] provided an alternative leadership, exercised controls and pressures on it, and in many instances overthrew it from power and replaced it'.[32]

To perform the roles it was assuming, the system needed to ensure 'plurality within the dominant party', which would make it 'more representative' and flexible. Simultaneously, the party should be 'prepared to absorb groups and movements from outside' in a manner that would 'prevent other parties from gaining in strength'. As it gathered more power to itself, the dominant party would also institute 'internal checks to limit the use of this strength'.[33]

These features that Kothari saw as vital to the sustenance of the Congress system unravelled following the mid-1960s. An economic crisis that upset early hopes of the Nehruvian years was a significant contributor to a political shake-out. The Congress lost power in a number of key states in 1967, retaining only a parlous grip at the Centre. In 1974, in a decennial reappraisal, Kothari insisted that despite setbacks, the basic features of the system remained intact. The losses and gains incurred in 1967 and through subsequent contests were 'part of the corrective framework of the dominance system'. The Congress system, moreover, was not one of dominance alone; it was much more a 'system of competition' and still more, 'a system of responding to changes in public opinion.'[34]

There had been certain states where the Congress was reduced to irrelevance, and even in the absence of a party of consensus at the national level, the system would endure. The Congress would ensure the sustenance of the system, if compelled to, by 'integration' with other parties, creating coalitions that would contain a 'polar confrontation'. Alternately, it could invoke the 'federal leverages available to the dominant party', i.e. assert administrative authority in a manner that safeguards its pre-eminence.[35]

Kothari's revised formulations may have been appropriate to the situation that emerged with sweeping Congress victories in general elections to Parliament and the state legislatures between 1971 and 1972. But they were upended, even while being written, with the economic stresses generated by successive monsoon failures and a global oil price shock, engendering strife across several parts of the country. Subsequent events, including the declaration of a nationwide Emergency, the suspension of civil liberties and the spectacular electoral debacle that the Congress went down to in 1977, seemed to suggest the end of the system put together by India's first prime minister and restored to a semblance of stability by his daughter in 1971.

A quarter century later, Yogendra Yadav offered another kind of retrospect of that decade. Indira Gandhi had seemingly restored Congress dominance in 1971, but the party she led to victory was a radically altered formation, which had to 'negotiate a new terrain of electoral politics.' These shifts, in turn, were a consequence of the 'first democratic upsurge in the late 1960s', which had brought in large numbers from the 'middle castes' or the 'other backward classes' (OBCs), into active electoral competition.[36]

Successive national general elections—in 1971, 1977, 1980, 1984—produced decisive victories for either the Congress, or in one instance, a conglomerate of anti-Congress forces. Yet, these were no mere variants on the Congress system. The Congress continued being the dominant pole of electoral competition, but in place of the earlier subtlety of building coalitions from the ground upwards, 'elections turned into plebiscites where the effective unit of political choice was the entire nation, sometimes split along north-south lines'. A typical election verdict involving the Lok Sabha through this period took the form of a 'nation-wide or sometimes state-wide wave for or against the Congress'.[37]

If Indian democracy was all about the Congress system through its first two decades, it acquired a new shape through the following two. Yadav sees the latter period as distinct enough to merit the tag of a 'second electoral system'. And then, between the 1989 and 1991 contests came a powerful stimulus for change in the conjunction of three forces: Mandal, Mandir and market.[38] Mandal spoke of an assertion of middle-caste power that crystallized in an active campaign for assured representation in the executive apparatus. Mandir was about the resurgence of an older brand of nationalism, briefly exiled from the Congress mainstream under Nehru and Indira Gandhi, which involved the exclusion of minority faiths and the assertion of an invented *Hindu* identity for the Indian nation.

As the epic confrontation between Mandal and Mandir was just beginning, the older benevolence of the Indian state with its promise of development for all was rapidly dissipating. In its place came a hard-nosed turn to the market. There would no longer be a representative State that involved all to act as the arbiter of distributive justice, except at the margins of deprivation and historical injustice. The market would, from 1991 onwards, be the final judge and arbiter.

The contest for legislative and executive power drew in larger numbers at just the time that space for policy interventions ensuring a fair distributive bargain began to sharply constrict. As Yadav puts it: 'Just when the lower order had some access to political power, the most significant economic decisions were removed from the political agenda'.[39] The outcome was growing volatility in electoral competition, as unstable coalitions formed and fissured from one contest to another, with alliance partners unable to gain promised advantages from power. The state of the Indian polity through the 'third electoral system', as Yadav has termed this phase, represented, in an especially sharp form, the collision between political equality as embodied in the universal franchise and the 'self-reproductive processes of the structure of socio-economic inequality'. The two had, for long, been in conflict, though neither had ever been able to 'tame the other'.[40]

The years since were a time of multiplying political parties and shifting alliances. Is there a term that could adequately describe India's politics between 1989 and 2014, i.e. from the time a general election for the first time threw up a hung parliament to the restoration of a single-party majority? Perhaps through the six general elections fought between 1989 and 2014 (both years excluded), the parts had begun to determine the destiny of the whole. National politics became an amalgam of state-level elections, driven by the fierce competition between castes and factions for control over the levers of power. As the grand ambitions of development of the Nehru years yielded in stages to an acceptance of the market as the final authority in matters economic, two coalitions emerged, which could not be described in terms of ideology, since this was also a time of convergence.[41] Aside from a brief interlude between 2004 and 2009, when the left had significant influence at the level of the central government, the idiom of governance generally followed the diktat of the market.

What changed in 2014? For one, there was a global economic meltdown in 2008, which lapped up against Indian shores from about 2010, in the shape of serious inflationary pressures. This also coincided with revelations, through media exposés, of a degree of financial misfeasance that the incumbent government had indulged in to keep its coalition intact. Public discontent fused with the urge for a strongman at the helm, somebody who would offer sufficient contrast to the soft-spoken and seemingly effete prime minister at the time.

Campaigning through Networking

India, in 2014, saw a campaign that used network connectivity to forge new ideas of political identity and create a fresh alignment of power. The general election to the Lok Sabha was the setting for this unique experiment. It was a contest in which the right-wing nationalist party, the BJP, began with a distinct advantage in terms of media endorsements. The incumbent Congress party was exhausted after 10 years in power, for part of which time it had the good fortune to capitalize on an economic boom. But as preparations began for the 2014 contest, the good times were at an end and resentment over allegations of political corruption ran high.

Quickness of reflex was among the distinctive features of the BJP campaign, led by Narendra Modi, then the chief minister of Gujarat, and a politician who had, for long, been under a shadow for his abetment of a wave of communal violence in 2002.[42] The winds had shifted in the 12 years since, and the media and the voluble Indian middle class that had seen its revolution of rising aspirations falter under Congress rule were keen to find a new standard-bearer. Modi's campaign was, with some justice, labelled the 'maximum campaign'.[43] And its outcome in May 2014 was a triumph on a scale that had been denied to any individual or party since 1984.

A striking feature of the campaign was its immersive character, its ability to invite a large section of an angry and aggrieved electorate into a big tent where Modi would talk to them directly in an idiom that reflected their frustrated aspirations. The statistics of the campaign suggest nothing so much as a methodical and calculated pursuit of power: well over 400 rallies personally addressed by Modi during a seven-month span and another 900 through three-dimensional holographic projection. In the six-week period between the first and last phases of polling, Modi travelled 3,00,000 kilometres to address nearly 200 rallies. Meanwhile, vans fully equipped with audiovisual technology traversed the far reaches of the country, conveying a message of better times to come. This was carried out in tandem with an advertising blitz that saturated every conceivable form of media, whether print, TV, radio, online and outdoor, with Modi's image and the assurance that he would be the one to restore a sense of 'national prestige'.[44]

The visible optics of the campaign were so overpowering then that few found any occasion to look into the largely inscrutable world of social media.[45] Yet, that was an active arena of political mobilization, and soon after taking office, Modi signalled his enthusiasm for social media at a meeting with Facebook's chief operating officer, Sheryl Sandberg. According to an entry in Modi's personal website, Sandberg congratulated him on his 'exceptional use of Facebook to connect with voters'.[46] Soon afterwards, Modi reportedly instructed colleagues in the party and government to use social media to get the word out but to stay clear of direct interactions with traditional news media.[47] Though never fully articulated, a feature of the strategy was Modi's refusal, all through his first term, to 'face a single uncensored interview or press conference'.[48]

Modi's first term was also a time of accelerated change in the information ecosystem. Network technologies enabled new bonds of identity, affording fresh opportunities for the acute political operative. The widening disparities occasioned by the drift away from welfare state politics were a threat to social order, but they also afforded opportunities for creating new patterns of electoral competition. There is, as some have observed, a horseshoe symmetry between populism of the Left and the Right.[49] On both sides of the political spectrum, populism seeks to redress widening disparities and provide a fair deal for those at the bottom of the scale of income and wealth. On the Left, populism creates the 'us and them' duality in correspondence with the scale of income and wealth. On the right, populism wedges itself into other fault lines of ethnicity and race, for instance, and seeks victory through division.

Soon after the last ballot was cast in the 2019 general election, the seventeenth to the Lok Sabha, *Columbia Journalism Review* posted an article on its website, rich with cross references, titled 'Results expected in India's "WhatsApp election"'. Exit poll results released after a 38-day campaign and seven rounds of polling indicated a surprisingly comfortable win for the incumbent prime minister. Yet, for all the issues at stake, the most riveting aspect of the election was 'the rampant proliferation of disinformation and hate speech online'. It was a situation that 'traditional media', a significant presence in the public sphere, bore part responsibility for. By far the greater aggravation, though, had come from the social media platform Facebook and its wholly owned messaging service WhatsApp.[50]

Three days later, after a victory even more decisive than the forecast, Modi addressed the senior leadership and newly elected members of his party and its coalition partners. Alongside the call to duty, the main theme of his 75-minute speech in Hindi, Modi issued several explicit warnings about the media. Print media and TV may seem a good way to project ideas onto the public stage, he said, but there is a risk of falling victim to its 'magnetic power'. The media speculation that had emerged in a mere matter of days since the election results, about the possible constitution of the Cabinet, was 'motivated by ill intentions and aimed at creating divisions.'[51]

The signals were clear: the prime minister of the world's largest democracy, in his second term, would sustain the contentious relationship with the media established through the first. At first glance, the reasons seem unclear. Modi's 2019 victory, even more than the previous one, was greeted in several quarters of the business press as a sweeping triumph of brand management.[52] A successful brand strategy, as every marketing text teaches, involves creative media strategies. The difference, though, is that in the case of Modi and the 2019 election, traditional media was disdained as an enclave of privileged elites. Social media was where the 'real people' were afforded an opportunity to make their voices heard.

Always a powerful political force, populism has gained a new impetus in the network society. Anti-elitism is one element of the mix that creates a successful model of populist politics. Another is an aversion to pluralism or social complexity. Populism believes that every problem has a straightforward solution and celebrates the simple, matter-of-fact approach. Accommodating diversity on any matter is a pointless indulgence. An element that provides fertile soil for populism would be a degree of socio-economic differentiation, with large gaps between various groups. An 'us versus them' duality is easy to conjure out of this mix, alongside the populist assertion of a monopoly in terms of representing the 'people'.[53]

For all its insistence on the will of the people, populism is exclusivist. As Jan-Werner Muller notes, 'only some of the people are really the people' and they 'speak with one voice and issue something like an imperative mandate that tells politicians exactly what they have to do in government'.[54] The media, especially the older legacy news outlets, are disdained in this perception as a body that creates an unwanted interface between the people and its leaders, distorting the pristine nature of the relationship.

As the 2019 campaign drew to a close, Modi made a seeming exception to his policy of avoiding media interviews to appear on camera for a news channel. He constantly referred, through the interview, to a sheaf of papers, found, on closer examination, to list a rehearsed catalogue of questions and answers.[55] His only major interview with a print media outlet through the first term was on the eve of the penultimate round of voting in 2019. The *Indian Express*, which was granted this interview, is a long-established newspaper with a reputation for adversarial journalism. That was the high watermark of the Modi transparency regime, with no sign of prior clearance or consultation over the questions that would be posed.

In substance, the interview was a story of Modi challenging every question rather than answering. He queried the newspaper's editorial priorities, its choice of news to feature as also the audience it catered to. There was a time, he said, when a journalist spoke through his work and sought to maintain an objective façade, but now he was betrayed by his social media presence. Among the questions posed was one on the agenda that remained unfulfilled, despite the comfortable majority that Modi enjoyed in the Lok Sabha. Modi's response was: 'Getting the Indian Express to be objective in criticism of Modi'.[56]

Modi also coined a syllogism—the 'Khan market crowd', referring to an upmarket location in the Indian capital city—to sum up his disdain for the cosmopolitan Indian who had never quite accepted him. Referring to himself in the third person, as he often did, Modi spoke of how that crowd would not be able, despite all its intent and desperate efforts, to 'dismantle his image', which was the outcome of several decades of toil and striving.[57]

The People, True and False

Populism claims the mantle of speaking in the true voice of the people. Just as insistently, it assumes for itself the right to determine what is the *truth* the people alone are privy to. Truth is often regarded as a metaphysical construct, though it has a more pragmatic dimension as a process of accurately recording perceptions and ensuring they become part of an agreed social record. Agreement over facts and their generalization into higher truths is generally regarded as an indispensable part of the foundations of a well-ordered society. But then if facts are a matter of perception, that would open the doorway to a troubling relativism. Every person's fact could differ from every other. Perceptions are moulded by culture, and observations of fact are conditioned by the cultural artefact of language. Is truth, then, culturally determined?

It is a dilemma that recalls Hannah Arendt's classic essay from 1967. 'Truth and politics' was a theme she was drawn to by the response to her landmark 1963 book on the trial in Jerusalem of the Nazi killer Adolf Eichmann. That book, written from eyewitness observation, spoke what she thought were undisputable truths. But the response ranged from puzzlement at her motivations to outright mendacity in discrediting the facts she relied on. Thinking back, Arendt made what seemed a vital distinction. 'Factual truths', for her, bore reference to observations by living subjects of constantly changing reality. 'Rational truths', on the contrary, were part of the received wisdom. Few could question the latter, such as the proposition that two and two made four. But factual truth was always prone to challenge as being no more significant than opinion.[58]

Truth and politics, Arendt conceded, had always been 'on rather bad terms with each other' and 'truthfulness' was never counted 'among the political virtues'. This reality had a profound bearing on the practice of politics, since 'facts and events', the outcome of the collective life of humanity, were the 'very texture of the political realm'.[59] James Madison, one among seven founding fathers of the US constitution, said about governments that finally they all 'rest on opinion'. Yet, an individual's opinion tended to be 'timid and cautious' in its expression, and only acquired 'firmness and confidence in proportion to the number with which it is associated'.⁶⁰ Numbers could be a guarantee of strength, though not of authenticity. Indeed, the whole procedure, for Arendt, seemed thoroughly unsatisfactory, since there was nothing that prevented a majority 'from being false witnesses'. Indeed, 'the feeling of belonging to a majority may even encourage false testimony'.⁶¹

Could social media be the platform afforded, in the networked society, for harvesting attention and securing assent for a particular perception of reality? It is difficult to imagine social media as an autonomous force that works to similar effect irrespective of the milieu. The US is fertile soil, segregated by class and credentials into ghettos of privilege and deprivation by four decades of neoliberal economics. It is a context that enables particular classes to pretend that other worlds do not exist, that their perceptions, fortified in regular check-ins with social media, are all that matter.

Our Truth Is Greater than Yours

India, a social milieu with its own modes of sorting by class, caste and community affords new means of campaigning through connectivity technologies. The 2019 general election, in fact, tells a story of how the regime in power polished its image through the power of social media.⁶² This is a variant of the theme developed in Benedict Anderson's classic work on the origins of nationalism, *Imagined Communities,* which spoke of how the mass production of the written word by print capitalism was the foundation on which human societies expanded their boundaries beyond local contexts. Once bound both in time and space by oral communications and the relative brevity of individual and collective memories, human association could now embrace the concept of a nation.⁶³

Key to the imagination of the nation was a sense of shared time or simultaneity. Older conceptions saw time as succession, which fused a past and a divinely ordained future in an 'instantaneous present'. In place of this notion of 'simultaneity along time', capitalist modernity instituted, in Walter Benjamin's words, 'homogeneous, empty time', where simultaneity was 'marked not by prefiguring and fulfilment but by temporal coincidence and measured by the clock and calendar'.[64]

Anderson finds the new constructs of simultaneity in the novel, an art form uniquely connected to capitalist modernity, where an 'interior world' is connected to the 'exterior world' of the reader. The novel was a form of composition that required to be read rather than performed and was, in that fashion, dependent upon the mass production techniques that print capitalism permitted. The newspaper was another form of mass-produced commodity, a book produced on a 'colossal scale' but with no expectation of anything but 'ephemeral popularity'. This property of 'obsolescence of the commodity on the marrow of its printing', imparted to the newspaper a unique status as a marker of simultaneity in the human experience. The significance of the 'mass ceremony' of newspaper reading, which Hegel likened to the morning prayer, is 'paradoxical' in Anderson's terms:

> It is performed in silent privacy, in the lair of the skull. Yet each communicant is well aware that the ceremony he performs is being replicated simultaneously by thousands (or millions) of others of whose existence he is confident, yet of whose identity he has not the slightest notion. Furthermore, this ceremony is incessantly repeated at daily or half-daily intervals throughout the calendar. What more vivid figure for the secular, historically clocked, imagined community can be imagined?[65]

The network society permits the affirmation of simultaneity and shared meanings through every instant, as messages often crowd into an individual's attention span with little respite. The algorithms that social media platforms use in selecting and targeting messages create echo chambers where every individual gains the validation he seeks. If the nation is a daily referendum, the network society supports an incessant chorus of either approbation or disapprobation, depending on where the balance of political power lies.

As cycles of information gathering and dissemination contract, trust in the newspaper and other players that collectively are known now as 'legacy media' has collapsed. The internet was seen, in early years, as the great new hope, which would enable every user to choose just the right mix of news feeds. Far from creating an ecosystem in which all voices would emerge and be heard, the new web architecture is creating a silo for every user, where he would be assured of his personal need for validation. At a time when nations are dealing with a crisis of internal cohesion, the bonds formed in the virtual world are an aggravating rather than ameliorative factor.

Time is a reality lived individually and collectively. As shared experiences embedded in collective memory, time is also continually mined for a sense of self and identity. The past is never quite past, and the unending present is where community lives are forged and reproduced through infinite numbers of quotidian acts. Industrial modernity, among the accompaniments to nationalism, unfolds in what has been called 'homogeneous empty time', an experience measured out in the uniform tempo of clocks and calendars.[66] Since modernity began its worldwide spread, the emptiness of time has been filled in by the rhythms of commodity production and relations of exchange that girdle the globe.

Globalization in its most intensive phase, beginning in the 1980s, yoked every nation to that pulse but for a few who stayed out of its embrace. And then in 2020 came the novel coronavirus, a lethal virus that captured the cycle of time, with its exponential multiplication. As one nation after another chose standstill as a survival imperative, time effectively was frozen to slow down and then pause the exponential viral growth. That required the dilation of social spaces, the severance of bonds built over the years. For the first time since the world's billions were told that they shared a common rhythm, they had to detach from the flow of time, severing complex linkages as the world pivoted towards fragmentation.

Just behind the crushing anxiety about surviving the virus, there was a sense of deep foreboding about the economic future. Capitalist reproduction stood still, its engines stilled by the paralysis of time. There was an expectation among the greater optimists that once the pandemic was seen off, the engines would spark back to life. That hope may well be futile, since waves of globalization, as they recede, leave a terrain pockmarked by inequality.

Mainstream economics speaks of two autonomous forces of supply and demand that determine an economy's equilibrium. It omits the basic point that demand is a function of supply—generated by the engagement of workers, farmers, traders and business owners—in daily acts of capitalist production. It is the entitlement each of these stakeholders gains through a contract—arrived at prior to the production cycle—that determines how well they cope with a slowdown, or in current circumstances, standstill. The progressive skew of the distributive bargain over the decades of globalization now places billions among the world's working poor at risk of ruin.

Capital is embedded time, in which the contemporary world inherits the labour of past generations. Capitalism is also a morality play—of progress driven by the innovative, who enrich themselves while carrying all along. Rising inequalities and the frequent financial shake-outs that drive those on the downside of the distributive bargain to penury are viewed as minor perturbations, as the system moves inexorably towards greater opportunity for all. The creation of wealth is seen inherently as an act of benevolence and as reward for the virtuous act of waiting. Unlike those of lesser virtue, who consume their earnings with little regard for the future, the capitalist is willing to wait for his reward in the future.

That mantra was the capitalist justification until instant gratification became an enshrined value in the 1980s. From then on, the investor in the financial markets did not need to wait, since he was guaranteed overnight rewards. Instruments of bewildering complexity were created to bridge today's gratification with ironclad assurances of rewards in future.

As the US, centre of the global capitalist order, floundered for a credible response to the contagion sweeping its territory, it had few options but to create future claims on its resource, in dollar-denominated debt, that it may never be in a position to honour. Countries of lesser privilege, such as India, had little choice but to shut down entirely, freezing the passage of time in the hope of a reawakening soon, with all the distributive rules of the game intact.

An economy entering a 'stationary state' was a dreaded prospect for the classical economists who witnessed the early turmoil and dislocations of industrial modernity. By the mid-nineteenth century, though, John Stuart Mill could contemplate the standstill with equanimity as a state that would be regenerative, restoring humanity to the wisdom of a situation 'in which, while no one is poor, no one desires to be richer, nor has any reason to fear being thrust back by the efforts of others to push themselves forward'. The increase of wealth could not be 'boundless' and there had to be a 'stationary state' that could conceivably be postponed but, inevitably, had to follow the 'progressive state'. This did not imply a stasis in human improvement but rather afforded an opportunity for collective recuperation from the 'normal state' that industrial capitalism imposed, 'of struggling to get on', of 'trampling, crushing, elbowing, and treading on each other's heels'.[67]

Classical political economy, which theorized upon the material substratum of the nation, was built upon the premise of an innate ethical sensibility. Concurrent with Mill's generation, though, there was another sensibility gaining ground, which adapted Darwinian evolution into a harsh vision of the individual struggling against society. That hidden streak of capitalism was awakened afresh in the decades of globalization. In 2020, with the onset of the greatest global health crisis in over a century, anxieties multiplied over the cohesion of the international order.

The fear of being left behind in the race towards social achievement could motivate political assertion in ways that disregard conventional norms of liberal democracy. Identity conflicts gain greater vigour, and claims to 'belonging' could be asserted in ways that threaten minorities that have carved out a niche, not always a secure one, but one that is integral to the daily life of the nation. Populist politics seeks to recruit some of these insecurities into the cause of majoritarian assertion in nation states otherwise sworn to abide by the liberal credo.

In an essay written shortly after his book on nationalism, E.J. Hobsbawm proposed that research needed to focus more closely on the tendency for nations to turn themselves into '*mono-ethnic, mono-linguistic* and *mono-cultural* territories'. This growing trend of insisting on narrower definitions of national identity, pointed to one of four possible end points: 'mass assimilation or conversion by state force, mass expulsion of populations or "ethnic cleansing", genocide or the creation, *de facto* or *de jure*, of an apartheid system which turns non-members of the dominant group into foreigners or a legally inferior underclass of sub-citizens'.[68]

This transformation of nationalism has acquired a new momentum since Hobsbawm wrote. Experiences of genocide, ethnic cleansing and apartheid are fresh in public memory, though perhaps banished to a zone of denial, with the comfortable assumption that liberal democratic political systems would be resilient against a drift towards the extremes. That state of blissful denial has been rudely dispelled in the third decade of the twenty-first century.

In the US, minority privileges are enshrined in the system of elections and the constitution of the legislature. The people do not elect the US president; they elect an electoral college that then elects the president. It was a system unique to the early days of the US as a republic and has since been kept afloat on the ballast of racism and the political fiction of state's rights. The US, over the last several elections, has manifested a marked polarization between 'red' and 'blue', a situation aggravated by the structure of the upper legislative chamber, which gives the red states, sparsely populated and socially less diverse, the same number of seats as the blue, where economic buoyancy has attracted immigrants and created a measure of diversity.

With a self-designated role as the interpreter of the Constitution in accordance with an 'originalist' reading, the Supreme Court of the United States (SCOTUS) is another redoubt of conservative thinking. Originalism is a curious judicial doctrine that accords primacy to the intent of the text as written centuries back, with little regard for how those principles have gained in nuance with the passage of time. Three of the nine judges on SCOTUS were appointed by a president who lost the national popular vote in 2016. Two others were appointed by a second-term president who won his first term after a split SCOTUS, by a margin of one, transformed defeat in the national vote into a victory, in the Bush v. Gore case of 2000.

In sharply polarized times, India's system of elections, based on a simple plurality in territorially defined single-member constituencies, could inflate the popular endorsement politicians claim from electoral verdicts. Since India adopted the Westminster system as its preferred model of democratic practice at Independence, a certain equableness was maintained by a mutually agreed compact among all political parties to play within a set of rules. In a vast and diverse country, it was understood that no elected government would take policy into the extreme zones, when sections of the citizenry could get alienated from the national mainstream. The 2014 election was a watershed, and polarization based on religion has been the dominant theme since. Once the politics of rage and resentment becomes the winning ticket for any party, multiple other fissures are likely to emerge.

The politics of polarization falls on the fertile economic soil of growing inequality. The years of neoliberalism following India's own close encounter with a debt-induced meltdown in 1991 have been ambiguous in terms of progress on poverty. Official estimates, as presented in the annual Economic Survey tabled by the finance ministry in Parliament, claim a steady decrease in the incidence of poverty, in terms of both the ratio and the absolute number. But over the first decade since liberalization, the task of estimation was complicated by certain changes in methodology.

Simply for this reason, official claims that India had made significant inroads in the battle against poverty in the years of liberalization proved contentious. Angus Deaton, later a Nobel laureate for his work on poverty, was prepared to concede that there had been a fall in the poverty ratio, though of not sufficient magnitude to make a dent in the absolute number of the poor. Others such as Abhijit Sen argued that the decade following 1995 had been a lost decade in the war against poverty, with the number of the poor having increased.[69]

Roughly about that time, a consensus emerged on income and wealth inequality having increased in India.[70] The years of high growth that followed may have reduced poverty, but then came the global financial meltdown of 2008, with the possibility that many millions globally, as also in India, may have plunged afresh into penury. In the years since, the official statement from the Indian government on the state of the economy has addressed the issue of inequality typically by noting very cursorily where the Gini coefficient—the most widely accepted measure—stands in India. Reassurance is sought in other countries being at a much worse level in the inequality index.[71]

Inequality is often regarded as an inescapable consequence of how people adapt to the need to keep the nation afloat. Some excel, the others follow. When does inequality become the active denial of rights? As the economist Reetika Khera points out, it took a long while for India to ensure that all women enjoy maternity benefits. Yet, the benefits delivered to those at the bottom of the income scale were inconsequential and given grudgingly. There are some who enjoy 'world-class maternity benefits', when the 'same level of benefits has been denied for so long' to all, even resisted as a universal right. So, that raises the question of what kind of society it is that provides 'more and more for the privileged but grudges every penny set aside for those in greater need?' It is one that functions as a 'nanny state for the rich but wants the poor to be *aatmanirbhar*—self-reliant'.[72]

Substantive equality in terms of economic status is a goal that may seem too far. But what about formal equality? A challenge that looms large ahead of Indian democracy is the restoration of equality in voting rights, of establishing afresh the principle that every vote cast would have roughly the same probability of influencing the pattern of political representation. India's situation, in some senses, is the reverse of what the US faces. Because of the perceived problem of overpopulation after roughly the first quarter century of India's independence, representation for every state in the Union was frozen in accordance with the 1971 Census. This decision was implemented under the 42nd Amendment to the Constitution, under the ill-remembered Emergency, though it was not reversed in the repair job carried out by the successor regime. The rationale was simple: there was a national interest in population stabilization, which meant that increasing political representation for states registering a growth in numbers would be a perverse incentive.

Ambedkar had, as far back as 1955, endorsed the principle

of 'culture' as a basis for the internal organization of nations. Culture, he believed, was a binding force, and the integrity of the nation as a whole was maintained by the coherence of its parts. He also warned that yoking distinct cultural units together, despite their differences, could pose a threat to the integrity of the whole. States that had gone through social reform and learnt to accept diversity would be uncomfortable sharing governmental cycles with others that remained impervious to these.[73]

The pause in the drawing of parliamentary constituencies anew, in accordance with population in each state, will expire in 2026. In the decades since it was imposed, certain states have had rapid population growth, while others have reached the threshold of the demographic transition when birth and death rates are roughly matched. If the ceiling of 552 seats in the Lok Sabha were to be maintained, the share of Uttar Pradesh today would go from 80 to 88, Bihar and Jharkhand together would go from 54 to 61, and all other states in the north would gain in representation. Gujarat and Maharashtra would gain one seat each, and West Bengal would lose two. The five southern states, Tamil Nadu, Kerala, Karnataka, Andhra Pradesh and Telangana, would lose a total of 18 seats: falling to 111 against their current total of 129 Lok Sabha seats.[74]

India's constitution mandates, under article 82, that seats in Parliament should be allocated between the states after every census. This issue was deferred first in 1976 and then again in 2002, for another quarter century. The linguistic reorganization of states was the cement that held the Indian Union together through the 1950s and afterwards. The principle was not always implemented consistently, and adjustments were always possible to deal with specific contingencies. But the unity of the whole has been safeguarded by the coherence of the parts.

Identity as a construct could become predatory at some point, demanding the extinction of rival constructs. Anthropologist Arjun

Appadurai puts it thus: predatory identities are socially constructed and emerge out of a mobilization requiring the 'extinction of other, proximate social categories, defined as a threat to the very existence of some group, defined as a "we"'.[75] A modern nation, once constituted in terms of an ethnos, or ethnic identity, could seamlessly transition into a predatory state, which requires the extinction of another collectivity for its own survival. Majoritarian morality emerges from the anxiety of incompleteness: the sense that the nation remains unfulfilled till it embodies a pristine identity handed down from primordial times. As majoritarianism becomes a political project, it creates the anxiety of purity, of how to ensure that the nation remains unsullied by alien implants that recall historical traumas. India's effort at self-purification involves the isolation of the Islamic faith today. But that quest for an impossible object is, if nothing else, mutable. It could soon turn in upon and consume the ideal of the nation itself.

Notes

1. Appiah, K. Anthony, *The Lies That Bind: Rethinking Identity: Creed, Country, Colour, Class, Culture,* Liveright, New York, 2018, p. 21.
2. 'The President's Address to the Nation Announcing Steps to Limit the War in Vietnam and Reporting His Decision Not To Seek Reelection', The American Presidency Project, https://bit.ly/38K9GMI. Accessed on 26 May 2022.
3. Krugman, Paul, *Peddling Prosperity: Economic Sense and Nonsense in the Age of Diminishing Expectations*, W.W. Norton, New York, 1994, p. 15.
4. Blyth, Mark, *Austerity: The History of a Dangerous Idea*, Oxford University Press, 2013, p. 120.
5. Ibid.
6. Quoted in: Ibid. 126.
7. Krugman, Paul, *Peddling Prosperity: Economic Sense and Nonsense in the Age of Diminishing Expectations*, W.W. Norton, New York, 1994,

p. 32.
8   Ibid. 24.
9   Stein, Judith, *Pivotal Decade: How the United States Traded Factories for Finance in the Seventies*, Kindle edition, 2010, location 5197. As Alasdair Roberts (*The End of Protest: How Free-Market Capitalism Learned to Control Dissent*, Kindle Edition, 2013, location 941) observes: 'In the early 1980s, the Reagan administration and Thatcher government both engaged in high-profile conflicts that signaled their determination to reduce the power of organised labor...In both cases, conservative leaders broke the union, and then consolidated their victories with changes in law that undercut the labor movement's ability to organize workers'.
10 Jack Welch, the CEO of the US corporate behemoth General Electric, was among the iconic management wizards of the time. His legacy has come in for a minute and unsparing examination in a recent book: Gelles, David, *The Man Who Broke Capitalism: How Jack Welch Gutted the Heartland and Crushed the Soul of Corporate America—and How to Undo His Legacy*, Simon and Schuster, New York, 2022.
11 We also learn that the Reagan years were a turning point in the emergence of an advocacy of untrammelled gun ownership as a basic right granted under the Constitution. This has since been enshrined in a judgment from the US Supreme Court and is believed to have been an essential ingredient in the a violent subculture that overlaps with white nationalism. See Waldman, Michael, 'How the NRA Rewrote the Second Amendment', Brennan Center for Justice, 20 May 2014, https://tinyurl.com/275859nu. Accessed on 23 June 2022.
12 Krugman, Paul, *Peddling Prosperity: Economic Sense and Nonsense in the Age of Diminishing Expectations*, W.W. Norton, New York, 1994, p. 130.
13 A recent work that represents an awakening is Sandel, Michael, *The Tyranny of Merit, What's Become of the Common Good*, Farrar,

Straus and Giroux, New York, 2020.
14. Stein, Judith, *Pivotal Decade: How the United States Traded Factories for Finance in the Seventies*, Kindle edition, 2010, location 5549.
15. The phrase was used by George W. Bush in a moment of attempted humour in October 2000, before he was elected president. But as with all such efforts at humour, it had a basis in fact.
16. Quoted in: Stein, Judith, *Pivotal Decade: How the United States Traded Factories for Finance in the Seventies*, Kindle edition, 2010, location 5754.
17. Roberts, Alasdair, *The End of Protest, How Free-Market Capitalism Learned to Control Dissent*, Cornell University Press, Cornell, 2013 (Kindle Edition), pp. 1315–20.
18. Anderson, Perry, *Americana*, Three Essays Collective, Gurgaon, 2015, p. 22.
19. Stiglitz, Joseph, *Freefall: Free Markets and the Sinking of the Global Economy*, Penguin, USA, 2009, p. 189; Roberts, Alasdair, *The End of Protest, How Free-Market Capitalism Learned to Control Dissent*, Cornell University Press (Kindle Edition), 2013, location 1133.
20. Boushey, Heather, *Unbound: How Inequality Constricts Our Economy and What We Can Do About It*, Harvard University Press, 2019, p. 30.
21. Roberts, Alasdair, *The End of Protest, How Free-Market Capitalism Learned to Control Dissent*, Cornell University Press, Cornell, 2013 (Kindle Edition), p. 1133.
22. Branko Milanovic, who tried to break down the newly emerging structures of inequality in a 2019 work, found that the big winners were 'global plutocrats'. And then came the 'new mass middle class of the emerging world, mainly in East Asia and India, who benefitted from the spectacular growth of their regions'. The big losers 'were Western middle-class workers whose incomes stagnated as the industries they worked in were hollowed out by foreign competition'. Quoted in: Ahamed, Liquat, 'The Rich Can't Get Richer Forever, Can They', *The New Yorker*, 26 August 2019, https://tinyurl.com/4d2hk3dn. Accessed on 27 May 2022. It should be

added here that the vast numbers of informal-sector workers in the developing countries, who normally do not feature in any such analysis, were perhaps the worst affected.

23 Fukuyama, Francis, 'Why Is Democracy Performing So Poorly?' *Journal of Democracy*, vol. 26, no. 1, January 2015, pp. 12–13.

24 Ibid. 19–20.

25 This is a matter addressed rather acutely by Raghuram Rajan in his book *The Third Pillar: How Markets and the State Leave the Community Behind* (HarperCollins, New Delhi, 2019).

26 An early work, published a year into the Trump presidency, portrayed several of the shenanigans occurring within the White House. See: Wolff, Michael, *Fire and Fury: Inside the Trump White House*, Little Brown, New York, 2018. The story of Trump's two impeachments is available from concurrent media coverage, as with Fandos, Nicholas, 'Trump Impeached for Inciting Insurrection', *The New York Times*, 22 April 2021, https://tinyurl.com/2p8dcatn. Accessed on 23 June 2022.

27 As early as 30 September, more than a month ahead of the election, the 'newspaper of record', the *New York Times* ('The Attack on Voting in the 2020 Elections', 30 September 2020, https://tinyurl.com/2p8w8uyr) was reporting as follows: 'As the 2020 presidential election nears, it is becoming clear that the Trump administration and the Republican Party are not just looking at but heavily investing in the largely nonexistent problem of voter fraud.'

28 'Trump election lawsuit "smacks of racism", Wisconsin Judge Says', Al Jazeera, 12 December 2020, https://tinyurl.com/435txtnn. Accessed on 23 June 2022.

29 Lecher, Colin, and Jon Keegan, 'Biden and Trump Voters Were Exposed to Radically Different Coverage of the Capitol Riot on Facebook', *The Markup*, 14 January 2021, https://bit.ly/3wURZmL. Accessed on 30 May 2022.

30 Castells, Manuel, *Communication Power*, Oxford University Press, Oxford, 2013, p. 12, p. 23; These themes are also explored in

some detail in Muralidharan, Sukumar, 'Chapter 4', *Freedom, Civility, Commerce: Contemporary Media and the Public*, Three Essays Collective, Delhi, 2018.

31. Vaidhyanathan, Siva, *Anti-Social Media: How Facebook Disconnects Us and Undermines Democracy*, Oxford University Press, 2018, p. 15.
32. Kothari, Rajni, 'The Congress "System" in India', *Asian Survey*, vol. 4, no. 12, December 1964, pp. 1163–64.
33. Ibid. 1164–65.
34. Kothari, Rajni, 'The Congress "System" Revisited: A Decennial Review', *Asian Survey*, vol. 14, no. 12, December 1974, p. 1041.
35. Ibid. 1042.
36. Yadav, Yogendra, 'Electoral Politics in a Time of Change', *Economic & Political Weekly*, vol. 34, no. 34–35, 21 August 1999, https://bit.ly/3t0JUKH. Accessed on 30 May 2022.
37. Ibid.
38. Ibid.
39. Ibid.
40. Ibid.
41. Introduction, *Party Competition in Indian States: Electoral Politics in Post-congress Polity*, Suhas Palshikar, K.C. Suri, Yogendra Yadav (eds), Oxford University Press, Delhi, 2014.
42. The Gujarat violence has been extensively reported and analysed. Aside from media reports, one of the first records of the violence was the report of a Concerned Citizens' Tribunal, led by a distinguished former judge of the Supreme Court, V.R. Krishna Iyer, and comprising two other senior jurists, P.B Sawant and Hosbet Suresh, along with former IAS officer and social activist Aruna Roy, retired IPS officer K.S. Subramanian, and academics Ghanshyam Shah and Tanika Sarkar. See the full text of the report here: https://tinyurl.com/55dbpk3s.
43. Muralidharan, Sukumar, 'Modi, media and the feel-good effect', *Himal Southasian*, 30 June 2014, https://bit.ly/3a828mX. Accessed on 30 May 2022.

44 Ibid.
45 Safi, Michael, 'India's ruling party ordered online abuse of opponents, claims book', *The Guardian*, 27 December 2016, https://bit.ly/3lXtajU. Accessed on 30 May 2022.
46 'Prime Minister Narendra Modi Meets Facebook COO Sheryl Sandberg', Narendra Modi, 3 July 2014, https://tinyurl.com/2s4dyfkm. Accessed on 23 June 2022.
47 'India's Modi bypasses mainstream media and takes to Twitter', Index on Censorship, 27 August 2014, https://tinyurl.com/2p8dkdme. Accessed on 23 June 2022.
48 Finnigan, Christopher, 'The new Indian election: Free but not fair', South Asia Centre, London School of Economics, 10 May 2019, https://tinyurl.com/4vfdture. Accessed on 23 June 2022.
49 Groshek, Jacob, and Karolina Koc-Michalska, 'Helping populism win? Social media use, filter bubbles, and support for populist presidential candidates in the 2016 US election campaign', *Information, Communication and Society*, vol. 20, no. 9, June 2017, pp. 1389–1407.
50 Allsop, Jon, 'Results Expected in India's "WhatsApp election"', *Columbia Journalism Review*, 22 May 2019, https://bit.ly/3t3Vt47. Accessed on 30 May 2022.
51 The full speech can be viewed on the Youtube channel of India's upper house of parliament, dated 25 May 2019, https://www.youtube.com/watch?v=8XIqnmtowns. The specific quotes mentioned above can be found at minutes 38:50, 40:44 and 46:08.
52 Goyal, Sandeep, 'Opinion: The rise and rise of brand Modi, how winner takes all', *mint*, 24 May 2019, https://bit.ly/3asDSfs. Accessed on 6 June 2022.
53 Muller, Jan-Werner, *What is Populism?* Penguin Random House, 2016, p. 15, p. 25.
54 Ibid. 21, 31.
55 'Modi's media interview triggers new questions', *Business Standard*, 13 May 2019, https://bit.ly/3z7dW3B. Accessed on 30 May 2022.
56 '7 Takeaways From Modi's Interview to Indian Express', *The Quint*,

12 May 2019, https://bit.ly/3z4Tb8q. Accessed on 30 may 2022.
57   Jha, Raj Kamal, and Ravish Tiwari, 'Prime Minister Narendra Modi Interview "Khan Market gang hasn't created my image, 45 years of tapasya has...you cannot dismantle it"', *The Indian Express*, 13 May 2019, https://bit.ly/3POhCNq. Accessed on 30 May 2022.
58   Arendt, Hannah, 'Politics and Truth', https://tinyurl.com/yzderzxv, p. 2. Accessed on 30 may 2022.
59   Ibid. 3.
60   Quoted in: Ibid. 4.
61   Ibid. 10.
62   The story is told with varying degrees of elaboration in 'Nationalism a driving force behind fake news in India, research shows', BBC News, 12 November 2018, https://bbc.in/3xlv2td. Accessed on 6 June 2022; 'News and Information over Facebook and WhatsApp during the Indian Election Campaign', Programme on Democracy and Technology, 13 May 2019, https://bit.ly/3NUeDkH. Accessed on 6 June 2022.
63   Anderson, Benedict, *Imagined Communities: Reflections on the Origin and Spread of Nationalism,* Verso, London, 1983, p. 24.
64   Ibid.
65   Ibid. 35.
66   Ibid.
67   Mill, John Stuart, *Principles of Political Economy: With some of their applications to Social Philosophy,* Sir William James Ashley (ed.), Longmans, Green & Company, London, 1921, p. 752.
68   Hobsbawm, E.J., 'The State, Ethnicity and Religion', *On Nationalism*, Little Brown, London, 2021, p. 216.
69   The debate is presented in all its essential details in Deaton, Angus and Valerie Kozel, 'Data and Dogma: The Great Indian Poverty Debate', Princeton Univrsity, 2004, https://tinyurl.com/2xwfub83. Accessed on 6 June 2022.
70   Himanshu, 'Recent Trends in Poverty and Inequality: Some Preliminary Results', *Economic & Political Weekly*, vol. 42, no. 6,

February 2007, pp. 497–508, https://tinyurl.com/mwvhax4u. Accessed on 23 June 2022.
71 See the Ministry of Finance, *Economic Survey, 2015–16,* where the issue of inequality is grudgingly addressed on page 210 of Volume 2 by presenting it as one among many parameters on which India is assessed against global standards.
72 Khera, Reetika, 'Unfair Share: India is in deep denial about inequality', *The Caravan*, 1 February 2002, https://tinyurl.com/yckjerh4. Accessed on 6 June 2022.
73 Ambedkar, B.R., 'Thoughts on Linguistic States', *Dr Babasaheb Ambedkar, Writings and Speeches,* Volume I, Vasant Moon (ed.), Education Deprtment, Government of Maharashtra, Mumbai, 1979, pp. 148–50.
74 The figures have been diligently calculated and presented in Vaishnav, Milan and Jamie Hintson, 'India's Emerging Crisis of Representation', Carnegie Endowment for International Peace, 14 March 2019, https://bit.ly/3mgt4Ur. Accessed on 6 June 2022.
75 Appadurai, Arjun, *The Fear of Small Numbers: An Essay on the Geography of Anger*, Duke University Press, Durham, 2006, pp. 51–52.

ACKNOWLEDGEMENTS

Mid-2019 was a key moment in the transit of this book from idea to reality, thanks to a group of young historians I have the good fortune of working with. Meetings of this group were frequent through the months before the long lockdown, and members were continually prodding each other, including those rather long in the tooth, to subject their ongoing and planned work to unrestrained and vigorous criticism. That was a promising start, though this work may have taken a rather more leisurely course had not a commissioning editor from Rupa, entirely out of the blue, messaged me with an enquiry about a possible book on the exact same themes. Pure coincidence, as I later found out, since the editor had come across a rather brief book review I had written some months before, and was cold calling to check if a longer work may be in prospect.

This work began under these twin impetuses and has since been sustained on the support received from a number of friends and associates. For all of them I will reserve my special words of thanks for our next personal encounters.

The ideas I have put down here did not spring full-blown in the last three years. They have been long in the making and some have been road-tested in works published earlier. Permission to reuse material and ideas from these earlier works is gratefully acknowledged.

Mallika and Shobhana were constant companions as this work took shape, and Vinod and Lakshmi kept encouraging from afar. My mother was delighted to hear that the venture was underway but did not live to see it completed. In deepest love and gratitude, I dedicate this book to her memory and my father's.

INDEX

Abdullah, Sheikh, 69, 86, 88–91
Age of Consent Bill agitation, 125
Allahabad High Court, 50
All India Congress Committee (AICC), 90, 91
All-India Muslim League, 133
All-Parties Conference, 143
Ambedkar, B.R., viii, xiv, 12, 14, 26, 27, 32, 49, 64, 65, 122, 125, 134, 135, 147–157
Anderson, Benedict, 168, 236, 237
Anti-colonial movements, 197
Anti-Congress sentiment, 94
Anti-elitism, 233
Antisocial Media, 225
Appadurai, Arjun, 245–246
Appiah, Anthony, 210
Armistice Day, 67
Aryan
  supremacy, 126
  theory, 128
  theory of race, 127
Arya Samaj, 74, 126, 132, 134, 135
  approach, 134
Asom Gana Parishad (AGP), 43
Ayodhya, 15–19, 31, 33, 41, 50–54, 79, 102–103, 105–107
  mobilization, 106

moment, 16
petition, 50
Babri Masjid, 31, 51, 54, 103
Bahujan Samaj Party (BSP), 41, 106, 107
Bajrang Dal, 8
Bannerjee, Surendranath, 129
Basu, Amrita, 82
Beveridge Report, 200
Bhakra Nangal Dam, 96
Bharatiya Janata Party (BJP), 17, 33–34, 37–41, 43–47, 70, 103–104, 106, 108, 230
  campaign, 230
Bharat Mata Mandir, 102
Bharat Sadhu Samaj (BSS), 92
Biden, Joe, 224
Birla, Ghanshyam Das, 148
Boer War, 197
Bose, Subhas Chandra, xiv, 144, 148
Bourdieu, Pierre, 210
Bourgeois society, 156, 178, 192
Brahmin–Baniya club, 39
Brass, Paul, 104
British
  colonialism, 121, 123, 135
  colonies, 198
  crown, 29, 121
  empire, 119
  Raj, 30, 68, 118, 131

rule, 157
Bush, George W., 218–219, 222, 242
Capital accumulation, 180–181
Capitalism, 145, 172, 180, 212, 236–237, 239–241,
Castells, Manuel, 224
Caste oppression, 27–28
Chandavarkar, Narayan, 134
Charlu, P. Ananda, 129
Churchill, Winston, 200
Citizenship (Amendment) Act (CAA), 41–44, 46
Civic equality, 180
Civil Rights Act, 83
Civil society, ix, 19, 101, 104, 108, 141, 156, 158, 168, 183, 186, 190–193, 221, 224
Columbia Journalism Review, 232
Columbus Day, 15
Communal antagonism, 85, 137
Communal Award of 1932, 148
Communication Power, 224
Competition and Concord, 177
Congress-dominated system, 150
Congress of Berlin, 195–196
Congress system, 225– 228
Constituent Assembly, viii, 25–27, 29–31, 52, 64
Corn Laws, 181
Counter-revolution, 201
Covid-19 pandemic, 10, 11, 223
Critique of Hegel's Doctrine of the State, 191

Critique of Practical Reason, 186
Dalit political movements, 154
Dalrymple, William, 73
Dandi March, 144
Darwinian evolution, 241
Das, Chittaranjan, 143
Dawn, 68
Delhi High Court, 48
Democratic incumbency, 217
Democratic recession, 221
Depressed Classes Association, 134
Desai, Morarji, 98
Deutsch, Karl, 169
Dufferin, Viceroy, 122
Dutch colonies, 198
Economic
  survey, 243
  theory, 180–182, 214
  turbulence, 211
Electoral contests, 105
Electoral Minorities, 49, 50
Engels, Friedrich, 171
European
  colonialism, 198, 200
  enlightenment, 189, 199
  modernity, 155, 156
  powers, x, 197
Facebook, 224–225, 231–232
First World War, 169, 172, 197
French colonies, 198
French nation, 5–6, 14, 25, 176
French Republic, 176, 177
French Revolution, 4–5, 173,

174, 175, 177
Fukuyama, Francis, xi, xii, 221
Gadgil, N.V., 79–80
Gait, E.A., 131–132
Gandhi, Indira, 91, 92, 97, 98, 101, 227, 228
Gandhi, Mahatma, xiv, 26, 68, 69, 79, 80, 118–120, 130, 135–146, 148–157
Gellner, Ernest, 100
Ghare Baire, 136
Ghatak, Ritwik, 66
Ghosh, Aurobindo, 138
Gini coefficient, 219, 243
Golwalkar, M.S., 138
Great War, 197
Guha, Ramachandra, 85
Habermas, Jürgen, 28, 193
Harijan Sewak Samaj, 147–148, 150
Harvey, David, 180
Hind Swaraj, 118, 120, 135, 138
Hindu
 communal majority, 157
 nationalism, 126–127, 130–134
 revivalism, 127, 138
 scriptures, 150, 152
Hinduism, 26, 105, 126, 131, 133, 134, 142, 145, 151, 155,
Hindu Mahasabha, 81
'Hindu-Muslim dispute', 53
Hindus, A Dying Race, 133
Hindus and the Coming Census, 133

Hindu society, 153
Hindutva, 8–10, 13, 16–18, 33, 85, 105–108, 123, 138
Hindutva political agenda, 106
Hobbes's work, 156
Hobsbawm, E.J., 16, 168, 171, 173, 195, 200, 241
Imagined Communities, 236
'imagined community', 168
Indian community, 118
Indian Constituent Assembly, 25
Indian constitution, 10, 15, 20, 27–28, 45, 101
Indian Councils Act of 1892, 122
Indian democracy, 54, 228, 244
Indian Express, 234
'Indian Home Rule,' 136
Indian judicial process, 48
Indian National Congress, 125, 128
Indian nationalist project, 120
Indian Republic, 33, 52
Indian Social Reforms Conference, 125
International Monetary Fund (IMF), 202
Islamic revival, 125
Jamia Millia Islamia, 46
Jat-Pat-Todak Mandal of Lahore, 151
Johnson, Lyndon, 211, 215
Kafka, Franz, 172
Kant, Immanuel, 184–188, 191

Karachi Congress (1931), 145
Kashmir Valley, 86, 101
Kenya African Union, 199
Keynes, John Maynard, 212, 213
Khare, N.B., 78
Khera, Reetika, 244
Kothari, Rajni, 225–227
Krugman, Paul, 212–214, 217, 219
Kundera, Milan, x–xi, 172
League of Nations, x, 197, 198
Legislative Assembly, 94, 95
Legislative consensus, 28
Lenin, Vladimir Illyich, 172
Liberal-democratic framework, 12
Liberation Day, 72
Lok Sabha, 33–37, 40–41, 105–107, 228, 230, 232, 234, 245,
Lower-caste liberation movements, 155
Lower House of Parliament, 17
Madison, James, 235
Madras High Court, 36
Malaviya, Madan Mohan, 130
Mamluk tribes, 6
Mandal, B.P., 38
Mandal moment of 1990, 105
Martyrs' Day, 70
Marx, Karl, 191–192
Mehta, Pherozeshah, 128–129
Mill, John Stuart, 171, 240
Ministry of Home Affairs (MHA), 87, 93, 96, 98, 102
Ministry of Women and Child Development, 45
Modi, Narendra, 35, 37, 39, 43, 46, 66, 230– 234
Modi government, 33, 36, 41, 44
Mohammad, Bakshi Ghulam, 85
Mohammadan Anglo-Oriental Defence Association, 123
Mughal
 empire, 120
 rulers, 51
Mukherji, U.N., 133–134
Munshi, K.M., 81
Muslim community, 50, 65, 99, 122, 131
Muslim League, 29, 65, 130, 133
Muslim refugees, 70, 72
Nagari scripts, 123
Naidu, Sarojini, 2
Nanda, Gulzari Lal, 86, 88, 92
National Assembly, 174
National Crime Records Bureau, 83
'National Egoism', 140
Nationalism, ii, 2, 6, 138, 141, 168, 170, 199
National politics, 229
National Register of Citizens (NRC), 42– 44, 46
 process, 43
Nehru, Jawaharlal, xiv, 28, 31,

53, 65, 130, 131, 144
Nehru, Motilal, 130, 143
Neoliberalism, 221–222, 243
Network technologies, 231
Nixon, Richard, 215
Noorani, A.G., 74, 76
North-Western Provinces, 122
Obama, Barack, 219, 223
October Coup: A Memoir of the Struggle for Hyderabad, 73
Organic Swaraj, 143
Organization of the Petroleum Exporting Countries (OPEC), 201
Orion, 127
Orwell, George, 2
Other Backward Classes (OBCs), 35, 39– 41, 227
Ottoman Empire, 195
Oudh Municipalities Act, 122
Pal, Bipin Chandra, 127, 138
Pandit Sundarlal Committee, 75
Pant, Gobind Ballabh, 31, 52, 54, 81
Partition Horrors Remembrance Day, 66
Partition refugees, 87
Pashtun tribes, 71
Patel, Sardar Vallabhbhai, 30, 80
Patidar agitations, 37
Patil, S.K., 92
Patriotism, 1, 2, 6
Pax Soviet-Americana, 200
Philosophy of Right, 187, 189

Phule, Jyotiba, 128, 155
Phule, Jyotirao, 125
Political boundaries, 181
Poona Pact, 149
Poonch jagir, 71
'Private art', 189
Productive process, 182
Radcliffe, Cyril, 66
Raghubar Dayal Commission, 94, 95
Rai, Lajpat, 126–128, 131–132, 138
Rajagopalachari, C., 89
Rapid Survey of Children, 45
Rashtriya Swayamsevak Sangh (RSS), 74, 101
'Rational truths', 235
Reagan–Thatcher revolution, 201
Reign of Terror of 1793, 67, 175
Renan, Ernest, 13–14, 79
Republican Party, 223
Republic Day, 8, 15
1848 revolutions, 194
Ricardo, David, 181
Robinson, Joan, 213
Rohingya Muslim refugees, 42
Round Table Conferences, 26
Roy, Srirupa, 82
Russian revolution, 197
Samajwadi Party (SP), 41, 106,
Sandberg, Sheryl, 231
Savarkar, Vinayak Damodar, 118
Scheduled Castes (SCs), 40, 83

Scheduled Tribes (STs), 40, 83
Schumpeter, Joseph, 212, 213
Second World War, x, 44, 70, 168, 169, 193, 198, 199, 200, 210, 211, 220
Secularism, 16, 29, 33, 76, 104, 145
Self-reproductive processes, 229
Sen, Abhijit, 243
Shaheen Bagh, 47
Shastri, Lal Bahadur, 53, 87, 91
Shirer, William L., 148
Shock, Volcker, 215, 216
Sieyes, Abbe, 182
Simon Commission, 143
Singh, Karan, 70
Smith, Adam, 11, 178, 181–184, 188
Smith, Anthony D., 169
Social Conference, 125
Social Darwinism, 201
Socially and Economically Backward Classes (SEBCs), 35, 36, 64
Social media, 224–225, 231–234, 236–237
Soviet Union, 144, 201, 218
Spanish Civil War, 197
Srinivas, M.N., 32
State Legislative Assembly, 54
Stiglitz, Joseph, 219
Sundarlal Committee, 75, 76
Suppressed cultures, 169
Supreme Court, 13, 28, 33–36, 42, 46, 50, 51, 52, 64, 79
Swadeshi movement, 136–138, 140
Syrian Arab territories, 197
Tagore, Rabindranath, xiv, 120, 136–141, 156
Thapar, Romesh, 89–90
The Arctic Home in the Vedas, 127
The Destruction of Hyderabad, 76
Theosophical Society of Colonel Olcott, 127
The Theory of Moral Sentiments, 11
The Wealth of Nations, 11
'Third electoral system', 229
Third Estate, 174, 183
Thompson, E.P., 141
Tilak, Bal Gangadhar, 123, 138
To Eternal Peace, 186
Traditional polities, 209
Trump, Donald, 47, 221, 223
United Nations Commission for India and Pakistan (UNCIP), 72
'Universalism', 194
Urdu Defence Association, 123
US deficit, 220
US monetary authority, 215
Uttar Pradesh Legislative Assembly, 106–107
Victory Day, 67
Violence, 78
Vishwa Hindu Parishad (VHP), 102

Watergate scandal, 211
Welfare State, 193, 200–201, 215, 217, 231
White House, 217, 223
Wilkinson, Steven, 104, 107
World Bank, 202
Yadav, Yogendra, 227–229
Young India, 143

www.ingramcontent.com/pod-product-compliance
Lightning Source LLC
Chambersburg PA
CBHW030104170426
43198CB00009B/490